PUBLICATIONS OF
THE MANCHESTER CENTRE FOR ANGLO-SAXON STUDIES

Volume 3

King Harold II and the Bayeux Tapestry

Harold II is chiefly remembered today, perhaps unfairly, for the brevity of his reign and his death at the Battle of Hastings. The papers collected here seek to shed new light on the man and his milieu before and after that climax. They explore the long career and the dynastic network behind Harold Godwinesson's accession on the death of King Edward the Confessor in January 1066, looking in particular at the important questions as to whether Harold's kingship was opportunist or long-planned; a usurpation or a legitimate succession in terms of his Anglo-Scandinavian kinships. They also examine the posthumous legends that Harold survived Hastings and lived on as a religious recluse. The essays in the second part of the volume focus on the Bayeux Tapestry, bringing out the small details which would have resonated significantly for contemporary audiences, both Norman and English, to suggest how they judged Harold and the other players in the succession drama of 1066. Other aspects of the Tapestry are also covered: the possible patron and locations the Tapestry was produced for; where and how it was designed; and the various sources – artistic and real – employed by the artist.

PUBLICATIONS OF
THE MANCHESTER CENTRE FOR ANGLO-SAXON STUDIES

ISSN 1478–6710

Published Titles

1. *Textual and Material Culture in Anglo-Saxon England: Thomas Northcote Toller and the Toller Memorial Lectures*, ed. Donald Scragg
2. *Apocryphal Texts and Traditions in Anglo-Saxon England*, ed. Kathryn Powell and Donald Scragg

King Harold II and The Bayeux Tapestry

edited by

GALE R. OWEN-CROCKER

THE BOYDELL PRESS

First published 2005
The Boydell Press, Woodbridge

ISBN 1 84383 124 4

The Boydell Press is an imprint of Boydell & Brewer Ltd
PO Box 9, Woodbridge, Suffolk IP12 3DF, UK
and of Boydell & Brewer Inc,
668 Mt Hope Avenue, Rochester, NY 14620, USA
website: www.boydellandbrewer.com

A CIP catalogue record for this book is available
from the British Library

Library of Congress Catalog Card Number: 2004022191

Printed in Great Britain by
Cromwell Press, Trowbridge, Wiltshire

Contents

Illustrations

Plates

Illustrations of the Bayeux Tapestry (Plates 1–24) are reproduced by special permission of the City of Bayeux. They appear between pages 73 and 90.

Figures

Figures 4–6 were interpreted and digitized by Katrina Keefer. Figures 7–8 were measured by Richard Crocker and digitized by Abdullah Alger. Other figures were drawn by the authors unless otherwise stated. Figures 12–24 were digitized by Abdullah Alger.

Contributors

Shirley Ann Brown, York University, Toronto, Canada

H. E. J. Cowdrey, St Edmund Hall, Oxford

Gillian Fellows-Jensen, University of Copenhagen, Denmark

Cyril Hart

Chris Henige, University of Wisconsin-Whitewater, USA

N. J. Higham, University of Manchester

Ian Howard

Catherine E. Karkov, Miami University, Oxford, Ohio, USA

Sarah Larratt Keefer, Trent University, Peterborough, Canada

Michael Lewis, British Museum, London

Stephen Matthews

Gale R. Owen-Crocker, University of Manchester

Preface

Harold II (Harold Godwinesson) was king of England for just nine months: from his coronation the day after the death of Edward the Confessor, 5–6 January 1066, until he was killed and the English defeated at the Battle of Hastings on 14 October of the same year. Harold was far from being the only candidate for the English throne when King Edward died childless, but his credentials are undeniable. His accession can be seen as the culmination of a long career, which had brought him to the position of leading ealdorman and effective governor of England. He was related closely by marriage to Edward the Confessor and by blood to the royal house of Cnut. Successful in both diplomacy and war, Harold steered the country through unprecedented internal and external turmoil and after his death he was not forgotten either in secular narrative or in the traditions of the Church which he had used his great wealth to endow.

The embroidered frieze known as the Bayeux Tapestry is one of the most important records for Harold's last two years, leading up to his accession and the battle in which he lost his throne and, apparently, his life. Inevitably the Tapestry has been treated as a historical source, but it is idiosyncratic, sometimes contradictory of other sources and structured to present a coherent narrative. Its messages remain ambiguous to modern commentators as it suggests both Anglo-Saxon and Norman attitudes to the events of 1064–6, in a tension between Norman patronage and English workmanship.

This volume, which brings together the career of King Harold II and the graphic depiction of his life, originated in a conference held by the Manchester Centre for Anglo-Saxon Studies in April 2002, one of a series on Anglo-Saxon kings. It was directed jointly by David Hill and Gale Owen-Crocker and included an excursion led by David Hill, which visited York, Riccall, where Harold Hardrada of Norway landed with an invasion force, and nearby Stamfordbridge, where Harold II defeated Harold Hardrada, together with his own brother, Tostig Godwinesson, on 25 September 1066, the climactic triumph of his kingship. The article by Sarah Keefer and the Introduction by H. E. J. Cowdrey have been added to those first delivered as papers at the conference. Both are developed from papers read at International Medieval Congresses at Kalamazoo, Western Michigan, University.

The editor gratefully acknowledges the financial support of the British Academy towards the conference, and of the University Small Grants Fund, the Faculty of Arts Research Fund and the Research Committee of the School of English and American Studies, University of Manchester, towards the publication.

Gale R. Owen-Crocker
Manchester 2004

Abbreviations

AM	manuscript in the Arnamagnæan Collections (in Copenhagen and Reykjavik)
ANS	*Anglo-Norman Studies*
AntJ	*Antiquaries Journal*
ArchJ	*Archaeological Journal*
ASC	The *Anglo-Saxon Chronicle*
ASE	*Anglo-Saxon England*
Barlow, *Vita Ædwardi*	*The Life of King Edward who Rests at Westminster*, ed. Frank Barlow (London, first published 1962, revised edition 1992). Page numbers are from the revised edition.
Bernstein, *Mystery*	David J. Bernstein, *The Mystery of the Bayeux Tapestry* (London, 1986)
BL	British Library
Brilliant, 'Stripped narrative'	Richard Brilliant, 'The Bayeux Tapestry: a stripped narrative for their eyes and ears', first published in *Word and Image* 7 (1991), 93–125, and here cited in the reprint in Gameson, *Study*, pp. 111–37
Brooks and Walker, 'Authority and interpretation'	N. P. Brooks and H. E. Walker, 'The authority and interpretation of the Bayeux Tapestry', first published in *Proceedings of the Battle Conference on Anglo-Norman Studies* 1 (1979), 1–34 and 191–9 and here cited in the reprint in Gameson, *Study*, pp. 63–92
CCCC	Cambridge, Corpus Christi College manuscript
Dodwell, 'BT and the French secular epic'	C. R. Dodwell, 'The Bayeux Tapestry and the French secular epic', first published in *Burlington Magazine* 108 (1966), 549–60 and here cited in the reprint in Gameson, *Study*, pp. 47–62
Dodwell and Clemoes, *Hexateuch*	C. R. Dodwell and Peter Clemoes, *The Old English Illustrated Hexateuch*, Early English Manuscripts in Facsimile 18 (Copenhagen, 1974)
Gameson, *Study*	*The Study of the Bayeux Tapestry*, ed. R. Gameson (Woodbridge, 1997)
Gks	manuscript in the Old Royal Collection of the Royal Library Copenhagen
HÞ	*Hemings þáttr Áslákssonar*, ed. Gillian Fellows Jensen, Editiones Arnamagnæanæ Series B3 (Copenhagen, 1962)
Ohlgren, *Illustration*	*Anglo-Saxon Textual Illustration: Photographs of Sixteen Manuscripts with Description and Index*, ed. Thomas H. Ohlgren (Kalamazoo, 1992)
Stenton, *BT*	*The Bayeux Tapestry: a Comprehensive Survey*, ed. Frank Stenton *et al.* (London, 1957, revised 1965)
Wilson, *BT*	D. M. Wilson, *The Bayeux Tapestry* (London, 1985)
Wormald, 'Style and design'	Francis Wormald, 'Style and Design', in Stenton, *BT*, pp. 25–36

1

King Harold II and the Bayeux Tapestry: a Critical Introduction*

H. E. J. COWDREY

A SURPRISING feature of the Bayeux Tapestry is the amount and the continuity of the attention that is given to Harold II. Of the three kings with whom it is concerned – Edward the Confessor, Harold, and William the Conqueror – it is Harold, not William, who is most often referred to. In the seventy-three scenes usually acknowledged in the Tapestry,[1] there are certain or probable representations of Harold in twenty-six, but of William only in twenty. In the Latin captions, up to the appearance of the comet (Wilson, *BT*, Plates 1–32), Harold's name figures fourteen times to William's ten; thereafter William's appears nine times to Harold's seven. Stenton commented that the Tapestry was 'throughout . . . intimately connected with the course of Harold's personal fortunes'.[2] Francis Wormald commented yet more strongly that, as many scholars have remarked, 'in the unfolding of the story Harold's part is even more important than that of the Conqueror himself. It is a history of the former's fall even more than of the latter's triumph. Harold's disaster is caused by the breaking of his oath to William. Before that he is a successful figure. After the coronation his troubles come, ending in defeat and death.'[3] The presentation of Harold in the Tapestry clearly merits full and careful attention.

The basic facts about Harold's life may be briefly indicated.[4] He was probably born between 1020 and 1026, the second son of the powerful Godwine, earl of Wessex and his Danish wife, Gytha. In 1051 a political crisis led to the expulsion of Godwine and his family. While Godwine was exiled to Flanders, Harold fled to Ireland; but in 1052 the Godwines returned and were reinstated in their power and possessions, Edward the Confessor having dismissed his Norman supporters. In 1053 Godwine died and, his eldest son having also died, Harold became earl of Wessex. He

* This paper develops arguments set out in H. E. J. Cowdrey, 'Towards an interpretation of the Bayeux Tapestry', first published in *ANS* 10 (1988), 49–65 and reprinted in Gameson, *Study*, pp. 93–110, from which pagination is taken in this paper; see also *The Anglo-Norman Anonymous*, XV. no. 3 (1997), 7–8.

1 Thus Stenton, *BT*. These scenes correspond to the numbering on the modern backcloth on which the Tapestry is mounted.

2 Stenton, *BT*, p. 24, n. 19, cf. p. 15.

3 Wormald, 'Style and design', p. 33.

4 For details of the sources for Harold and the principal modern discussions, see R. Fleming, 'Harold II', in *Oxford Dictionary of National Biography* (Oxford, 2004), XXV, 365–62.

remained the principal figure in the kingdom until King Edward died on 5 January 1066. On the day following, Harold was crowned king. He ruled strenuously and on 25 September he inflicted a total defeat upon the armies of Harold Hardrada, king of Norway, and his own brother, Tostig, earl of Northumbria, at Stamfordbridge; but on 14 October he was himself defeated at Hastings by William, duke of Normandy, being killed in the battle. On 25 December, William was crowned king at Westminster. The first of Harold's two marriages, to Edith 'Swan-neck', had the character of concubinage; he had numerous offspring by her. However, he married secondly Ealdgyth, daughter of Ælfgar, earl of Mercia, by whom a son was born to him posthumously. Despite Harold's power as earl of Wessex, there are many uncertainties in the chronology of his life. Thus, the date even of the travels in Normandy of which the Tapestry makes much is not clear, though there are indications that it should be assigned to 1064.[5] When information is not plentiful and its interpretation uncertain, the Tapestry itself is a major factor in determining historians' views of Harold.

There can be no gainsaying Wormald's view that, at least in the main story of the earlier part of the Tapestry (Wilson, *BT*, Plates 1–27) – the margins may be reserved for later consideration – Harold is a successful figure, indeed that his character is consistently noble, virtuous and laudable. The question is worth asking whether or not the impression of Harold that one receives from the main story is consistent with what may be gathered from other evidence, especially from written sources favourable to him,[6] and whether the depiction in the Tapestry leaves major aspects of Harold's dealings as earl of Wessex without consideration. The focus must be upon the image presented rather than upon the factual record, which is somewhat meagre.

The image presented in the first part of the Tapestry implies that he was a man of impressive personal presence and dignity who was of acknowledged loyalty, prowess and probity. Several depictions of him convey his impressiveness: for example he rides to Bosham in front of his retinue with a hawk on his fist and hounds running ahead of him (**Plate 1**); even in captivity to Count Guy of Ponthieu his dignity is retained (**Plate 3**); on campaign in Brittany he serves Duke William well (**Plate 9**), and after William has given him arms (**Plate 10**), he rides nobly (Wilson, *BT*, Plates 24–5). During his brief enjoyment of regality he will be invested with due majesty (**Plate 14**). This is consistent with the written sources. Even for the hostile Norman sources, William of Jumièges and William of Poitiers, Harold was the Confessor's most eminent subject in wealth, honour and power.[7] In England, the *Life of Edward the Confessor* was almost unqualified in its praise: Harold was the eldest and wisest of Godwine's sons; he was a new Judas Maccabeus. Handsome and gracious in his person, he was well able to withstand physical adversity. Famed for the power of his body and mind, he had qualities of patience, mercy and kindness, though to malefac-

5 See Stenton, *BT*, p. 14.

6 As illustrated below, favourable sources include the *Anglo-Saxon Chronicle*, the *Life of King Edward*, John of Worcester and (later) the *Waltham Chronicle*. Norman sources, especially William of Poitiers, are predictably hostile. William of Malmesbury is also critical.

7 William of Jumièges, VII. xiii (31): *The Gesta Normannorum Ducum of William of Jumièges, Orderic Vitalis, and Robert of Torigni*, ed. Elisabeth M. C. van Houts, 2 vols (Oxford, 1992–5), II. 158–61. William of Poitiers, I. xli: *The 'Gesta Guillelmi' of William of Poitiers*, ed. Ralph H. C. Davis and Marjorie Chibnall (Oxford, 1998), pp. 68–71.

tors he was duly stern.[8] John of Worcester, another favourable source, claimed that such good qualities were also evident in Harold as king.[9] The *Waltham Chronicle* shows the continuation of such a picture of Harold as a fine soldier, tall, strong and handsome, who was in all respects outstanding; as king he was *egregius rex*.[10] The Tapestry implies that Harold was, or seemed to be, an altogether loyal subject of the Confessor. Thus, in the opening scene he obediently receives the king's instructions before setting out for France (Wilson, *BT*, Plate 1); upon returning he duly reports to the king (**Plate 12**) and at the king's death-bed he appears to accept the king's special charge to him (**Plate 13**). The written sources are impressively unanimous in reporting Harold's loyalty to him during his years as earl of Wessex. Most strikingly, the *Anglo-Saxon Chronicle* concludes its (metrical) obituary of the Confessor by applauding Harold's services: Harold was 'A noble earl who all the time/ Had loyally followed his lord's commands/ With words and deeds, and neglecting nothing/ That met the need of the people's king'.[11] Such exemplary loyalty was elsewhere noticed and never contradicted.[12]

Such qualities were matched by Harold's deeds and life-style. The Tapestry depicted his courage and skill in warfare which won him Duke William's recognition during his campaign in the Breton marches (Wilson, *BT*, Plates 18–24). During the Confessor's reign, Harold served conspicuously and successfully in the Welsh marches, especially against the formidable Welsh prince Gruffydd ap Llywelyn (1039–63) and his son. Described by John of Worcester as *strenuus dux*, he was credited with exceptional success in subduing the Welsh marches.[13] As king, Harold exhibited leadership at the battles of Stamfordbridge and Hastings.[14] William of Malmesbury referred to Harold's travels in Ponthieu and Normandy with which the Tapestry begins (Wilson, *BT*, Plates 4–17).[15] In preparation for his journey, Harold in

8 *Vita Ædwardi*, I. v: Barlow, *Vita Ædwardi*, pp. 46–51. The importance of this source arises from its very early date, probably 1065–6 for Book I and perhaps 1067 for Book II (pp. xxix–xxxii) and from its dedication to Queen Edith, the Confessor's widow and Harold's sister. The author admits that Harold was 'too ready with his oaths': I. vii, pp. 80–1.

9 John of Worcester, 1066: *The Chronicle of John of Worcester*, ed. R. R. Darlington and P. McGurk, 3 vols (Oxford, 1995–), II. 600–1.

10 *Waltham Chronicle*, XIV, XXI: *The Waltham Chronicle*, ed. Leslie Watkiss and Marjorie Chibnall (Oxford, 1994), pp. 26–7, 56–7.

11 *ASC* 1065 CD: *The Anglo-Saxon Chronicle: A Revised Translation*, ed. Dorothy Whitelock with David C. Douglas and Susie I. Tucker (London, 1961), pp. 139–40.

12 Especially *Vita Ædwardi*, I. v: Barlow, *Vita Ædwardi*, pp. 50–1. John of Worcester, 1064–5: Darlington and McGurk, *John of Worcester*, II. 596–7. *Waltham Chronicle*, XV: Watkiss and Chibnall, *Waltham Chronicle*, pp. 26–7. Cf. William of Poitiers, I. xli: Davis and Chibnall, *Gesta Guillelmi*, pp. 70–1.

13 *ASC* 1055 C, 1063 DE, 1065 CD: Whitelock, *Chronicle*, pp. 130–1, 136–8. John of Worcester, 1055–6, 1063, 1065: Darlington and McGurk, *John of Worcester*, II. 578–81, 592–3, 596–7. *Vita Ædwardi*, I. v, II, *Poeta*: Barlow, *Vita Ædwardi*, pp. 64–5, 86–7. William of Malmesbury, II. clxxxxix. 1: *William of Malmesbury Gesta Regum Anglorum*, ed. R. A. B. Mynors, R. M. Thomson and M. Winterbottom, 2 vols (Oxford, 1998–9), I. 356–7.

14 *ASC* 1066 CDE: Whitelock, *Chronicle*, pp. 140–5. John of Worcester, 1066: Darlington and McGurk, *John of Worcester*, II. 604–5. Cf. William of Poitiers, II. xxii: Davis and Chibnall, *Gesta Guillielmi*, pp. 134–7.

15 William of Malmesbury, II. ccxxviii. 3–6, II. ccxxxvi. 3: Mynors *et al.*, *William of Malmesbury*, I. 416–19, 440–1. Cf. William of Jumièges, VII. xiii (31): van Houts, *Gesta*, II. 158–61. William of Poitiers, I. xlii–xliii, II. xii: Davis and Chibnall, *Gesta Guillelmi*, pp. 68–73, 120–1. Guy of Amiens,

the Tapestry shows the piety appropriate to his rank and duties by praying at Bosham church (**Plate 1**). His piety was elsewhere acknowledged. He established a community of secular canons at Waltham Cross, endowing it generously with land and relics; according to the *Waltham Chronicle* he prayed there before the Battle of Hastings.[16] In the Tapestry, Harold lived sumptuously according to his station, feasting (**Plate 1**) and travelling with the apparatus of hunting which was the passion of the nobles of his day (**Plate 1**, cf. **3**, **7**). With comparable panache, in 1065 he planned to entertain the king to a hunting expedition in the Welsh marches, based on a building at Portskewet which was evidently intended to be a permanent hunting lodge lavishly provisioned with appropriate victuals.[17] In the main story of the early part of the Tapestry, a picture of Harold is presented which tallies closely with what can be gathered about him and his public image from written sources; it is difficult to suggest anything about him that cannot be directly or indirectly related to that picture. It is as though, by accident or by design, the Tapestry is concerned to exhibit Harold as he was widely understood and publicized to have been, especially in sources favourable to him; but there is another side to the picture. In two ways, the Tapestry seems to have been concerned to show that the image of Harold as a *chevalier sans peur et sans reproche* was a false one, and that the underlying reality was far different.

The first apparent line of attack has been much discussed; it is that the borders of the Tapestry repeatedly hint that the image was radically flawed from the start. The *dux Anglorum* (as the Tapestry chose to call him, **Plate 1**) is not as he seems to be; this is a man to beware! The character assassination (for that is what it is) seems to begin as early as Harold's stop-over at Bosham. While he and a companion devoutly pray, two birds in the lower margin posture aggressively, their heads grovelling on the ground (**Plate 1**). Whereas Harold feasts nobly, in the margin two crafty wolves lick their paws so they can hunt in the deceitful manner of their kind (**Plate 1**). From Harold's departure from Bosham to his capture by Count Guy of Pontieu, the lower margin alludes to nine of Aesop's fables. The 'morals' of these fables are not ethical but prudential: look out! hidden dangers beset the unwary from the ways of the crafty and deceitful (Wilson, *BT*, Plates 4–11).[18] In due course, as Count Guy leads Harold to Duke William, Harold rides as a noble should ride; he is a paragon of chivalry; but in the lower margin an obscene sketch seems to reveal his *luxuria*: he is a lecher, who cannot be trusted (**Plate 7**).[19] In such ways, the lower border seems to nag away

lines 295–300: *The Carmen de Hastingae Proelio of Guy Bishop of Amiens*, ed. Frank Barlow (Oxford, 1999), pp. 18–19. The *Anglo-Saxon Chronicle* has no annal for 1064, the most likely date for Harold's journey, but for a later, English view, see Eadmer, I: *Eadmeri Historia Novorum in Anglia*, ed. Martin Rule, Rolls Series, 81 (London, 1884), 7–8.

16 *Waltham Chronicle*, XIV–XVIII, XX: Watkiss and Chibnall, *Waltham Chronicle*, pp. 24–39, 44–51. William of Malmesbury, II. ccxlvii.1: Mynors *et al.*, *William of Malmesbury*, I. 460–1.

17 *ASC* 1065 CD: Whitelock, *Chronicle*, p. 136.

18 For further discussion of the use of the fables see Cowdrey, 'Towards an interpretation', pp. 99–100. Among several more recent treatments, see Bernstein, *Mystery*, pp. 82–7, 124–35: J. Bard McNulty, *Visual Meaning in the Bayeux Tapestry: Problems and Solutions in Picturing History* (Lewiston, NY, Queenston, Ont., and Lampeter, 2003), pp. 23–36. Scholars disagree on the number of fables in the Tapestry. The count of nine corresponds to Hélène Chefneux, 'Les Fables dans la Tapisserie de Bayeux', *Romania* 60 (1934), 1–35, 153–94.

19 William of Poitiers described Harold as '*luxuria foedum*', though it is not clear whether he had in view

against Harold, and to hint at what he is really like. When Harold returns to England, the denigration seems to break from the borders into the main story. To introduce the return, Aesop's fables reappear in the upper border. The wolf taunts the crane for a help that the crane has imprudently provided and we recall William's gift of arms to Harold (**Plate 10**); and the crow which is perched in a tree and courting admiration is placed above Harold, as he rides (**Plate 12**). Harold, it will be recalled, will soon be displayed in false regality; but like the crow he will soon be discredited (Wilson, *BT*, Plates 31, 32–3). The foreshadowing of this débâcle is the prelude to Harold's return to Edward the Confessor at Westminster (**Plate 12**). At this point his quality as a man of shame is brought firmly into the main story. Like his attendant, he is crooked and hunchbacked. What the Tapestry wishes to be recognized as Harold's true character in not merely hinted in the borders but placarded in the main story. In effect, the Tapestry seems to present visually and at length the picture of Harold that William of Malmesbury summarized in a few words:

> That truth may not be concealed, according to the public figure that [Harold] cut, he would have governed the kingdom with prudence and power if he came by it lawfully. For during Edward's lifetime whatever wars were started against the king he subdued by the strength of a [Harold] who sought to exhibit himself to his countrymen at large, but after the fashion of one who was himself panting after the kingdom with itching hope (*in regnum scilicet spe prurienti anhelans*).[20]

The good appearance masks a very different reality.

There seems also to have been a second line of attack on Harold's character which has attracted less notice but which may be no less significant. It has already been noticed that the crooked and hunchbacked Harold who returns from Normandy to Edward the Confessor (**Plate 12**) is an icon of his own flawed character. It may appear to be a contradiction of what has been said above that once already Harold has appeared in a somewhat similar, hunchbacked posture (Wilson, *BT*, Plates 9–10). It was when he stood before his chance captor, Count Guy of Ponthieu; and there is much in common between this scene in Ponthieu and Harold's later return to the Confessor in England. Although he is only a count, Guy sits in a similar posture of authority to Edward. The count gestures with his right hand much as the king gestures. In both scenes, Harold stands near the door with just one close companion; and in both scenes, Harold and his companion are bowed down by some kind of dishonour. At Ponthieu, however, it is not any moral or culpable dishonour of conduct or character. The clue is that Harold is vividly depicted as having to surrender the sword of which he has divested himself. With the sword he also surrenders his *cingulum militare* – the belt which from Roman times was the badge and the pride of knighthood. It was not Harold's fault if adverse winds at sea had blown him into Guy's captivity; there was no personal or moral stigma. The fact remained that

only his relationship with Edith 'Swan-Neck' or also with other concubines: William of Poitiers, II. viii: Davis and Chibnall, *Gesta Guillelmi*, pp. 114–15. See also *Waltham Chronicle*, XXI: Watkiss and Chibnall, *Waltham Chronicle*, pp. 54–5. Barlow plausibly suggests that the emphasis in the *Vita Ædwardi* (I. v) upon his brother Tostig's exemplary chastity may imply a contrast with Harold: Barlow, *Vita Ædwardi*, pp. 50–1.

20 William of Malmesbury, II. ccxviii. 8: Mynors *et al.*, *William of Malmesbury*, I. 420–1.

circumstances had led to his surrendering to the count his sword and with it the belt that was the outward and visible sign of his military capacity and honour. Therefore, however blameless he might be, his back is bowed in token of chivalric dishonour.

The surrender cries out to be brought into relation with another scene which is surely its companion-piece – that in which, just after he leaves Brittany, William gives arms to Harold after his good service there (**Plate 10**). Commentators have tended to read quite a lot into William's giving of arms to Harold, especially in terms of what are described as 'feudal' customs and conventions. In the course of the Breton campaign he had shown sufficient valour to merit his being knighted in the field; but on the one hand, his surrender of the *cingulum militare* to the count of Ponthieu shows that, as the Tapestry understood it, he was a knight already. On the other, his role during the Breton campaign as the Tapestry exhibits it calls for careful study. If he played an active part in the actual fighting, the Tapestry disregards it. His heroic act in rescuing two Norman knights from the quicksands near Mont-Saint-Michel (**Plate 9**) was performed before the fighting, in which he is not shown as taking part. It is highly significant that, between the professionally shameful disarming of Harold by Guy of Ponthieu and the professionally honourable arming of Harold by William of Normandy (Wilson, *BT*, Plates 9–10; **Plate 10**), although Harold is treated with due regard especially by the duke, he is never identified in a fighting role nor does he wear the armour and bear the arms that befit his rank; the shield that he carries when rescuing William's men from the quicksands is manifestly that of one of those rescued (**Plate 9**). No doubt Harold merited the gift of arms by his companionship of the duke on campaign and by afterwards rescuing his men; but as the Tapestry wishes matters to be seen, the gift was William's subsequent act of personal generosity in replacing bounteously the arms that Harold had been compelled to surrender to his vassal Guy of Ponthieu. For William's bounty was great indeed. He gave Harold the panoply of a noble warrior – helmet, hauberk, sword and lance with pennon (**Plate 10**); and more: he restored him to honour as a fighting man. The scene that follows drives this point home. Harold, who has faced the hazards of the Breton campaign dressed in mufti, now accompanies his benefactor Duke William on the relatively safe journey through Normandy to Bayeux in the panoply of arms and armour, which William also wears. The armed parade to Bayeux is highly significant. William has indeed restored Harold to the company of the military class; and, this having been done, Harold forthwith, in the Tapestry, swore his famous oath to William at Bayeux (or Bonneville-sur-Touques?)[21] (**Plate 11**).

If it is right thus to relate to each other the two powerful scenes of Harold's surrender of his arms to Guy of Ponthieu and of his receiving arms from William as he left Brittany, there may be seen one more way in which the first part of the Tapestry is designed to undermine Harold's character. For Harold owed to Duke William's magnanimity and generous gift such arms as those with which he fought against him at Hastings (Wilson, *BT*, Plate 56). If Harold's perjury to William after his oath taken upon relics in Normandy brought its nemesis, his fate was the more

21 For the whereabouts of the oath-taking see Cowdrey, 'Towards an interpretation', in Gameson, *Study*, p. 94 and n. 4.

richly deserved by reason of his ingratitude to William who had restored to him the military standing that he had perforce surrendered in Ponthieu.

In these ways, two lines of attack on Harold's conduct and character come together in the hunchbacked figure who returns to King Edward at Westminster (**Plate 12**). In the second portion of the Tapestry, which deals with events from Harold's return to the appearance of the comet (Wilson, *BT*, Plates 28–33), Harold's perjury and the nemesis to which it leads become a main, if not the main, topic of the central band of the Tapestry. It has been discussed in some detail elsewhere;[22] it may suffice for now to notice how, in order to heighten the drama and to indicate the inexorable sequence of events, the timescale is foreshortened. Events from Harold's return, which cannot have been later than 1 August 1065 and which probably occurred in the previous year, until the appearance of the comet in April 1066, are telescoped about the death of the Confessor and the crowning of Harold on 5–6 January 1066. The last scene shows Harold as having been quickly stripped of regality and of the power to rule (Wilson, *BT*, Plates 32–3). One subject in this sequence of events perhaps merits amplification: it is that of whether, on his deathbed, the Confessor altered his earlier intention by providing that Harold should succeed to the English kingdom. Such may be the significance of the gesture whereby Edward extends his right hand to touch Harold's; Edward's death then opens the way for the crown to be given to Harold (**Plate 13**). Such an interpretation is widely adopted by modern commentators, and it is undeniably supported by a number of sources.[23] Yet the *Life of King Edward* avoids any suggestion that Edward committed the kingship to Harold. Its testimony must be taken seriously, because of its early date, its being written for Queen Edith who was present at the deathbed, and its supplying information that in detail clarifies the evidence of the Tapestry.[24] It purported to give Edward's last words, as follows:

> Porrectaque manu ad predictum nutricium suum fratrem Haroldum, 'Hanc', inquit, 'cum omni regno tutandam tibi commendo, ut pro domina et sorore ut est fideli serves et honores obsequio, ut, quoad vixerit, a me adepto non privetur honore debito.'
>
> (And extending his hand to his aforesaid protector [the queen's] brother Harold, 'Her [Edith]', he said, 'I commend to you with all the kingdom for safeguard, that you should serve and honour her as lady and sister, as she is, with faithful service, so that as long as she shall live she may not be deprived of any honour derived from me.')[25]

The critical words in this passage – 'protector (*nutricium*)' and 'Her I commend to you with all the kingdom for safeguard (*Hanc cum omni regno tutandam tibi*

22 See Cowdrey, 'Towards an interpretation', in Gameson, *Study*, pp. 97, 101–3.

23 *ASC* 1066 E, cf. 1065 CD: Whitelock, *Chronicle*, pp. 139–40. John of Worcester, 1066: Darlington and McGurk, *John of Worcester*, II. 600–1. William of Poitiers, II. xii, xxv: Davis and Chibnall, *Gesta Guillelmi*, pp. 118–19, 140–1. Eadmer, I: Rule, *Eadmeri*, p. 8. *Waltham Chronicle*, XIV: Watkiss and Chibnall, *Waltham Chronicle*, 24–7, but cf. XX, pp. 44–5. William of Malmesbury is studiously non-committal, writing only that the English said that Edward made a deathbed gift of the kingdom to Harold: William of Malmesbury, II. ccxxviii. 7, II. xxxviii. 1–4, III. ccxl. 2: Mynors *et al.*, *William of Malmesbury*, I. 418–21, 444–7, 452–3.

24 Especially the names of those present: *Vita Ædwardi*, II. xi: Barlow, *Vita Ædwardi*, pp. 118–19.

25 *Vita Ædwardi*, II. xi: Barlow, *Vita Ædwardi*, pp. 122–3.

commendo)' – must be understood in the light of a similar phrase in the account of the death of Harold's father Earl Godwine in 1053; at his obsequies the people fall into lamentation, remembering with sighs and abundant tears this the father, this the protector, of itself and the kingdom (*hunc patrem, hunc nutricium suum regnique*).[26] In their context, these words are as far as could be from implying that Godwine had sought the kingdom for himself; since his return from exile he and his sons had supported the king and given peace to the land. The similar phrases in Edward's deathbed charge can only mean that, for the *Life*, Harold was not himself given the kingdom but that, faithful to his promises to Duke William, Edward placed it under Harold's protection to be conveyed, as he too had promised upon oath, to William.

It must be conceded that the deathbed scene in the Tapestry will bear either interpretation – either that Edward gave the kingdom to Harold who proceeded to coronation, or that Edward charged Harold to protect the kingdom as his father had done, and to bring about William's succession; whereupon, having accepted Edward's charge, Harold forthwith did nothing of the sort but seized the kingdom for himself with the aid of his English supporters. However, in the Tapestry, the second interpretation has something to commend it. Not only does it compound Harold's guilt by having him deceive the dying Edward as well as Duke William, but it adds point to the reversal of the order of events. After Edward's body has been carried out for burial (Wilson, *BT*, Plates 29–30) there follows a scene in which Edward makes his deathbed dispositions, superimposed upon a representation of him as dead (**Plate 13**). In the next scene, Harold is given the crown (**Plate 14**). Harold receives it from two English followers, and the one offering the crown points downwards towards the dead Edward, not upwards to the deathbed scene. Harold's crowning follows from Edward as dead, not from Edward as alive and making his final testament. Significantly, both Harold and his other retainer hold large battle-axes. Harold owes the crown to no circumstances that have gone before but to a seizure of power facilitated solely by his own English followers. Next he sits in regality (**Plate 14**) but under the comet the emptiness of his power is manifest (Wilson, *BT*, Plates 32–3). The evidence of the *Life* of the Confessor may thus provide a vital clue to how the Tapestry presents the sequence and the significance of events.

The third portion of the Tapestry extends from the communication to William of the news of Harold's succession to the crown to the defeat of Harold at Hastings (Wilson, *BT*, Plates 33–73); the end of the Tapestry is lost through damage. It too has been discussed elsewhere.[27] So far as Harold is concerned, there is a marked change in the presentation of him after the adverse tone of the earlier sections. Harold's perjury and its penalty remain indelibly in the viewer's mind as a strong memory. The purpose of the Tapestry is no longer to moralize by showing Harold as a wicked man who pays the price of his duplicity. It is to tell a story of well-planned and hard-fought warfare for the most part waged honourably and valiantly by both sides even though the outcome is foreshadowed (Wilson, *BT*, Plates 31–3). Harold is four times described as *rex*, even in the scene showing his death (Wilson, *BT*, Plates 53–4, **Plate**

[26] *Vita Ædwardi*, II. v: Barlow, *Vita Ædwardi*, pp. 46–7.

[27] See Cowdrey, 'Towards an interpretation', in Gameson, *Study*, pp. 97, 103–7.

20, Wilson, *BT*, Plates 64–5, **Plate 23**). William, it should be noticed, remains *dux*; no doubt this does no more than use his correct title until his own coronation at Christmas 1066, but it serves to underline the renewed respect with which Harold is treated. The emphatic image of him before the battle is that of a noble warrior (**Plate 20**). Yet there is a final, telling detail. If, as is more than likely, the prostrate figure whose leg is being shamefully hacked by a Norman knight is indeed Harold, whose death is twice indicated in the arrow incident and in the mutilation, the two scenes point the nemesis that has overtaken him. In the latter Harold not only lies with his two hands limp and powerless but his battle-axe falls to the ground while his scabbard hangs uselessly down (**Plate 23**). The arms by which he came by the crown – the axe that he held and the sword that was proffered to him (**Plate 14**) – have been of no avail to save him.

It may be asked what light such a presentation of Harold sheds on the purpose of the Tapestry and of the public to which it was addressed. At first sight, the designer of the Tapestry seems to have had an eye to those in England who, after 1066, continued to honour Harold and his memory and to be restive against the regime of William the Conqueror. He seems to have focused on the memory of Harold as English sources were preserving it and to counter it by showing Harold in his true colours. This would correspond with the theory that the Tapestry was designed and executed in England and that its being taken to Normandy was a consequence of the fall from royal favour of Bishop Odo of Bayeux. On the other hand, it can be argued that the concentration, in the first part of the Tapestry, on events in Normandy indicates the envisaging of a public in the duchy. The Tapestry, after all, not only exhibits Harold as flawed by duplicity and perjury, but also proclaims Duke William's magnanimity, political authority, and military qualities; it establishes the moral and legal rightness of his claim to the crown of England.

It may be concluded that no clear answer emerges to the question of the purpose and public of the Tapestry, which keeps its secrets so far as these subjects are concerned. For the changed presentation of Harold in the third, longest, and visually most memorable portion of the Tapestry so that he is once again the noble warrior suggests that its overriding purpose was to tell a story – that of preparation for and the fighting of a great battle. The story is told for its own sake, and it is directed to all viewers, Normans, English and others, who will draw their differing conclusions according to their standpoint. Important though the first two portions are, they are preludes to the story of the battle, setting the stage and preparing observers for the hard-fought contest, waged heroically on both sides. The Tapestry thus succeeds in presenting Harold as the strong and powerful figure that English sources disclose him as being and nevertheless a flawed character who rightly experienced nemesis for his perjury and ingratitude to William; at Hastings he at once suffered a defeat which was made inevitable by his turpitude and also presented the Normans with a redoubtable opponent whose eventual defeat was the supreme triumph of their arms. For one thing is left in no doubt: the magnitude and decisiveness of the Norman achievement. Upon this the whole story of the Tapestry is centred.

The foregoing discussion has been concerned with the two topics of Harold and the Bayeux Tapestry considered together; the articles that follow for the most part consider them separately. The first four of them are about Harold. N. J. Higham and

Ian Howard write about the succession to the crown. For Higham this, rather than Harold's oath and perjury which are so prominent in the Tapestry and other propagandist sources, was throughout Harold's adult life in fact the mainspring of the English political process. He concedes that there is no clear evidence from earlier than the crisis of wintertide 1065–6 for Harold's candidature. Before it there can be little more than speculation. Nevertheless, the key issue of the decades before the Norman Conquest is how the over-mighty family of the Godwines interacted with the kingship at the centre of the political establishment. Harold's hasty coronation in January 1066 was less a sudden triumph than the ultimate realization of an ambition for the crown which had for long been harboured by a faction leader renowned for his subtlety and ability to keep his own counsel. Higham makes clear, however, and the point should perhaps be emphasized, that Harold's political role was not one of mere opportunism. As he interestingly documents, the greater families prudently refrained from pressing their differences to the point of out-and-out conflict, since they did not wish the country to be the more laid open to foreign invaders because they had destroyed each other. Like others, the Godwines were concerned to interact with a kingship and an Anglo-Saxon state which were institutionally strong and should not be lightly undermined. Harold's own personal wealth was important as conferring not only power but also credibility. By contrast with his main English contestant for the kingship, Edgar the Ætheling, he no doubt stood further from the claim of being of royal kin, but on grounds of age, resources and military qualities he more fully embodied the *utilitas* – the effectiveness and usefulness – for which contemporaries looked in the important elective element of eleventh-century kingship. The qualities that the Bayeux Tapestry conceded to Harold, and which other sources also highlighted, help to explain why he was able to come by the crown.

Higham discusses the succession mainly in terms of English history and politics; believing that historians have underestimated the Danish element in English affairs in the eleventh century, Howard seeks to correct the balance. He argues that Harold became king in 1066 not because he was the son of Earl Godwine but because through his Danish mother he was a descendant of the Gormsson kings in Denmark. As such he had a legitimate title to the English crown. There is admittedly little, if any surviving evidence to suggest that, *à propos* of the events of January 1066, either friend or foe referred to Harold's Danish descent; and as Howard illustrates, from an English point of view the Gormsson family did not have an encouraging record to which Harold might appeal. However, the elective element in Harold's succession was probably paramount. Such is suggested by the Bayeux Tapestry's location of Harold's receiving the crown between Edward's death with its pieties and Harold's own sitting in sacral regality. The crown-giving is wholly secular. Under the caption 'Here they [unidentified] have given to Harold the king's crown', two laymen with battle-axes give the crown to Harold, also in everyday dress and holding a battle-axe (**Plate 14**). Harold received the crown because of the choice of his followers in recognition of his military, political and personal suitability. Howard registers the valuable point that, so far as descent was concerned, Harold and his supporters may have taken into account his Danish family background and relationship to Cnut's line.

Two further studies of Harold have as their subject the legends of his survival after the Battle of Hastings. For the most part, historians have considered that, after his death there, he was buried in the collegiate church of the Holy Cross, Waltham, which he had founded.[28] Such is the record of the *Waltham Chronicle*, according to which, at the canons' request, Duke William allowed them to retrieve the body and give it honourable burial in their church. The *Chronicle* dismissed stories that Harold had survived to dwell in a hermit's cave at Canterbury or that when he died he was buried at Chester;[29] but such legends persisted. Gillian Fellows-Jensen discusses and edits three versions in Icelandic sources. Stephen Matthews considers the *Vita Haroldi*, an early-thirteenth-century compilation which historians have often dismissed as a historical romance of little value. From the angle of inquiry into the actualities of Harold's life and death this is scarcely to be denied; but, with its eulogy of Harold as earl and king to which Higham refers in his paper and with its presentation of Harold after Hastings as a devout hermit living near Dover who eventually died at Chester, the *Vita* is appropriately described by Matthews as belonging to a genre of 'secular hagiography'. Such legends of exemplary life, death and benefit to others could be both persistent and dangerous. One remembers Earl Waltheof, executed by William the Conqueror for his association with the rebellion of the earls in 1075 and quickly the subject of a cultus at Crowland Abbey.[30] Any such cultus must be forestalled by whatever undermining of character as Norman and Anglo-Norman sources brought to bear upon Harold. Of this, the Bayeux Tapestry is an example: its effect, and perhaps in part its intention, was to discredit a dangerous cult amongst a subject people. The survival stories disclose something of the thought-world of Norman and even Angevin times.

This thought-world is further explored in the rest of the papers in this book, which concern the Bayeux Tapestry. Sarah Larratt Keefer's subject is the horses of the Tapestry which have hitherto been relatively little written about. She begins by registering the important point that, since ancient times, depictions of such galloping horses as are a feature of the Tapestry have necessarily been artistically stylized and far from naturalistic. In general, therefore, the horses of the Tapestry offer abundant comment, direct or implied, on the persons and events that are depicted; they comment on both Normans and English. Thus, the changing fortunes of figures such as Harold are reflected in the mounts they ride – stallion, mare, gelding, mule – and the spurs and accoutrements they wear. The priapic stallions of the Tapestry behave in ways not known to nature; they refer less to the generative powers of the horse than to military prowess, valour and perhaps ambition of the rider. Keefer pays special attention to the mounted figure of Odo of Bayeux when, during the Battle of Hastings, holding a staff (*baculum tenens*), he encourages his young men in the fight (**Plate 22**). She considers that the *baculus* in Odo's hand implies a confusion of spiritual and secular; like the masculinity of his stallion, it symbolizes 'an *auctoritas* that is either out of control or being used for a self-driven goal instead of its appropriate one'. One can easily agree that the Tapestry assigns prominence to Odo, its probable patron, in the enterprise of invading England; arguably the Tapestry displays him in a clear and

28 For legends about Harold's burial see Watkiss and Chibnall, *Waltham Chronicle*, pp. xliv–xlvi.

29 *Waltham Chronicle*, XXXI: Watkiss and Chibnall, *Waltham Chronicle*, pp. 50–7.

30 For Waltheof see H. E. J. Cowdrey, *Lanfranc: Scholar, Monk, and Archbishop* (Oxford, 2003), pp. 189–91.

consistent way as acting upon a deliberate and open separation of spiritual and secular powers which he himself would have recognized and proclaimed. This is nowhere more clearly indicated than by Odo's own seal:[31] on the obverse, Odo is shown on horseback with coif (or conical helmet), staff,[32] and kite-shaped shield; on the reverse he is shown standing, tonsured, and holding in his left hand a crozier. In 1082 when Odo had fallen from royal favour, the distinctness of Odo's two powers could be used against him, when Archbishop Lanfranc is said to have advised King William to imprison him: 'You will not be seizing the Bishop of Bayeux but putting under guard the earl of Kent.'[33] At the time when the Tapestry was probably designed, that event was in the future; but in the Tapestry, Odo is arguably depicted as already acting with a division of powers that would have been acknowledged by most churchmen and lay persons in the Anglo-Norman lands.

The presentation of Odo in the Tapestry is more comprehensively discussed by Gale R. Owen-Crocker, especially in relation to his half-brother, Duke William. Odo has a prominence which is not evident in the Latin captions of the Tapestry, where William's leadership is duly acknowledged, nor, indeed, in the frequency with which Odo appears; for he does so only rarely (**Plates 15**, **16** twice, **22** and perhaps, as Owen-Crocker suggests, **9**). By implication, however, he has a leading role in counsel, feasting and warfare. In the scene in which counsel is taken about the building of invasion ships (**Plate 15**), for example, Odo sits higher than William, and it is Odo who seems to be instructing the shipwright. It is not surprising that this and other representations of Odo should display the invasion as in some respects a family consortium between William and his half-brothers Odo and Count Robert of Mortain, for such evidence as the ship-list of the Conqueror illustrates the scale of the brothers' stake in the enterprise.[34] Nevertheless, the prominence of Odo is by no means to the visual advantage of William; it suggests that the Tapestry sustains an undertone of rivalry between William and Odo.

Owen-Crocker further develops the case for this by suggesting that Odo's prominence is systematically pointed up by parallel interrelationships between the depictions of Odo and Harold, so that the fortunes of Odo form a sort of antitype to those of Harold. These interrelationships are so complex as to prompt the original suggestion that the Tapestry was designed as the inside of a square with approximately equal sides. The parallels visible across the square thus enhance the sequential relationships of adjacent scenes which have hitherto been the main way in which the Tapestry has been interpreted. The consequential possibility that the Tapestry was originally hung in a square building, such as a castle keep, with a spiral staircase in one corner, is developed by Chris Henige's paper, which proposes the Norman keep, with wooden walls, of Dover Castle as a potential *locus*. Since Dover Castle was subject to Odo's

31 *Sir Christopher Hatton's Book of Seals*, ed. L. C. Loyd and Doris Mary Stenton (Oxford, 1950), No. 431, p. 301 and Plate VIII.

32 The object that Odo is holding is not a sword, since it lacks the cross-guard that was necessary to protect the swordsman's hand. It is comparable to the *baculus* of the Bayeux Tapestry (**Plate 22**).

33 William of Malmesbury, IV. cccvi. 3: Mynors *et al.*, *William of Malmesbury*, I. 544–5.

34 Elisabeth M. C. van Houts, 'The ship list of William the Conqueror', *ANS* 10 (1988), 159–83, esp. 179.

authority as earl of Kent, the prominence that he was given visually and subliminally is readily explicable.

This suggestion calls for careful consideration. The developing narrative of the Tapestry inevitably encourages a sequential interpretation from scene to scene, and it is challenging to envisage a design that would also call for the viewer's eye constantly to cross from side to side of a square setting. Some of the parallels claimed by Owen-Crocker and Henige are *prima facie* more convincing than others. So far as Dover is concerned, the state of the keep in William the Conqueror's time is far from clear; one also asks whether the exhibition of the Tapestry is compatible with the military design, purpose and furnishing of a castle keep; and would the interior of a Norman keep have had enough light to view the Tapestry? Further discussion will no doubt clarify such matters.

The remaining four articles are concerned with particular, but important, subjects concerning the Tapestry; consideration is given to the borders which have received much attention in recent decades. Catherine E. Karkov studies how women are presented in the Tapestry as an aspect of its overall composition. She duly notes the paucity of references to them: only three women, all of them English, figure in the main story – the mysterious Ælfgiva (**Plate 8**), Queen Edith at the deathbed of her husband Edward the Confessor (**Plate 13**) and the unnamed woman who, after the Norman landing in England, flees with her child from a burning house (**Plate 17**); the margins yield only three further examples. The Tapestry belongs firmly to Marc Bloch's 'first feudal age', which in literary terms was an age of epic not romance.[35] It was very much a men's age in power, thought and feeling, so that the scant reference to women should occasion no surprise. Leaving aside Ælfgiva, it is worth noting that Edith is performing the acknowledged woman's duty of her age in mourning her dying husband; although special significance may attach to the gesture by which she emphatically points to her left hand: if the left hand is a symbol of the crooked and deceitful, she may be referring to the conduct of her brother Harold.[36] The fleeing Englishwoman is perhaps an example of the remarkable determination of the designer of the Tapestry to exhibit warfare in all its aspects – the cruelties and acts of dishonour as well as its glories, heroism and success.[37]

The comparability between the Tapestry and epic, especially the *chansons de geste* such as the *Chanson de Roland*, is the subject of Shirley Ann Brown's paper. She makes the important point that, in form, the relations between the main story and the borders in the Tapestry is like that between the *récit*, or main story, of epic convention and the *chant*, or commentary, which reflects upon the moral significance of the *récit* and which occasionally looks forward to future consequences. In substance, there is a similarity between the Tapestry and the *Chanson de Roland* in their characterization of the respective hero-villains Harold and Ganelon. This reinforces the argument that,

35 For the contrast between the first and second feudal ages, see M. Bloch, *La Société féodale*, 2 vols (Paris, 1949), I. 95–115: for the transition from epic to romance, see e.g. R. W. Southern, *The Making of the Middle Ages* (London, 1953), pp. 219–57.

36 See Cowdrey, 'Towards an interpretation', p. 102.

37 The hacking of the body of Harold by a Norman knight (**Plate 23**) is an example of knightly dishonour. Cf. William of Malmesbury, III. ccxliii: Mynors *et al.*, *William of Malmesbury*, I. 454–7.

in the Tapestry, the *récit* in which Harold is for long a noble character is progressively undermined by a *chant* that hints at the perfidy which led to his downfall. In this connection Brown offers an attractive discussion of the chained bear in the lower margin of a scene in which Duke William's messengers hasten to Count Guy of Ponthieu to negotiate Harold's release from captivity. Brown notes that, in the *Chanson de Roland*, the bear provides a metaphor for violence and betrayal. In the Tapestry it refers to Harold in respect of both character and predicament, for the bear, captive and defenceless, is being baited by a knight with sword and shield (**Plate 6**),[38] rather as Harold was subject to Count Guy's *force majeure* from which Duke William is delivering him. It might be added to Brown's discussion that the case for the bear as a reference to Harold is reinforced if related to the recent disarming of him by Guy after his capture (Wilson, *BT*, Plates 9–10). The dramatic tension is heightened because the bear, its teeth muzzled by its bonds, is being baited by an armed knight; its predicament comments on Harold's specifically between his disarming by Count Guy and his being re-armed by the generosity of Duke William (**Plate 10**). Perhaps the reversal of the order of events by which the dispatch of the messengers (**Plate 5**) is placed after their arrival in Ponthieu (Wilson, *BT*, Plates 10–13) is designed to add emphasis to William's generosity to Harold which he will disregard; and, if as is likely, in the light of usual practice, the bear has been blinded, can there be a distant foreshadowing of Harold's deserved wound in the eye at Hastings (**Plate 23**)? However this may be, Brown has demonstrated the effectiveness of the bear as marginal comment; but the very suggestiveness of the image also carries a warning against the danger (into which Brown does not fall) of allowing speculation about details of the Tapestry to run too far by building too much upon a small base or by letting imagination run away.

For some time now, historians have been aware of the importance of manuscripts associated with the Canterbury monasteries of Christ Church and St Augustine, especially the latter, as sources for the visual detail of the Tapestry and therefore of evidence connecting it with Canterbury. A fresh vein of evidence is explored by Cyril Hart. Showing admirably how evidence should be used, particularly for the understanding of the margins but also sometimes for visual detail in the main story, he establishes beyond reasonable doubt that certain Canterbury manuscripts of the so-called *Cicero-Aratea* and an accompanying planisphere were known to the Tapestry's designer. The case for a Canterbury origin for the Tapestry is thereby further strengthened.

Finally, Michael Lewis proposes a comprehensive consideration of the Tapestry as evidence for eleventh-century visual culture. This involves comparisons between material culture as depicted in the Tapestry with that found in contemporary art and that known through archaeological survival. He takes the three examples: conical helmets, details of ship design and the depiction of church buildings. It emerges that each subject must be explored according to its own peculiarities; thus, there is a strong case for crediting the Tapestry as a source for military helmets; in depicting

38 The baiting of a bear by a knight is unusual if not unique in medieval art and literature. A bear is baited by a man with a club in London, BL, MS Arundel 91, fol. 47v (**Fig. 15(d)**) but baiting is usually by dogs.

churches, established conventions of visual representation tended to prevail over direct observation. At present scholars would do well to guard against drawing overall conclusions about the Tapestry's factual reliability as evidence.

As in this case, so in general, although the articles hereafter assembled do not achieve full and final solutions to the subjects that are discussed, they do serve to illustrate respects in which the many problems that the study of the Tapestry raises may be addressed. They point the need for further careful observation and discussion of one of the richest and most fascinating documents of medieval history which is likely to provoke lively debate for many years to come.

Part I

King Harold II

2

Harold Godwinesson: the Construction of Kingship

N. J. HIGHAM

> To review the actions of the most illustrious and rightfully appointed King Harold, at this time duly and lawfully crowned, is nothing else than to display to pious minds a most brilliant reflection of a divine serenity and meekness.[1]

WITH these words the author of the early-thirteenth-century *Vita Haroldi* set himself to tell the story of one to whom he referred as 'Harold, Servant of God, formerly King of the English'. He wrote, of course, in the interest of Waltham Abbey, a house which Harold had effectively re-founded around 1060 and which consequently viewed him as its most prominent early patron. At Waltham, Harold's reputation clearly mattered, and he was portrayed both as a rightful king and subsequently, having miraculously survived Hastings, as a righteous hermit.

That this author should have felt it necessary to so defend Harold's reputation speaks volumes for the impact of William's biographers and propagandists, who, in the years following Hastings, set about undermining the legitimacy of his kingship. It is a portrait of the morally flawed ruler doomed by God's vengeance at his oath-breaking that emerges from these histories. Harold was, in the words of William of Jumièges, 'perjured in the fealty which he had sworn to the duke'.[2] William of Poitiers proclaimed him an 'insane Englishman' who had 'seized the royal throne with the plaudits of certain iniquitous supporters and thereby perjured himself', referring again to the same oath to William. Harold's greed had caused the tragedy of Hastings, he was both a fratricide and a usurper, and the appearance of Halley's Comet in the spring of 1066 was direct proof of God's wrath at his presumption.[3] The infamous oath, and so the charge of perjury, is particularly prominent in the Bayeux Tapestry's

1 *Vita Haroldi: the Romance of the Life of Harold, King of England*, ed. Walter de Gray Birch (London, 1885), p. 12, translation pp. 12–13. For a modern translation of the whole text, see Michael Swanton, *Three Lives of the Last Englishmen* (London, 1984), pp. 3–37. For a fresh discussion, see Stephen Matthews, 'The content and construction of the *Vita Haroldi*', in this volume. For the story of Harold's survival, which is a central feature of this text, see also Gillian Fellows-Jensen, 'The myth of Harold II's survival in the Scandinavian sources', in this volume.

2 William of Jumièges, *Gesta Normannorum Ducum*, ed. J. Marx (Rouen and Paris, 1914), p. 133; the translation is by Reginald Allen Brown, *The Norman Conquest: Documents of Medieval History* (London, 1984), No. 23 at p. 14.

3 Guillaume de Poitiers, *Histoire de Guillaume le Conquérant*, ed. and trans. Raymonde Foreville (Paris, 1962), pp. 204–8; the translation is by Brown, *Norman Conquest*, No. 49 at p. 26.

story of Harold's visit to William's court (**Plate 11**).[4] Here too, the narrative undermines the Anglo-Saxon's legitimacy as a crowned king, and so justifies the bloody campaign which brought William to the throne. Eadmer, writing at Canterbury in the 1090s, also emphasized Harold's oath to William concerning the succession. In consequence, the Norman victory was due to 'the miraculous intervention of God, who by punishing Harold's wicked perjury shewed that He is not a God that hath any pleasure in wickedness'.[5] Even the *Vita Ædwardi Regis*, commissioned by Queen Edith, remarked on the lightness with which Harold was prepared to support his own testament with his oath, even while elsewhere portraying him more generally as an outstanding military leader and civil governor, while other authors were less veiled in their condemnations once he was dead.[6]

Harold's oath to William mattered, clearly, and it has ever since cast a long shadow over his reputation. In the interests of balance, however, it might just be worth reminding ourselves of two things. Firstly, several near-contemporary authors did not mention it at all, and some even went out of their way to eulogize Harold and defend his kingship, as did John of Worcester,[7] for example. Secondly, most, if not all, of the eleventh-century élite perjured themselves at some time or another.[8] The accusation in most instances tells us far more about the perspective of the author than about the perpetrator, for such charges were a normal part of the stock in trade of political commentary at this date. Oaths mattered, certainly, as various late English law codes affirm,[9] but perjury was clearly not particularly uncommon. Had Harold survived Senlac Hill, this instance would have either been excluded from history, or discounted as made under duress. Emphasis on the oath was, therefore, very much an exercise in the construction of memory for political and dynastic advantage in the aftermath of victory.[10]

4 As Wolfgang Grape, *The Bayeux Tapestry* (Munich, 1994), p. 117.

5 Eadmer I. ix; G. Bosanquet, *Eadmer's History of Recent Events in England* (London, 1964), p. 9.

6 *Vita Ædwardi*, VII: Barlow, *Vita Ædwardi*, p. 81. 'Harold, rather too generous with oaths (alas!), cleared this charge too with oaths'; *Vita Ædwardi*, V: Barlow, *Vita Ædwardi*, pp. 48–52. A more damning charge is that of Orderic Vitalis (III. ii. 118), who accused Harold of having 'betrayed his faith to his lord [William] through greed for the kingdom': *Orderic Vitalis: Historia Ecclesiastica*, ed. and trans. Marjorie Chibnall, 6 vols (Oxford, 1969–80), II (1969). 137.

7 John of Worcester, 1066: *The Chronicle of John of Worcester*, ed. R. R. Darlington and Patrick McGurk, trans. Jennifer Bray and Patrick McGurk, 3 vols (Oxford, 1995–), II (1995). 601, which stresses Harold's legitimacy as king and virtue as ruler. To the author of the *Carmen*, Harold's principal crime was his fratricide, and oath-breaking passed unmentioned: Guy of Amiens, lines 130–9: *The Carmen de Hastingae Proelio of Guy Bishop of Amiens*, ed. and trans. Catherine Morton and Hope Muntz (Oxford, 1972), p. 11.

8 See, for example, Harthacnut's oath-breaking in 1041: *ASC* 1041 C (Abingdon Chronicle): *The Anglo-Saxon Chronicle MS C*, ed. P. W. Conner, *The Anglo-Saxon Chronicle: A Collaborative Edition*, ed. David Dumville and Simon Keynes (Cambridge, 1996). For translation see *The Anglo-Saxon Chronicle, Abingdon Manuscript (C)*, ed. and trans. Michael Swanton, p. 162. *John of Worcester*, for 1065 (Darlington and McGurk, p. 599), stresses the treachery with which Queen Edith ordered the killing on behalf of Tostig of northern nobles who had assembled in his chamber at York *sub pacis federe* ('under cover of a peace treaty').

9 See, for example, the Laws of Cnut, 36: *English Historical Documents*, ed. Dorothy Whitelock (London, 2nd ed., 1979), I. 460.

10 For a discussion of the construction of political memory in the late Anglo-Saxon period in western Europe, see Patrick Geary, *Before France and Germany: The Creation and Transformation of the Merovingi* (Oxford, 1988).

If we set aside this matter of Harold's perjury, therefore, how should historians view his path towards kingship? Over the last century or so, perceptions of his career have fluctuated wildly, from those who saw in Harold the last defence of Englishness against the iniquitous foreigner, to those for whom he was first and foremost a usurper who had attempted to deny the rightful heir.[11] If we look to modern works for guidance, the only recent book-length study of Harold, published in 1997, does confront the stereotype offered by William's apologists, but follows something of the line of the *Vita Haroldi*, as noted already. Ian Walker's Harold, not unlike that of Edward Freeman, is a brave and loyal, if somewhat greedy, servant of King Edward, whose designs on the crown irrupted only very late in the day. The stimulus was his recognition of the

> ruthless ambition and dangerous claims to the throne of England of William of Normandy, the knowledge of which transformed Harold's intentions and brought him to consider for the first time the possibility of his own succession to the throne.[12]

His act was a usurpation in this reconstruction, but only as regards his exclusion of Edgar the Ætheling, not William, and the decision to take the throne is construed as a patriotic one, made by a public-spirited man.

Whatever one might make of Edgar's claim – and it certainly seems to have been taken seriously between 14 October and the submission at Berkhamstead[13] – there is a danger here of portraying Harold in too naïve a light and as an unwitting victim of circumstances. There again, Walker's argument that Harold was imbued with remarkable personal qualities,[14] sits ill with the figure whom he portrays as so out of touch with contemporary politics that he had not even considered William's candidacy before visiting Normandy.[15] We fall, in addition, into the trap of telling history as if it were primarily composed of the deeds of successive great men.[16] This is, of course, a common weakness of historical biography, which focuses on the individual to the exclusion of the context, but this compulsion to portray Harold in a favourable light has led his story to be immunized against the more prosaic realities of power politics in the eleventh century, to which we might profitably return.

What can we say, therefore, about the construction of Harold's kingship, and, in particular, the genesis of his ambition to obtain the throne? Our problem is clearly one of evidence. Only in the winter of 1065–6 can we clearly identify Harold's candidature; prior to that, we can do little more than speculate. That said, the late emergence

[11] Contrast the general approach of Freeman (Edward A. Freeman, *Norman Conquest*, 2 vols (Oxford, 3rd ed., 1877), II *passim* but particularly 41–4), with David Douglas, *William the Conqueror* (Berkeley and Los Angeles, 1964), p. 182.

[12] Ian Walker, *Harold: the Last Anglo-Saxon King* (Stroud, 1997), p. 199.

[13] Use of the term *ætheling* presumably also reflects recognition that the king's half-great-nephew was king-worthy.

[14] Largely dependent, of course, on the pen portrait offered in the *Vita Ædwardi*, V.

[15] A view which is directly contradicted by the description of Harold in the *Vita Ædwardi*, V (Barlow, *Vita Ædwardi*, p. 51), as having 'studied the character, policy and strength of the princes of Gaul not only through servants but also personally . . .' so that 'he acquired such an exhaustive knowledge of them by this scheme that he could not be deceived by any of their proposals'.

[16] Walker, *Harold*, p. 201.

of evidence of Harold's ambition does not of itself constitute evidence of the lateness of that ambition, and this is a trap into which historians have often fallen, to their cost. What I propose, therefore, is to outline what might be termed 'the long view' of Harold's career, and ultimately his candidacy for the throne, against a wider picture of eleventh-century power politics, in the expectation that his position may become more intelligible via that process. Within that vista, Harold was himself a relatively minor player until the early 1050s, but he was serving his political apprenticeship during the previous decade. Even in the 1030s, as a junior member of one of the most powerful families in the land, Harold was presumably beginning to realize what high position, great wealth and influence actually meant, and also how transient they could be. Events then will also arguably have impacted on his later political personality. I propose to focus, therefore, on the vulnerability of this great late Anglo-Saxon family, its territorial interests and political influence in the face of successive shifts in the tenure of the crown. The key issue is how the particular position of this over-mighty family interacted with kingship at the centre of the political establishment during the decades before the conquest, when Harold was constructing his career. I will argue that the issue of the succession to Edward the Confessor was the crucial political question of the day throughout Harold's adult life, and that we can to some extent reconstruct the factors which will have influenced his thoughts on the subject over a lengthy time-scale. I will additionally argue that it is Harold's political career that should engage us, and that his eventual bid for the throne should be viewed very much in the context of his and his family's search for security, for themselves, for their political power and for their vast wealth. The late Anglo-Saxon period is littered with figures who had risen to positions of influence and wealth but had then signally failed to secure it for their successors. Godwine and Harold were among the most successful such men,[17] but the meteoric nature of Godwine's rise made the family exceptionally vulnerable. It was almost inevitable that any king intent on actually ruling would be drawn into confrontation at some point with so over-mighty a subject. As the author of the Worcester Manuscript of the *Anglo-Saxon Chronicle* remarked regarding the dynasty's expulsion by King Edward in 1051:

> It would have seemed remarkable to everyone who was in England, if anyone earlier told them that it should turn out thus, because he was formerly so very much raised up, as if he ruled the king and all England; and his sons were earls and the king's favourites; and his daughter was married and espoused to the king.[18]

Firstly then, let us turn to the family's experience of royal succession in the eleventh century. Tenure of the throne was highly contested throughout, and was by no means the sole preserve of one narrowly-defined lineage. Rather, there was a compar-

[17] For concise resumés of the careers of both Godwine and Harold, see Ann Williams' entries in *The Blackwell Encyclopaedia of Anglo-Saxon England*, ed. Michael Lapidge, John Blair, Simon Keynes and Donald Scragg (Oxford, 1999), pp. 212–13 and 228–9, which particularly highlights the 'immense wealth' which Harold had accrued as earl. His estates as earl at the start of 1066 are illustrated by David Hill, *An Atlas of Anglo-Saxon England* (Oxford, 1981), p. 103.

[18] *ASC* 1052 D (= 1051): *The Anglo-Saxon Chronicle MS D*, ed. G. P. Cubbin, vol. 6 of *The Anglo-Saxon Chronicle: A Collaborative Edition*, ed. David Dumville and Simon Keynes (Cambridge, 1996); Swanton, *Chronicle*, p. 176.

atively dispersed set of potential claimants, which brought a dangerous unpredictability to the issue.[19] Royal deaths and even serious illnesses, from Swein's in 1014 and Æthelred's in 1016, normally precipitated a struggle for the succession, with considerable dangers for any member of the élite who supported the losing side, or even whose support for the victor was conditional. Eadric Streona had, under Æthelred II, held power and lands equivalent to Godwine's a decade later, but was just the most prominent of a series of casualties of dynastic conflict in the early years of Cnut's reign, which also claimed the lives of Earl Uhtred of Northumbria and members of the families of the ealdormen of Wessex and the Hwicce. Thereafter, even the mighty Earl Thorkell was exiled.[20] Clearly, no single family below the king was safe, however wealthy or politically influential they might have become.

Cnut's death in 1035 began an extended succession crisis which was not resolved finally until 1042,[21] with the unenthusiastic acquiescence of the élite in Edward's candidacy. These events did much to educate Godwine and his sons in the dangers inherent in proximity to the throne without real control over its tenure. There were recurring patterns, too, to these conflicts. Godwine's experience will have demonstrated forcibly the extent to which an early advantage lay with a candidate who was within the realm. A leader like Harold I ('Harefoot'), who acted swiftly to claim the crown, could secure coronation, take possession of the royal treasure, mints and tax raising powers, command the king's housecarls and officers and establish his patronage of the political establishment. Those with power bases which were more distant took longer to mobilize and had little prospect unless they came with significant forces and could secure a considerable measure of internal support. In the event of Edward's death, intervention from overseas might be as slow to arrive as that attempted by Harthacnut, which was delayed so long that all insular enthusiasm for his cause had long since evaporated.

Another factor was the unity of the insular establishment. It is arguable that the fluidity with which the crown passed into and out of the line of Cerdic during the eleventh century originated from an incipient dynastic struggle sparked off by Æthelred's intention to prioritize the claims of his younger sons by Emma of Normandy over his elder family, led by Athelstan (died 1014) and then Edmund Ironside.[22] Following his father's expulsion and ruin by Æthelred's close associates in 1009,[23] the young Godwine was party to these contests, initially as an associate of Athelstan,[24] and then of Cnut, and will have grasped the dangers inherent in factional conflict within England in the context of the succession. There is good evidence that the political community as a whole learned the lesson of internal dissension well and was keen to avoid open warfare. The *Anglo-Saxon Chronicle* (C) account of the 1051–2 crisis stresses the unwillingness of either side to press their differences to a battle because 'they did not want that this country should be the more greatly laid

19 The interfamily relationships of the aristocracy at the time are set out in Ian Howard, 'Harold II: a throne-worthy king', in this volume; see the genealogies at **Figs 2** and **3**, pp. 48 and 50.

20 Nicholas J. Higham, *The Death of Anglo-Saxon England* (Stroud, 1997), pp. 62–89 and *passim*.

21 *ASC* 1035–42 CD: Swanton, *Chronicle*, pp. 158–63.

22 Higham, *Death*, pp. 41–59.

23 *ASC* E: Swanton, *Chronicle*, p. 138.

24 *Anglo-Saxon Wills*, ed. and trans. Dorothy Whitelock (Cambridge, 1930), No. XX, pp. 56–62, at p. 60.

open to foreign nations, should they themselves destroy each other.'[25] The *Vita Ædwardi* expressed very similar sentiments in the context of the Northumbrian revolt in 1065.[26] That said, however, there was little unanimity among the senior aristocracy, and the major families necessarily saw succession crises both as grave risks but yet opportunities to enhance their power *vis-à-vis* rivals. Godwine is, of course, the supreme example of an English thegn who rose meteorically to enormous wealth and exceptional influence by virtue of having gambled on the success of a particular candidate. No-one gained more from the consequent proscription of suspect faction leaders. Nor, however, had anyone greater reason to fear that other claimants to his numerous estates and offices might obtain influence at the court of an in-coming king.

What is more, Godwine's handling of succession crises looks far from adept. Despite having been Cnut's premier earl since *c.* 1023, he proved incapable of controlling events during the interregnum of 1035–7. In reality, in the face of a well-supported local candidate, he was unable either to protect his ally, the dowager queen, or oversee the accession of their candidate, her son Harthacnut, and found himself having to accept all too belatedly the accession of Harold I across all England.[27] Godwine survived with his wealth intact, as far as one can judge, but he had been seriously wrong-footed and cannot have been trusted by the new king, who had received active support from rival earls. His tardy and presumably costly accommodation with Harold I, and his part-responsibility for Ætheling Alfred's death then lost him any advantage when his former allies finally acquired power at Harold's premature death. Harthacnut's invitation to his elder half-brother Edward, who was at this date still in Normandy, arguably reflects his distrust of all three of the earls, including the man whom his father had raised up as vice-regent and massively enriched, on whom Harthacnut had himself earlier relied.

Harthacnut's death on 8 June 1042, at only about twenty-two years old and unmarried, threw the regime into crisis once more. It should be no surprise that on this occasion Godwine supported a candidate who was already *in situ*, rather than once again attempting to hold England, or southern England at least, for a Scandinavian claimant. Even so, Godwine must have sold his support with considerable trepidation to the favourite son of the man who had beggared his own family three decades earlier, and whose full brother he had himself helped to destroy in a particularly brutal way in 1036.[28]

Edward was crowned, therefore, at Easter 1043, but paid so high a price for Godwine's support that his independence of action was seriously compromised. In the same year Swein Godwinesson began to attest charters as earl,[29] having been established in the southern marches towards Wales. Harold was, at least on occasion, in attendance on the king by 1044 and, alongside Beorn, Godwine's nephew by

25 *ASC* C: Swanton, *Chronicle*, p. 176.

26 *Vita Ædwardi*, VII: 'in that race horror was felt at what seemed civil war': Barlow, *Vita Ædwardi*, p. 81.

27 *ASC* C: Swanton, *Chronicle*, pp. 158–60.

28 *Ibid.*

29 Simon Keynes, *An Atlas of Attestations in Anglo-Saxon Charters, c. 670–1066* (Cambridge, 1995), unpaginated.

marriage, was provided with an earldom in either 1044 or 1045. By that year, the names of Godwine and his close kin regularly comprised four out of the six attestations of the king's earls.[30] The final act of this political settlement occurred in January 1045, when Edward married Godwine's daughter, Edith. The earl of Wessex therefore emerged from this last succession crisis with his power at court massively enhanced and with his family's influence and estates vastly augmented, over against Earls Leofric and Siward as well as the crown. However, his share of responsibility for Ætheling Alfred's murder necessarily made him vulnerable to royal vengeance, whenever that might seem appropriate to Edward. The construction of kinship by marriage with the king perhaps reduced the risk but only an unassailable position within Edward's administration, such that could permanently curtail the king's capacity to act against him, could provide any sort of guarantee of security.

Godwine had, therefore, recovered his influence at court and tied the new regime to himself and his family, but his position was based not on the sort of friendship and trust which had characterized his relationship with Cnut, but on a pragmatic settlement necessitated by a series of political accidents. The king and his premier earl had underlying differences which were fundamental, and personal as well as political.

The young Harold, who is unlikely to have been born before about 1026, was a beneficiary of this process but had every reason to appreciate its inherent tensions. The earldom of East Anglia had been in abeyance for a generation, since Earl Thorkell's tenure early in the 1020s. It was now reconstituted for Godwine's second son, with Beorn Estrithson holding another new earldom in the east Midlands. There was no obvious threat to the region, other than the possibility of Magnus of Norway's arrival in force in the Channel, which Edward and his supporters awaited in vain at Sandwich in 1044.[31] The new earldoms look less like the necessary delegation to royal officers of local powers than part of the price paid by Edward for Godwine's support. Edward, already forty in 1045, was probably not expected to reign for long and we can, perhaps, see in these dispositions how his new father-in-law was preparing to manage the next succession crisis to his family's advantage, either via the long minority of a grandson by Queen Edith or, failing that, the accession of another member of his own family: Beorn Estrithson, perhaps, who was Cnut's sister's son.[32]

Harold's political career emerged, therefore, from the ultimately successful management of a long and bruising succession crisis by his father in his family's interest. The whole was an exercise in political pragmatism and dynastic politics. It would be implausible to imagine that this lesson was lost on any intelligent observer, let alone the major beneficiaries.

Harold's rise was also at the expense of rival families, in particular that of Earl Leofric, whose power and influence in central England was under considerable pressure from all three of the new earldoms.[33] It is recent practice to portray the great earls of the period as mutually co-operative, rather than competitive, but the appearance of

30 *Ibid.*

31 *ASC* C: Swanton, *Chronicle*, p. 164.

32 For the relationship, see Howard in this volume.

33 For a map of the earldoms *c.* 1045, see Hill, *Atlas*, p. 105.

common purpose arguably masks deep divisions.[34] Earl Swein's invasion of southern Wales in alliance with King Gruffydd of Gwynedd in 1046 illustrates the competition for power and regional influence between the major faction leaders.[35] Swein had replaced Leofric's authority in Herefordshire and Worcestershire, precisely where his family's lands and power had been concentrated a generation earlier on the ealdormanry of the Hwicce, and Leofric is most unlikely to have welcomed this. Gruffydd had himself earlier killed Leofric's brother Edwin.[36] This alliance had a relevance, therefore, not just to Welsh affairs but also to the competition for power among the English earls, and signals the extent to which the Godwine family was making alliances and taking the offensive against its rivals.

The late 1040s were arguably a critical period in the development of thinking on the succession among Godwine and his sons. By the closing years of the decade, the queen's failure to produce an heir presumably meant that the old earl's hopes of a grandson on the throne were beginning to fade. The obvious alternative was a Danish candidate, but Swein Estrithson was driven out by Magnus of Norway in 1047 and was become a lame duck candidate. Earl Swein's visit to both Flanders and Denmark and his break there with his namesake just a few months earlier is most easily interpreted as a major shift by both the Godwine family and Count Baldwin in their thinking regarding the English succession.[37] The alliance between Wessex and Flanders was confirmed by Tostig Godwinesson's marriage to the count's half-sister, Judith, in or before 1051.[38] On his return to England in 1049, Earl Swein carried out the premeditated murder of his cousin, Beorn,[39] so making the split with Denmark irredeemable. What the family proposed instead regarding the succession is not recorded, but the options were few and must have been thought through in detail. They certainly did not favour any of Edward's French connections, and had good reason to be suspicious of his patronage of the incomers who had built castles within the earldoms of both Swein and Harold. In 1049, Edward supported a German attack on Flanders, implying that he recognized the danger posed to himself by the alliance of Godwine and Count Baldwin.[40] Strife between the king and the earl irrupted in 1051, ostensibly over promotions to the vacant sees of Canterbury and London, and a fracas between Edward's brother-in-law, Count Eustace of Boulogne, and the men of Dover,[41] perhaps over plans for another castle there. In the absence of the Godwine

[34] The first view is most particularly that of Frank Barlow, *The Godwins* (Harlow, 2002), *passim*. Contrast Eric John, *Reassessing Anglo-Saxon England* (Manchester, 1996), p. 175. Given their support for different candidates in the succession crisis of 1035–7, it is difficult to imagine Earl Godwine and his sons having any real friendship towards, or trust in, Leofric or Siward, although in practical ways co-operation was often necessary.

[35] *ASC* C: Swanton, *Chronicle*, p. 164.

[36] *ASC* 1039 C (Swanton, *Chronicle*, p. 160), to which reference was made again in the Worcester Manuscript, *ASC* 1052 D: Swanton, p. 176.

[37] *ASC* D: Swanton, *Chronicle*, p. 169.

[38] *Ibid.*, p. 175.

[39] *Ibid.*, pp. 168–71.

[40] *Ibid.*, pp. 166, 168.

[41] *Ibid.*, p. 172.

family in exile, Edward renewed high-level contacts with Duke William, apparently depositing Godwine's hostages with him and perhaps offering him the succession.[42]

Given the lack of any other credible internal candidate, the possibility must be entertained that Godwine was, by the beginning of 1051, considering the candidacy of one of his own sons, despite the embarrassment caused by Earl Swein's outlawry in that year.[43] The family's collective domination of southern England, their vast wealth, the alliance with Flanders and arguably with Henry I of France as well, all strengthened Godwine's position. Swein's newly established military reputation, added to the family's connections via Gytha with Cnut and via Edith with Edward, might well have been thought sufficient to sustain a credible candidacy had Edward died around 1050.[44] The balance of power in both Scandinavia and north-west France was such that intervention from overseas was unlikely. In that context, the attitude of the primate was critical. Godwine had enormous influence in Kent, of course, and powerful connections with Canterbury's clergy. When Archbishop Eadsige died in October 1050, the community attempted to elect Ælric, who was one of Godwine's relations.[45] However, in full council, the king appointed his Norman associate, Robert of Jumièges, whom he had previously made bishop of London. Edward's determination to deny Godwine a complacent family member as archbishop at Canterbury may well have had as much to do with the succession as with Godwine's acquisitiveness in Kent, for this post was crucial to any ambition which the earl may have entertained regarding the throne.

The family recovered from their exile in 1051–2, returning with the help of Count Baldwin, Henry I, Diarmid, king of Leinster and the Dublin Norse, plus the active support of the ship-men and thegns of the southern coastal shires.[46] Edward's alliance, constructed from the northern earls, various southern nobles, whom he had promoted, and his Norman connections, proved insufficiently cohesive or robust to exclude Godwine, and neither side was prepared to risk all-out war. Many of Edward's French friends were in turn forced into exile, Archbishop Robert among them, so undermining any potential French or Norman candidacy for the succession that Edward may have entertained. Even so, Edward's nephew, Ralf the Timid, and Odda of Deerhurst retained their new earldoms in the compromise settlement of 1052,[47] limiting Godwine to the eastern half of Wessex, where his dynasty had its deepest roots. Earl Swein absented himself on pilgrimage to Jerusalem, but this need not indicate any long-term withdrawal from recent ambitions. Rather, his journey

42 ASC 1052 D (= 1051: Worcester Manuscript) (Swanton, *Chronicle*, p. 176), claims that William visited Edward. It was a central feature of the Norman claim that Edward had offered William the succession and this is often interpreted as the likeliest occasion but there is no other evidence and the duke was on campaign far from the Channel throughout much of the year. William certainly held English hostages in 1066 but they could have been delivered to his custody by Archbishop Robert *en route* to Rome to collect his pallium, in which case that equally might have been the occasion on which the offer was made.

43 *ASC* 1048 E (= 1051; Peterborough Manuscript): Swanton, *Chronicle*, p. 174.

44 For Gytha's connection with Cnut, see Howard, in this volume.

45 Nicholas Brooks, *The Early History of the Church of Canterbury* (Leicester, 1984), p. 303.

46 *ASC* C: Swanton, *Chronicle*, p. 178.

47 For the relationship between Ralf and Edward, see Howard in this volume.

could be read as a particularly ostentatious search for absolution after Beorn's murder, or perhaps as Godwine's attempt to keep his unruly eldest son out of sight of the English court for the time being. His death *en route* could not have been anticipated but it was this unexpected incident, then Godwine's sudden demise in April 1053, which left Harold as the principal beneficiary of his family's recovery of power.

Harold became, therefore, earl of eastern Wessex in 1053, following a sequence of dramatic changes, both positive and negative, in his own political position since 1044, which can only have reinforced earlier lessons concerning the fragility of power beneath the crown. With only a single earldom now held by the family, his position at this point was far weaker than his father's had been at the beginning of the year, and any thoughts about the succession which he and his father may have entertained, had necessarily to be shelved. Odda held the south-west, Leofric and his son now held two great earldoms dominating central England, while Ralf held the south-western Midlands. In the north, Siward's successful invasion of Macbeth's Scotland in 1054, backed by a contingent of Edward's housecarls and a naval force, underlined the pretensions of another great family to influence and prestige. Harold and his remaining brothers were untried, but they had their father's political legacy and his well-founded affinity and probably the more regular attendance at court,[48] where Edith arguably also wielded considerable influence.[49]

Harold strove to restore the family's dominance, of course, and Edith arguably aided him, initially at least. Earl Siward was given precedence among the earls in the attestation list appended to an agreement between Bishop Wulfwig and Earl Leofric,[50] but the old earl died without adult male heirs in 1055 and Harold and/or Edith secured Northumbria for their brother Tostig. Also in 1055, Leofric's son, earl Ælfgar of East Anglia, was exiled,[51] presumably because he had resisted this decision, but his father, Leofric, retained a significant power. Moreover, Gruffydd ap Llywelyn secured the south of Wales in the same year, so effectively uniting the several petty kingdoms under his own rule. He now allied himself with Ælfgar, burnt Hereford and secured the earl's restoration,[52] and the two formed a marriage alliance via Ælfgar's daughter, Ealdgyth (sometimes Edith), so establishing a new, Mercian-Welsh coalition in opposition to the Godwinessons. On Earl Odda's death in August 1056,[53] Edward re-amalgamated western with eastern Wessex under Harold, perhaps to act as a counterweight to Ælfgar and his Welsh allies, whom he certainly had no reason to favour. Around 1056, therefore, under the king, power was relatively evenly divided between the two great dynasties of Godwine and Leofric, with Gruffydd in control of all Wales and newly linked to the latter's family by marriage to Ælfgar's daughter.

48 Note Godwine's death at court, while at supper with the King, Harold and Tostig, at Easter 1053 in Winchester: *ASC* 1053 C: Swanton, *Chronicle*, p. 182. John of Worcester, 1053: Darlington and McGurk, *The Chronicle of John of Worcester*, pp. 572–3.

49 Barlow, *Godwins*, p. 52.

50 Keynes, *Atlas*. Peter Sawyer, *Anglo-Saxon Charters: An Annotated List and Bibliography* (London, 1968), No. 1478, p. 413.

51 *ASC* D (Worcester Manuscript) (Swanton, *Chronicle*, p. 185), claimed that Ælfgar was 'wellnigh without fault'.

52 *Ibid.*, pp. 86–7.

53 *Ibid.*, p. 186.

Without the luxury of a 'king's party' of any real substance outside these power blocks, Edward was necessarily associated closely with the Godwinessons, who clearly relished the opportunity to portray themselves as his loyal subjects and supporters even while steering the regime in their own interests.[54]

By 1053, Edward and Edith were most unlikely to produce an heir. King Henry I of France's hostility to a Norman succession effectively neutralized Duke William. Once Godwine was dead, his family were, temporarily at least, ill-placed to try and secure the succession for one of their own. The English court seems, therefore, to have sought a compromise candidate acceptable to all of Edward, Siward, Harold and Leofric, around whom the establishment could close ranks. The mission to bring back from Hungary Edward's half-nephew, Edward the Exile, began in 1054 and culminated in 1057 with his arrival at London,[55] but he died virtually upon arrival. Edward the Exile left a son, Edgar, then aged only about five, who presumably became a ward of the crown. However, Harold's need for such compromises regarding the succession was diminishing, for Leofric, then Ralf, died in the same year, and Harold was presumably at least complicit in the outlawry of his rival Ælfgar, for a second time, in 1058.[56] The political situation changed dramatically in Harold's favour, therefore, between *c.* 1056 and 1059, less by virtue of his own actions than by an accumulation of political accidents which conferred on him the role of senior earl, plus facilitating the promotions of his brothers Leofwine and Gyrth to earldoms. With four earldoms held by the family, Edward the Exile will have seemed far less necessary to Harold than would have been the case in the political circumstances of 1054. Indeed, we should not necessarily assume that this in-comer would inevitably have succeeded had he lived and the Confessor died in the late 1050s.

The attestations appended to King Edward's charters in favour respectively of Bishop Ealdred and St Denis in 1059 graphically illustrate the new order, with Godwine's sons making up four out of five of the earls, the singular exception being Ælfgar, at number two.[57] Harold, his sister and his brothers were very much in control of the court and had secured influence throughout the bulk of England, with, in addition, many of the sees and major monasteries held in their interest by their clerical allies. It is in 1059 that we first see Harold attesting royal charters as premier earl, although his primacy arguably stemmed from Leofric's death in September 1057.

Had the Godwinessons succeeded in excluding the house of Leofric entirely, as they apparently intended, the succession was effectively theirs to bestow as they saw fit, and it is difficult to imagine any other candidate than one of themselves by this date, provided only that they could agree. However, the alliance of Earl Ælfgar with Gruffydd of Wales and a Norwegian fleet was sufficient for him to regain Mercia and demonstrate the potential for outside interference.[58] Leofric's family seems to have been too deeply entrenched in the patronage systems of the north-western Midlands

54 E.g. John, *Reassessing*, p. 186.

55 John of Worcester, 1057: Darlington and McGurk, *Chronicle of John of Worcester*, pp. 582–3.

56 *ASC* D: Swanton, *Chronicle*, p. 188.

57 Keynes, *Atlas*.

58 *ASC* 1058 D: Swanton, *Chronicle*, p. 188. The Welsh tradition suggests that Magnus and Gruffydd 'ravaged the kingdom of England', but that may be an exaggeration: *Brut y Tywysogyon*, ed. and trans. Thomas Jones (Cardiff, 1952), p. 14 [1056–1058].

to be excluded without recourse to a damaging civil war, which Harold apparently did not wish to set in motion. Although we have no way of knowing the detail, Ælfgar presumably had his own views on the succession and we can safely assume that he would not have shared Harold's agenda, any more than his father had earlier agreed with Godwine on such issues. His alliance with a Norwegian fleet commanded by Hardrada's son presages Harold Hardrada's descent on England in 1066, and the possibility that the Mercian earl intended to support an external candidate must be taken seriously.[59]

On the continent, the deaths of the count of Anjou and Henry I left William virtually unopposed in north-west France, and destroyed any real hope that Harold may have entertained of restraining the duke via the threat of invasion from his immediate neighbours. In England, however, Ælfgar's death around 1062 enabled Harold and Tostig to destroy Gruffydd in 1063 and both to enhance their own military reputations and establish princes beholden to themselves in Wales.[60] However, the regional dominance of the rival dynasty was such that Ælfgar's young son, Edwin, was appointed to his father's earldom, and he still retained some influence among the Welsh. Edward may well, of course, have seen the danger to himself and his kingship of removing the last serious bar to Harold's ambitions and acted accordingly. Although he had seriously weakened his rivals, therefore, Harold had still not disposed of Leofric's family and their potential to welcome into England an external candidate capable of fighting for the throne. Nor was the reduction of Wales secure in the long term, as the massacre of Harold's workmen at Portskewett in 1065 demonstrated.[61] The king was now elderly, and the issue of the succession was pressing, but there arguably seemed little likelihood of any agreement between Godwine's sons and Leofric's grandsons regarding this crucial matter.

Harold seems to have entertained several options as regards the succession at this date, and it is very much in character that he kept his deliberations to himself.[62] There were three potential internal candidates, the child Edgar, Tostig and himself. Harold was in a far stronger position then he had been around 1054, when he countenanced Ætheling Edward's return from exile, and there is no evidence that he seriously considered reviving the compromise which had then been on his agenda on behalf of the latter's young son. Nor had Edward made any obvious move to establish Edgar, who seems to have been placed in the Queen's care.[63] Tostig may have thought of himself as a potential candidate, and there are hints that Edith might have given her support,[64] but that can have had little appeal for Harold. His own candidacy was the obvious alternative from his perspective, given his personal standing and seniority as

59 Higham, *Death*, p. 143.

60 *ASC* 1063 E (Peterborough Manuscript): Swanton, *Chronicle*, p. 190. John of Worcester, 1063–4: Darlington and McGurk, *Chronicle of John of Worcester*, pp. 592–3, 596–7.

61 *ASC* 1065 D (Worcester Manuscript): Swanton, *Chronicle*, p. 191.

62 *Vita Ædwardi*, V: 'With anyone he thought loyal he would sometimes share the plan of his project, sometimes defer this so long, some would judge – if one ought to say this – as to be hardly to his advantage': Barlow, *Vita Ædwardi*, p. 49.

63 Barlow, *Godwins*, p. 59.

64 The *Vita Ædwardi*, VII (Barlow, *Vita Ædwardi*, pp. 76–83), implies that Tostig was favoured above his brothers by both Edith and Edward, but not necessarily as heir.

earl, his leadership of the family, his dynastic connections with both Cnut and Edward, his wealth and influence across so much of England,[65] and his close relations with many of England's senior churchmen. However, even if Tostig were acquiescent, Leofric's family retained the power to disrupt the internal unity which was a central requirement of any such plan. Harold had either to gain their support or risk their providing an entrée to an external candidate, with all the dangers that that would entail.

A very different option was to ally himself by marriage with William of Normandy, much as Godwine had done with Cnut and then Edward. He might then hope to be left as premier earl by a king whose other responsibilities would have required his frequent absence on the continent; but, as Godwine and his sons had discovered in 1051, marriages could be repudiated and even the most pliant king might attempt to assert himself.[66] The initiative would always lie with whoever held the crown. Harold will have been able to gauge the prospect for himself when he visited William's court, perhaps in or about 1064, and will arguably have concluded the duke to have been an ambitious and proud man, under whom the role of over-mighty subject could well be adjudged perilous. The risks were considerable in every case.

Harold's decision can be reconstructed from the outcome. At some point between 1063 and 1066, and probably later rather than earlier, Harold married Earl Leofric's grand-daughter, Edwin's sister, Ealdgyth, the widow of Gruffydd of Gwynedd. It is difficult to imagine a more cynical dynastic alliance, given Harold's own responsibility for her recent widowhood. Whether this was before or after the northern rebellion of the autumn of 1065 is unknowable, but at that point Harold's purpose at last becomes clear. To Edward's impotent indignation, he sacrificed the earldom of his brother Tostig in order to construct an alliance of mutual political interest with Leofric's grandsons. Edwin and Morcar gained power across the north, securing Northumbria, which had traditionally allied itself with their family earldom in matters of succession for a century and more. They gained also the reassurance of a marriage alliance with Harold, which might yield them in the future a nephew on the throne. He, of course, obtained their acquiescence in his candidacy for the throne, and, with Tostig forced into exile, could at last promote himself as the agreed internal candidate of the entire political establishment within England. Over the year 1066, the commitment shown by Edwin and Morcar to resisting invasion clearly justified his stance.[67] From this point, Harold could abandon the Norman connection with which he seems to have flirted while at William's court, and await the death of the old and failing king, confident that all the advantages of the internal candidate would be his when Edward died. None of this was lost, of course, on Edward himself, whose will had plainly not prevailed over those winter months.[68] Contemporary commentators

65 For the extent of the Godwinesson earldoms in 1065, see Hill, *Atlas*, p. 105.

66 Edward sent Edith to Wherwell nunnery when he exiled her kinsmen: *ASC* DE: Swanton, *Chronicle*, p. 176, replicating the practice of Edward the Elder and later Edgar.

67 The point is made very effectively by Orderic Vitalis, III. ii. 119: 'The Earls Edwin and Morcar, sons of the great Earl Ælfgar, were close friends and adherents of Harold and gave him every help in their power; for he had taken to wife their sister Edith [Ealdgyth]': Chibnall, *Historia* II. 139.

68 *Vita Ædwardi*, VII: Barlow, *Vita Ædwardi*, p. 80.

treated the whole matter of the death-bed bequest with great caution, as is graphically illustrated by the C and D manuscripts of the *Anglo-Saxon Chronicle* for 1065:

> However, the wise man [Edward] committed the kingdom to a distinguished man, Harold himself, a princely earl, who at all times loyally obeyed his superior in words and deeds, neglecting nothing of which the nation's king was in need.

Whether this should be read in terms of a regency or the kingship itself is, of course, highly debated,[69] but none could argue that Edward was ever likely to be enthusiastic about Harold's ambitions, and whatever legitimacy he ultimately lent his brother-in-law was from necessity, not of his own volition.

If we are to sum up then, how should we view the construction of Harold's kingship? We should certainly try to get behind the rhetoric resonating from both sides around the dispute between Harold and William in 1066, and view it instead as a political struggle contested by several powerful leaders, set against a complex and fast changing political backdrop which caused the advantage to slip backwards and forwards over time. Harold's aims grew out of the changing agendas pursued by Godwine and his sons across several decades. The principal purpose throughout was arguably both to maximise and to secure their vast wealth and territorial power, but that ambition was necessarily inseparable from the politics of the crown. The family was central to the royal succession from 1035 onwards, and the issue proved highly dangerous to them, bringing them to the edge of disaster on several occasions. This was the most substantial political matter of the day and no-one in Godwine's position could either ignore it or be ignored by the various contestants. Godwine presumably hoped, in 1043, that the marriage that he had engineered between Edith and Edward would eventually place his own grandson on the throne. When that aspiration failed, it would not have been a radical departure for him to consider one of his own sons as a claimant. After Beorn's murder, it is difficult to imagine Godwine supporting any other candidate, particularly once Edward had made clear his own preference for a Norman successor.

With both Godwine and Swein dead in the early 1050s, Harold pursued a pragmatic policy designed to re-build the dominance which his father had secured, and this he achieved in the winter of 1057. In the meantime, he was apparently content to put his weight behind the candidacy of Edward the Exile, through whom he could reasonably have expected to maintain his position and wealth, at least in the short term. The option to claim the throne himself may well have been under consideration by Harold and his closest associates even before the returning claimant had died, but we are not privy to their private discussions, any more than to his father's. We are, however, to his deeds. From 1055 onwards, the royal council acted against Harold's principal rival for power inside England, using legal practices to target earl Ælfgar, Leofric's son. Success could have secured Harold's position and enhanced his political power, including the power to seize the throne on Edward's death. This proved difficult, however, so, when the opportunity presented itself, Harold turned about face

69 See, for example, John, *Reassessing*, p. 188, who argued that Edward withheld support, versus Frank Stenton, *Anglo-Saxon England* (Oxford, 3rd ed., 1971), p. 580, who interpreted the deathbed bequest as valid. See also H. E. J. Cowdrey in the introductory article to this volume.

and constructed a settlement with Ælfgar's sons and the political communities of the northern earldoms, which was capable of delivering the same outcomes. He sacrificed to this purpose the rank and position of his brother Tostig, and with it any last chance of Flemish support, but William had arguably already worked to un-pick the alliance between the Godwine family and Flanders. Harold had learned to be pragmatic during a long apprenticeship, and his new strategy of accommodation worked well. Early in 1066, he achieved the crown with as much support from the political establishment in England as he could reasonably have hoped for, and with the acquiescence, or at least the appearance of acquiescence, of the old king.

Was Harold merely opportunistic in the late autumn of 1065, as most historians have assumed, or was his role in fact more sinister? There is some slight evidence that he was believed at the time to have actively encouraged the northern rebellion against Tostig. The author of the *Vita Ædwardi* is our only witness and he was understandably cautious in making such an accusation:[70]

> It was also said, if it be worthy of credence, that they [the rebels] had undertaken this madness against their earl at the artful persuasion of his brother, Earl Harold (which heaven forbid!). But I dare not and would not believe that such a prince was guilty of this detestable wickedness against his brother. Earl Tostig himself, publicly testifying before the king and his assembled courtiers, charged him with this; but Harold, rather too generous with oaths (alas!), cleared this charge too with oaths.

Clearly, the author both believed Harold to have fomented the rebellion for his own purposes and wished to persuade others of that fact, so placing responsibility for the collapse of the Godwinessons firmly on his shoulders. This presumably reflects Edith's view of events, and she was apparently partial to Tostig, so we cannot accept this entirely at face value. However, the accusation was arguably real enough, whatever the reality behind it, so it is fair to argue that Harold was suspected of designs on the crown even before the northern rebellion broke out. Had his marriage to Edwin's sister already occurred, such seems quite plausible, and in keeping with what else the *Vita* tells us about his character.

All the paths open to Harold had risks attached. Had he supported William's claim, there can be no certainty that he would have retained his wealth and influence once the new king established himself. Taken together, the lands of Harold and his siblings in 1066 were very similar in value to those of the crown,[71] and it is difficult to imagine that any incoming ruler would be comfortable with such a state of affairs. Nor would Edgar necessarily have been prepared to rule as his cipher once he had attained manhood. The strategy that Harold finally adopted had considerable

70 *Vita Ædwardi*, VII: Barlow, *Vita Ædwardi*, pp. 78–80. In contrast, Stenton (*Anglo-Saxon England*, p. 579) believed that the Northumbrian rebellion weakened Harold's candidacy, perhaps following Freeman, *Norman Conquest*, II. 503.

71 As illustrated by Hill, *Atlas*, p. 105, but an upward re-evaluation of royal assets in 1066 may be necessitated by new work by Stephen Baxter. See also Barlow, *Godwins*, pp. 60–61, who suggests the Godwines might have had more than the king. The combination of the estates of Leofric's grandsons with Godwine's sons exceeded those of the crown in value in 1066, which fact presumably influenced Harold's decision to ally himself by marriage with Earl Edwin.

strengths, delivering him an England comparatively united behind his own candidacy, with time to secure the benefits of the mantle of kingship before external candidates could intervene. Tostig's exclusion removed the one member of his own family who had the potential to contest his candidacy. The settlement with Leofric's grandsons and exclusion of Tostig effectively removed the need to raise Edgar to the throne as a neutral figure of unimpeachable royal descent. Harold moved with almost indecent haste to undergo the rite of coronation, he took over royal patronage and power, took immediate and effective control of the treasury and mints and in all respects positioned himself as king. His coronation should, however, be viewed less as a sudden triumph than as the ultimate fulfilment of ambitions long kept reined-in by a faction leader who was renowned for his subtlety and ability to keep his own counsel.[72]

There were factors, of course, that lay outside Harold's control. One was Edward's longevity, which required him continuously to rethink his position over a decade and more. Another was the situation in France, where, during the mid-1060s, the king was a minor under Baldwin's guardianship. A Norman invasion was therefore a real possibility, but the speed with which William might assemble and trans-ship his forces was unknowable (in the event it took nine months). In the circumstances, Harold did what he could, sending out spies to gather information along the Channel, and making ready forces with which to confront the expected invasion.

Despite the advantages of hindsight, it is difficult to propose any strategy better capable of guaranteeing the wealth, political power and eminence Harold already enjoyed during the last years of Edward the Confessor. His candidacy for kingship should be weighed not against some measure of principle, for few seriously doubt that he attempted a usurpation, but against his probable objectives and the available alternatives. Of course Harold's dynastic claim was fragile, albeit no more so than William's. Yet, even in these circumstances, the smoothness of his accession in January 1066 should be recognized as evidence of the political skills which he had brought to the construction first of his own dominance of Edward's court then, ultimately, of his candidacy to be accepted as Edward's heir. When he first adopted this strategy as his own must remain unclear, but the ideas underpinning it arguably stretch back to the machinations of his father in the 1040s, and perhaps even to a consciousness of Cnut's triumph in 1016.[73] In early January 1066, it must have seemed in England and across parts of the continent that his candidacy had a very good chance of success.

72 See note 62.

73 Harold had presumably heard numerous stories of Cnut's rise to power from his father and his associates, given that it was the foundation stone of his family's fortunes. For comments on Cnut's later reputation, with which Harold's might usefully be paralleled, see Jan Gerchow, 'Prayers for King Cnut: The Liturgical Commemoration of a Conqueror', in *England in the Eleventh Century*, ed. Carola Hicks (Stamford, 1992), pp. 219–38.

3

Harold II: a Throne-worthy King

IAN HOWARD

THE Danish Conquest of England was accomplished fifty years before the Norman Conquest but its socio-political consequences have received inadequate attention for a variety of reasons. One important result of this is that it is not fully appreciated that, fifty years after the Danish Conquest, William of Normandy conquered Anglo-Danish England not Anglo-Saxon England. In this important fact is to be found the answer to many of the problems associated with questions of royal legitimacy and the loyalty of the noble families in England during the period from the death of Edward the Confessor in 1066 to the death of St Cnut of Denmark some twenty years later in 1086.

The Norman Conquest is generally recognized as the watershed between Anglo-Saxon history and what must be termed 'English History' for want of a better description. The names of the English kings are numbered from the Norman Conquest so that, for instance, the Anglo-Saxon Edwards are ignored. The English noble families were wont to trace their ancestry to the Norman Conquest and English institutions were deemed to date from the same occurrence. That stark view of the Norman Conquest has been amended so that we now recognize that many established institutions, both social and economic, were taken over by the Normans and slowly transformed to suit changing circumstances; but few would question that Anglo-Saxon England came to an end in 1066 and that Harold II was the last Anglo-Saxon king. It follows from this that Harold was elected king because he was the leading member of the most powerful Anglo-Saxon family in England, a family that had striven to control the country for its own benefit throughout the long reign of King Edward the Confessor. Nick Higham argues the case for this traditional view of events very persuasively in this volume and elsewhere.[1] Yet the generally accepted view leaves too many unanswered questions and it seems particularly strange that the last Anglo-Saxon king should not have an Anglo-Saxon name and, indeed, may have been named after King Cnut's grandfather, King Harold Gormsson, sometimes known as 'Bluetooth'.[2]

1 N. J. Higham, *The Death of Anglo-Saxon England* (Stroud, 1997).

2 Harold's father, Earl Godwine, married the Danish heiress Gytha, a close relative through marriage of King Cnut and herself probably descended from the Danish and Swedish royal families. It is more than a coincidence that Earl Godwine's eldest children should be given the Danish names Swein, Harold, Tostig and Gunnhild. 'Swein' was King Cnut's father, 'Harold' was King Cnut's grandfather, and

For many years after the Battle of Hastings William the Conqueror struggled to control his new kingdom, yet he allowed the heir of the West Saxon house of Cerdic, the Ætheling Edgar, to survive as a member of his household and took him back into his household after he had allowed himself to be used as a figurehead during English rebellions. He treated Edgar rather like an unruly relative and there are parallels with William's treatment of his eldest son, Robert, who was also induced to rebel from time to time.[3] By contrast, William took very seriously the pretensions of King Swein Ulfsson of Denmark to the English throne. King Swein was half-hearted in his attempts to capture the throne of England[4] and he had a long history of campaigning on land and on sea with a singular lack of military success.[5] Yet many Englishmen, particularly in the north of England, were prepared to rise in his support and William's devastation of the north of England, in 1069–70, was aimed at extinguishing that support. After Swein's death, the threat of an invasion by his son, Cnut (the future St Cnut), was sufficient to make William go to extraordinary lengths to prepare his defences and it was probably the need to finance the defence of England that led to the creation of *Domesday Book*. William's reaction is in marked contrast to St Cnut's endeavours, since St Cnut was no more decisive than his father and his invasion force dispersed without attempting to conquer England. This raises a question as to why the kings of Denmark were able to exert such an influence on events in England, especially when they had such a poor and indecisive campaign record. Their influence pre-dates the Norman Conquest so that, during the reign of Edward the Confessor, the *Anglo-Saxon Chronicle* deemed it important to record that Edward had refused to provide King Swein Ulfsson with a fleet when he had requested one. The Chronicler does not explain why King Swein expected his request would be met; it assumes that his contemporaries would know.[6]

Our understanding of events is enhanced if it is acknowledged that William of Normandy conquered Anglo-Danish England, not Anglo-Saxon England. However, it is evident that William had a vested interest in disguising this fact. He was related to King Edward the Confessor but William's relationship was only of real value if Edward was regarded as the legitimate heir to the last Anglo-Saxon king, Æthelred II; not if Edward was the heir to his brother, the Danish King Harthacnut. This explains William's treatment of King Edward's great-nephew, the Ætheling Edgar. The

'Gunnhild' was the Danish name given to King Cnut's Slav mother; see Ian Howard, *Swein Forkbeard's Invasions and the Danish Conquest of England 991–1017* (Woodbridge, 2003), pp. 73–4 and p. 10, Fig. 2.

3 F. M. Stenton, *Anglo-Saxon England* (Oxford, 3rd ed., 1971), pp. 608–9.

4 Stenton, *Anglo-Saxon England*, pp. 603–5.

5 *Magnús konungs góða* (*King Magnus the Good*), XXV, XXIX–XXXIII: *Haraldz konungs harðràða* (*King Harold Hardrada*), XXXIV, XXXV, LVIII–LXIV: *Snorri Sturluson: Heimskringla, Nóregs Konunga Sogur*, ed. Finnur Jónsson (Copenhagen, 1911), pp. 436, 438–44, 467–70, 482–9. All references to *Heimskringla* are taken from this edition. There is also a multi-volume version with full critical apparatus: *Heimskringla, Nóregs Konunga Sogur af Snorri Sturluson including Fortolkning til Versene*, ed. Finnur Jónsson, 4 vols (Copenhagen, 1893–1901).

6 *ASC* 1049 D: *The Anglo-Saxon Chronicle MS D*, ed. G. P. Cubbin, vol. 6 of *The Anglo-Saxon Chronicle: A Collaborative Edition*, ed. David Dumville and Simon Keynes (Cambridge, 1996), p. 68. Swein asked for 'at least 50 ships' and the *ASC* says 'all the people opposed it'. This annal in the Worcester version of the Chronicle was prepared under the influence of Bishop Ealdred, see note 7, below.

Norman myths about the nature of the Conquest and William's claims to legitimacy were aided and abetted, quite unintentionally, by Bishop Ealdred of Worcester, who had a vested interest in supporting the Ætheling Edgar and whose views have influenced two of our main sources, The *Anglo-Saxon Chronicle* and John of Worcester's *Chronicle of Chronicles*.[7] This Ealdred, as archbishop of York, anointed both Harold II and William I.

However, since only members of the ruling family could expect to be elected king of the Anglo-Saxons until the Danish Conquest in 1016/1017, and only members of the ruling family had a claim to the throne of England after the Norman Conquest, it is entirely reasonable to argue that a relationship with the Danish Gormsson family was necessary to become ruler of Anglo-Danish England in the fifty-year period from the Danish Conquest until the Norman Conquest. In the following analysis, the royal succession in Anglo-Danish England from Cnut's conquest in 1016/17 is traced to show how by this criterion King Harold II had a legitimate title to the throne in January 1066. In so doing, it also demonstrates why Swein Ulfsson, king of Denmark, was regarded by many as the man with the most legitimate claim to be king of England both before and after the Norman Conquest.[8]

Sources of Information

It is sometimes said that history is written by the victors and it is true that much of our understanding of the Norman Conquest and William's claim to the throne of England is derived from Anglo-Norman sources. However, there exist two other information streams representing candidates whose claims to the English throne were set aside as a result of the Conquest. These may be termed 'Anglo-Danish' and 'Scandinavian' and they are examined here with a view to enhancing an understanding of the English succession dispute in 1066. The Anglo-Danish sources are for the most part contemporary with the events described. They include the *Encomium Emmae Reginae*, a politically motivated account of events inspired by Queen Emma; annals from the Worcester version of the *Anglo-Saxon Chronicle* which may have been commissioned by Bishop Ealdred of Worcester;[9] and extracts from a *Life* of King Edmund Ironside which may also have been commissioned by Bishop Ealdred.[10] This much-travelled

7 Bishop Ealdred's influence on Version D of the *Anglo-Saxon Chronicle* (London, BL, MS Cotton Tiberius B. iv) and on the *Life* of Edmund Ironside, extracts from which appear in John of Worcester's *Chronicle*, are discussed in Ian Howard, *The Conflict between King Edmund Ironside and Queen Emma: the English Succession Crisis 1014–1017*, forthcoming.

8 It is convenient, although inaccurate, to use the term 'king of England' before the Norman Conquest. Anglo-Saxon monarchs regarded themselves as kings of peoples, for instance Anglo-Saxons, Danes and Britons, and sometimes designated themselves emperor [*basileus*] of all the peoples in Britain. Likewise, Danish monarchs regarded themselves as kings of peoples, explaining why King Cnut could regard himself as king of Swedes, although his territorial authority did not extend into the regions we would regard as Sweden.

9 Cubbin, *MS D*, pp. lxxviii–lxxxi.

10 *Encomium Emmae Reginae*, ed. Alistair Campbell, Camden 3rd Series 72, Royal Historical Society (London, 1949), reprinted with a supplementary introduction by Simon Keynes (Cambridge, 1998). *The Anglo-Saxon Chronicle*, BL, MS, Cotton Tiberius B. iv (Cubbin, *MS D*: also *The Anglo-Saxon*

bishop was actively involved in the politics of the period and cannot be considered impartial. However, the same may be said of the sponsors of many of the sources upon which we have to rely for this and other periods of Anglo-Saxon history and it should also be said of our Norman sources.[11] The Scandinavian sources are represented by Snorri Sturluson's thirteenth-century sagas known as *Heimskringla*.[12] Snorri based his work upon earlier and sometimes contemporary records of events, although it should be acknowledged that the plausibility of the sagas is, at times, demonstrably contrived.

The period of English history known as Anglo-Saxon saw Northumbrian, Mercian and West Saxon hegemonies and concluded with what will be described in this paper as 'Anglo-Danish hegemony'. The proposition is advanced that King Æthelred II, sometime known as 'the Unready', was the last ruler to be elected king of all England because he was a member of the West Saxon House of Cerdic. From this proposition it will be demonstrated that Harold II Godwinesson was, by contemporary values, throne-worthy when he was elected king in January 1066, some fifty years after King Æthelred's death in April 1016. 'Throne-worthy' means that he was sufficiently a member of the ruling royal house to be a candidate for election as king. **Fig. 1** shows some of the complicated family relationships in Harold's pedigree. Each side of the square in the figure provides a simplified family tree. These four family trees show how Harold was related to the families that had an interest in the English crown.

1016: A Disputed Succession

It is true, of course, that King Æthelred had two sons, the Æthelings Edmund (Ironside) and Edward (the Confessor), who became kings. They were, in modern parlance, 'half-brothers'. Edmund's mother was Queen Ælfgifu. Edward's mother was a Norman, Emma, whom King Æthelred married in 1002. Confusingly, Queen Emma also used the English name 'Ælfgifu' for official purposes.

When King Æthelred died in April 1016 there were three claimants to the throne of

Chronicle according to the Several Original Authorities, I: Original Texts, ed. Benjamin Thorpe, Rolls Series (London, 1861), a comparative edition which remains the most effective way to examine versions of the *Chronicle* simultaneously). *The Chronicle of John of Worcester*, ed. R. R. Darlington and P. McGurk, 3 vols (Oxford, 1995–), II.

11 The Norman sources make the unlikely claim that the Normans influenced the election of King Edward to the throne of England by threatening intervention (William of Poitiers, XIV, quoted in R. Allen Brown, *The Norman Conquest* (London, 1984), pp. 19–20, section 33, from *Guillaume de Poitiers: Histoire de Guillaume le Conquérant*, ed. Raymonde Foreville (Paris, 1952), pp. 28–32): that King Edward promised the throne of England to Duke William (William of Poitiers, XLI–XLII; Brown, *Norman Conquest*, p. 22, section 36 and Foreville, *Guillaume de Poitiers*, pp. 100–6. William of Jumièges, XIII: Brown, *Norman Conquest*, p. 13, section 23, from *Guillaume de Jumièges, Gesta Normannorum Ducum*, ed. J. Marx (Paris, 1914), pp. 132–3), although the crown was, constitutionally, not his to give; and that Harold Godwinesson swore allegiance to Duke William during King Edward's lifetime (William of Poitiers, XLI–XLII: *jam satelliti suo accepto per manos*: Brown, *Norman Conquest*, p. 23, section 36, Foreville, *Guillaume de Poitiers*, pp. 100–6), although such an act should have been accounted betrayal and an act of rebellion by Harold against his king.

12 Jónsson, *Snorri Sturluson*.

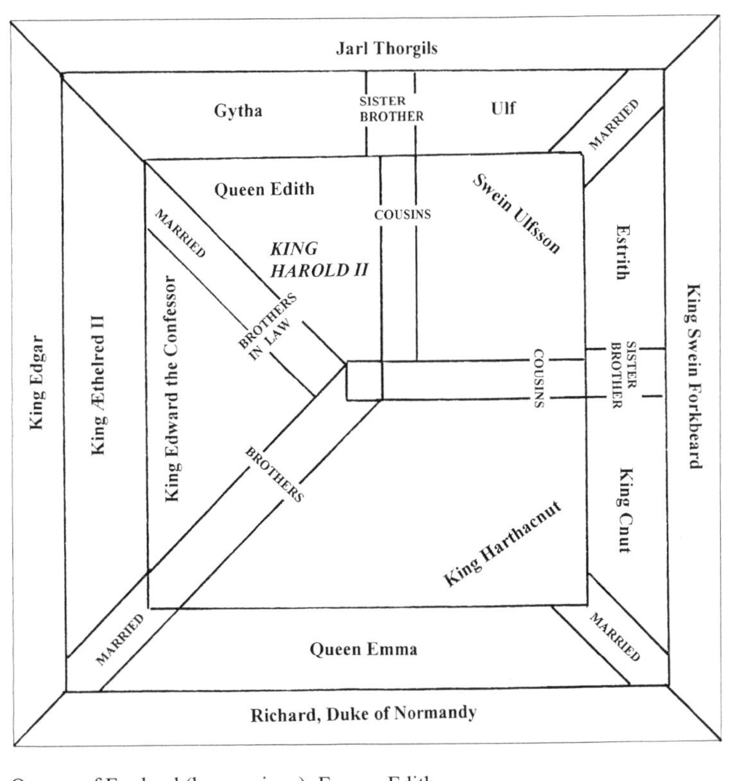

Queens of England (by marriage): Emma, Edith

Kings of England: Edgar, Swein Forkbeard*, Æthelred II, Cnut*, Harthacnut*, Edward the Confessor, Harold II

Pretender to the English throne: Swein Ulfsson*

* also king of Denmark

Fig. 1 Relationship to the English throne in the eleventh century

England: the Ætheling Edmund, the Ætheling Edward and King Cnut of Denmark.[13] King Cnut was the son of King Swein Forkbeard of Denmark who had conquered England in 1013. When Swein died in February 1014, King Æthelred recovered his throne. King Cnut invaded England in 1015 claiming that his father's conquest had given him a title to the English throne.[14] For some six months following Æthelred's death there was war in England between the supporters of these three pretenders. The final battle of this war took place at Ashingdon, after which there was an agreement dividing England in which Edmund was acknowledged as king of part of the

13 Despite an assertion in the *Encomium* (II. i–ii: Campbell, *Encomium*, pp. 14–19) that Cnut's brother, Harold, became king of Denmark after the death of their father, Swein Forkbeard, there is overwhelming evidence that Cnut became king of Denmark in succession to his father when King Swein died in February 1014. See Howard, *Swein Forkbeard's Invasions*, pp. 10, 67, 100–102, 133–4.

14 For an explanation of these events and the part played by King Cnut at this time see Howard, *Swein Forkbeard's Invasions*, Chapter 7, pp. 124–43.

country.[15] King Edmund died in November 1016, having never been king of all England. The marriage of the Ætheling Edward's mother, Queen Emma, to King Cnut effectively concluded the remaining dispute and King Cnut became king of all England. He ruled for nineteen years, until November 1035,[16] and an Anglo-Danish nobility prospered in that time, giving them a vested interest in the continuity of the new political order when Cnut died.

1035: A Disputed Succession

The succession crisis, which followed Cnut's death, is complicated. It will be described using Scandinavian sources to replace some of the *lacunae* in the account derived from Anglo-Saxon, Flemish and German (Saxony) sources. The important feature for the purposes of this paper is that it is evident that the Anglo-Danish nobility did not want a restoration of the House of Cerdic.

Cnut was survived by three sons, Swein and Harold by a marriage, in 1013, to Ælfgifu of Northampton and Harthacnut by a marriage, in 1017, to Queen Emma. There was a contemporary understanding that he had two other sons,[17] in modern parlance 'step-sons', the Æthelings Edward and Alfred, who were the sons of Queen Emma by her previous marriage to King Æthelred. Swein and Harthacnut were in Denmark when their father died and Snorri Sturluson's *Heimskringla* infers that they agreed to share the inheritance left by their father.[18] Snorri was not aware that Harold was regent in England for a period and so simply records that Harold succeeded King Cnut as king of England. He does state, however, that Harthacnut offered to divide his kingdom with Swein; an offer that was accepted. If Harold was regent in England, and England was divided, as it was,[19] it is logical to suppose that the agreement between Harthacnut and Swein extended to include England. Snorri quotes verses from Þjóðólfr and Bjarni Gullbrárskáld to support his account of events.

Harold was the only son in England at the time of Cnut's death when he claimed the regency of England on behalf of his brothers. The *Anglo-Saxon Chronicle* sources

15 *ASC* 1016 CDE says that Edmund succeeded to Wessex and Cnut to Mercia, or, as *ASC* D says, 'the north part' (Thorpe, *Chronicle*, pp. 284–5); London made peace independently.

16 *ASC* 1035 CD: Thorpe, *Chronicle*, pp. 292–3.

17 Thus Queen Emma's encomiast was referring to the æthelings Edward and Alfred, when he wrote that King Cnut and Queen Emma *alios uero liberales filios educandos direxerunt Normanniae*, 'sent in fact their other legitimate sons to Normandy to be brought up' (II. xviii: Campbell, *Encomium*, pp. 34–5. Campbell's translation).

18 Swein Cnutsson had been made king of Norway but fled to Denmark because he could not rely upon the loyalty of his Norwegian subjects when King Magnus the Good invaded Norway. He planned to return to Norway with a Danish army. For these events and the agreement between the two brothers, see *Magnús konungs góða*, IV–V: Jónsson, *Snorri Sturluson*, pp. 423–4.

19 *ASC* 1035–37 CDEF (Thorpe, *Chronicle*, pp. 292–5), infers or states that England was divided on Cnut's death, with the south of the country supporting Harthacnut's claims and the north supporting Harold Harefoot's claims. Only E and F refer to Harold being made 'regent'. All agree that Harold was *eventually* recognized as king, although the recognition is referred to in different annal years. The argument in this paper is that it makes sense of an otherwise obscure account in the sources if Harold claimed the regency of England on behalf of *both* his brothers but that Emma opposed him and wanted to represent Harthacnut herself.

make no reference to Swein Cnutsson's existence and, arguably, this makes the annal entries lack credibility. *Anglo-Saxon Chronicle*, version E, records Cnut's death in an annal for 1036. Since Cnut died on 12 November 1035, this annalist may be starting his year in September; alternatively, he may have chosen to record closely related events, which happened over a year-end, in one annal. *Anglo-Saxon Chronicle*, version E, says:

> Here [in this year] King Cnut died at Shaftesbury and he is buried in Winchester in the Old Minster; and he was king over all England for very nearly twenty years. And immediately after his death there was an assembly of the full *witan* at Oxford. And Earl Leofric and almost all the thegns [from] north of the Thames and the *liðsmen* in London chose Harold as guardian [regent] of all England, for himself and for his brother Harthacnut, who was in Denmark. And Earl Godwine and all the chief men in Wessex remained against it as long as they could, but they could not contrive anything against it. And it was then decided that Ælfgifu [Emma], Harthacnut's mother, should occupy Winchester with the king's bodyguards for her son, and hold all Wessex in hand for him; and Earl Godwine was their most loyal protector. Some men said about Harold that he was the son of King Cnut and Ælfgifu [of Northampton], Ealdorman Ælfhelm's daughter, but it seemed incredible to many men; and he was nevertheless full king over all England.[20]

This account jumps from Harold being regent to Harold being king over all England, without explanation. The *Anglo-Saxon Chronicle s.a.* 1035, versions C and D, do not discuss the issue of regency, though they cast doubt on whether Harold was truly the son of King Cnut. The *Chronicle* account certainly becomes more credible if we allow that Harold's elder brother, Swein, featured in the arrangements. This serves to explain the need for regency, the division of the country, and, later, Harold's claim to be king in his own right. The existence of an elder brother also reduces the political value of the claim that Harold was not Cnut's son, although some later English sources suggested that both Swein and Harold had been foisted on Cnut by trickery.[21]

Queen Emma disputed Harold's claim to the regency and, supported by Earl Godwine, asserted that she should act on behalf of Harthacnut. The country appears to have been divided between the parties at this point. Then Swein Cnutsson died, in the winter following Cnut's death,[22] and it became apparent that Harthacnut was unable to come to England for reasons which will be explained shortly. Harold asserted a title to kingship following his elder brother's death and, since he had not himself been party to the agreement with Harthacnut, before long he and his supporters were actively canvassing for Harold to be king of all England. That was not a practical possibility so long as the powerful Earl Godwine supported Queen Emma and Harthacnut. It seems likely that Queen Emma was uncertain of Godwine

20 My translation. See also *ASC* 1036 E (*English Historical Documents I, c. 500–1042*, ed. Dorothy Whitelock (London, 1955), 232, and nn. 4, 7), for evidence of a period of regency. See N. J. Higham, 'Harold Godwinesson: the Construction of Kingship' in this volume, for the families occupying the English earldoms at this time.

21 See John of Worcester, 1035: Darlington and McGurk, *John of Worcester*, pp. 520–3, an account which acknowledges the existence of Swein Cnutsson without considering his claim to share in Cnut's possessions in England.

22 *Magnús konungs góða*, V: Jónsson, *Snorri Sturluson*, p. 424.

and felt that the continued absence of Harthacnut from England was undermining her position. For whatever reason, Emma then committed a political blunder; she abandoned Harthacnut's cause and invited[23] her sons by King Æthelred, the Æthelings Edward[24] and Alfred, to return to England. When Alfred came to England, he and his followers were captured. Alfred was blinded and subsequently died from the ill treatment he had received.[25] Since Emma had effectively abandoned Harthacnut's cause, there would have been little point in Godwine adhering to it. He switched his support to Harold and was probably involved in the death of the Ætheling Alfred.[26] Thus, Harold Cnutsson, usually known as Harefoot, became king of all England and Queen Emma was driven into exile.

Seen through a prism of thirteenth-century Scandinavian sources, this explanation of events in England is entirely plausible. However, it has been demonstrated elsewhere that Scandinavian writers, especially Snorri Sturluson, manipulated their sources to achieve plausibility;[27] therefore these sources should be used with caution. The essential element in the story for the purposes of this paper is that the claims of the Æthelings Edward and Alfred to the throne of England were rejected violently and the Anglo-Danish nobility demonstrated that they wanted the succession to remain in the family of King Cnut: the Gormssons. There is support for this element of the story in versions of the *Anglo-Saxon Chronicle*.[28]

Harthacnut: King of Denmark and England

Following his father's death, Harthacnut had remained in Denmark because it was threatened with invasion by King Magnus the Good of Norway.[29] Although armies

23 *ASC* 1036 CD says that the Ætheling Alfred came to England to visit his mother (Thorpe, *Chronicle*, pp. 292–4). Emma's encomiast claimed that the invitation was a trick devised by King Harold Harefoot so that he could trap and kill Emma's sons (III. i–iv: Campbell, *Encomium*, pp. 38–43). However, it would be out of character for Emma not to have been involved in political manoeuvres at this time and Earl Godwine certainly changed sides, though his reasons for abandoning Emma are obscured by the different versions of the *Anglo-Saxon Chronicle* 1035–6 (see Thorpe, *Chronicle*, pp. 292–4).

24 Alfred came to England and it is possible that Edward came to England also, and was driven away: see Campbell, *Encomium*, p. lxvii. William of Poitiers, II–V: Foreville, *Guillaume de Poitiers*, pp. 4–12. John of Worcester 1036: Darlington and McGurk, *John of Worcester*, pp. 522–5.

25 *ASC* 1036 CD (Thorpe, *Chronicle*, pp. 292–4). Swanton (*The Anglo-Saxon Chronicle*, trans. and ed. M. J. Swanton (London, 1996), p. 160, n. 1) notes that Alfred's obit was celebrated at Ely on 5 February.

26 The evidence is in *ASC* CD 1036–7 (Thorpe, *Chronicle*, pp. 292–4) and in *Encomium Emmae Reginae*, III. i–vii: Campbell, *Encomium*, pp. 38–49. These sources indicate that he was involved in Alfred's capture and that he handed him over to the people who subsequently blinded him. The extant version of the *Encomium* was written before Harthacnut died in 1042, so it may pre-date the annals in *ASC* CD.

27 For examples see Howard, *Swein Forkbeard's Invasions*, Appendix 1, pp. 147–62.

28 *ASC* 1035–40 CDE: Thorpe, *Chronicle*, pp. 292–7.

29 In 1035, Magnus the Good drove Swein Cnutsson out of Norway. Swein went to seek assistance from his (half-)brother, Harthacnut, in Denmark. During the winter, the people of Norway and Denmark prepared for war. The issue was complicated by the death of Swein Cnutsson during the winter. Armies were raised for the war in 1036, but a battle was avoided because the kings' advisers preferred to negotiate a peace (*Magnús konungs góða*, I–VI: Jónsson, *Snorri Sturluson*, pp. 421–5). As a result of the peace accord, Harthacnut was relatively secure in his control of Denmark and would have been able to

were gathered, both sides preferred to avoid battle and negotiations took place during 1036 which led to a settlement of the dispute between Magnus and Harthacnut. Later, following Harthacnut's death, King Magnus and his successor, King Harold Hardrada, claimed that the terms of settlement included an agreement whereby Magnus should succeed to the throne of Denmark if Harthacnut died before him. Also, Magnus and Harold Hardrada extended their understanding of this agreement to include the kingdom of England as well as Denmark.[30] Again, we may question the Scandinavian sources and we are entitled to suspect that Magnus and Harold Hardrada were being imaginative in describing and expanding the terms of whatever peace accord had been agreed. The important feature for present purposes is that the kings of Norway behaved as though there was such a treaty. It is, in fact, tempting to speculate whether Harthacnut was suffering from a fatal illness and that those around him knew it. Both Magnus in Scandinavia and Queen Emma in England behaved as though they expected that Harthacnut would not live very long.[31]

Because of the agreement with King Magnus, Harthacnut was able to leave Denmark and become king of England when his brother, Harold, died, in 1040.[32] He brought his mother, Queen Emma, back from exile and then, presumably persuaded by his mother, he invited his brother, in modern parlance 'half-brother', the Ætheling Edward, to return to England. At about this time, during Harthacnut's lifetime, Queen Emma commissioned political propaganda, which has come down to us in the extant version of the *Encomium Emmae Reginae*. This propaganda states that England, like Heaven, is ruled by a Trinity with a common purpose: Queen Emma and her two sons, Harthacnut and Edward:

> Obeying his brother's command, he [Edward] was conveyed to England, and the mother and both sons, having no disagreement between them, enjoy the ready amenities of the kingdom. Here there is loyalty among sharers of rule, here the bond of motherly and brotherly love is of strength indestructible. All these things

go to England in 1037. However, during 1036 in England, Earl Godwine became a supporter of Harold Harefoot and the Ætheling Alfred was killed (*ASC* CD 1036: Thorpe, *Chronicle*, pp. 292–4). Therefore by the time Harthacnut was free to travel to England, Harold Harefoot was securely established there as king.

30 Snorri describes how Magnus claimed the throne of England in a letter written to King Edward the Confessor threatening Edward with an invasion if he did not surrender England to him: *Magnús konungs góða*, XXXVI: Jónsson, *Snorri Sturluson*, pp. 445–6.

31 Campbell, *Encomium*, p. lxviii, notes that William of Poitiers makes clear that Harthacnut's death was not unexpected by himself. Arguably, the marriage agreement of Cnut's daughter, Gunnhild, and Henry, king of the Germans (eldest son of the Emperor Conrad who became the Emperor Henry III) presupposes that Harthacnut was slowly dying and that Gunnhild would pass on a title to the throne of Denmark, and with it control of the western Baltic, through a son of her marriage. Harthacnut may have been suffering from an illness such as tuberculosis: see Howard, *The Reign of Æthelred II (the Unready)* (Woodbridge, forthcoming). (Conrad's ambition in this direction was thwarted by Gunnhild's unexpected death from a fever caught in Italy, in 1038.)

32 From about 1037 Harthacnut was free to consider undertaking an expedition out of Denmark (n. 29, above). According to Emma's encomiast, Harthacnut was preparing for an invasion of England and had joined his mother at Bruges (III. viii–xii: Campbell, *Encomium*, pp. 48–53). There is support for this in *ASC* 1039, 1040 CD (Thorpe, *Chronicle*, p. 296). It is likely that Harthacnut had assembled an invasion fleet but the disposition of the fleet during 1039/1040 is uncertain.

> were granted them by Him, who makes dwellers in a house be of one mind, Jesus Christ, the Lord of all, who, abiding in the Trinity, holds a kingdom which flourishes unfading. Amen.[33]

The *Encomium* makes clear the claim, soon to be put into effect because of Harthacnut's death, that Edward should be regarded as throne-worthy because he was Harthacnut's brother. The *Anglo-Saxon Chronicle* also recognizes the importance of Edward's relationship with Harthacnut, whilst making an aside about him being King Æthelred's son who had been driven into exile, suggesting surprise at Harthacnut's invitation:

> And soon in that year came Edward, his brother on the mother's side, from beyond the sea – King Æthelred's son, who was earlier driven out of this [home-] land many years before, and nevertheless was sworn in as king; and then he dwelt in this way in his brother's household as long as he lived.[34]

Edward (the Confessor): King of England

Edward did become king when Harthacnut died, in 1042.[35] There seems to have been a smooth transition of authority and this may have been because Edward was already involved in the government of England as the *Encomium* says. However, *Heimskringla* suggests that Edward was not associated with Harthacnut as ruler of England and Snorri Sturluson, in *Heimskringla*, puts these words into King Edward's mouth:

> My brother Harold was king whilst he lived. But when he drew his last breath, then Harthacnut, my brother, [came] from Denmark to rule and then thought it [the] only right brotherly division between us two that he would be king over both England and Denmark; but I should have nothing to rule over. Now he died; then it was the counsel of all the people of the country here to take me for king here in England.[36]

The use of the term 'brother' by Snorri may cause confusion. Harold and Harthacnut were 'brothers' because Cnut was their father. Harthacnut and Edward were 'brothers' because Emma was their mother. Harold and Edward were not blood relatives; but they were, in our parlance, 'stepbrothers' through the marriage of Cnut and Emma.

Whichever version of the relationship between Harthacnut and Edward is most persuasive, Edward became king and cemented an accord with Earl Godwine by marrying the earl's daughter, Edith. In *Heimskringla*, Snorri Sturluson says her name is an anglicized version of the Scandinavian 'Gytha' and that she was named after her mother, Gytha Thorgilsdaughter.[37] Significantly, Queen Edith was the niece of King Cnut, the cousin of Swein Ulfsson and the granddaughter of Jarl Thorgils, of whom

33 *Encomium*, III. xiv: Campbell, *Encomium*, pp. 52–3. Campbell's translation, p. 53.

34 *ASC* 1041 CD: Thorpe, *Chronicle*, pp. 296–8. My translation.

35 *ASC* 1042 CD: Thorpe, *Chronicle*, p. 298.

36 *Magnús konungs góða*, xxxvii: Jónsson, *Snorri Sturluson*, p. 446. My translation.

37 *Helga Óláfs Konungs* (*St Olaf's saga*), CLII: Jónsson, *Snorri Sturluson*, pp. 346–7. As with sons, it was

more below. Edith's marriage to King Edward was also significant in that the sons of Earl Godwine became King Edward's brothers-in-law. By this marriage, Edward associated himself firmly with the Anglo-Danish establishment and ensured that his sons, if any, would be descended from Jarl Thorgils and would be related to the Danish royal family.[38]

Swein Ulfsson

The smooth transition of authority took place partly because there was no obvious candidate available in England other than Edward. That is not to say that a more throne-worthy candidate did not exist; one did, although he was not in a position to claim his inheritance. His name was Swein Ulfsson; often referred to in English history books as Swein Estrithsson, after his mother. It is necessary to delve back into Danish history to understand Swein Ulfsson's importance and why his candidature was not supported in England at this time.

There were three particularly important families in tenth- and eleventh-century Denmark, the Thorgilssons, the Strut-Haroldssons and the Gormssons. It was the Gormssons who had provided the kings of Denmark, through the direct male descent, for five generations. The Strut-Haroldsson family played an important part in Scandinavian and English history but does not have a direct bearing upon the present argument.[39] The Thorgilssons are fundamentally important to it, however.

Jarl Thorgils is an enigmatic figure who features in the Scandinavian sagas as a dynastic link between the ruling families of Denmark and Sweden. *Knytlinga saga* explains how a daughter of King Harold Gormsson, Thyra, was married to Styrbjörn of Sweden, the son of King Olaf Bjarnarson and nephew of King Eric the Victorious, kings of Sweden.[40] Jarl Thorgils was the son of this marriage, so he was a direct descendant, through the female line, of King Harold Gormsson, and was also related to the Swedish royal family. Jarl Thorgils was the father of Eilaf, Ulf and Gytha. The *Chronicle* of John of Worcester, which was written in the twelfth century but is based on earlier sources, explains the male ancestry of Earl Björn Ulfsson,[41] and, in so

customary to name daughters after their fathers. An anglicized version of her name has been preferred here to the Old Icelandic '*dóttir*'.

38 The Anglo-Danish establishment in England would have believed that a son of this marriage was descended from King Harold Gormsson.

39 Sigvaldi Strut-Haroldsson was the leader of the famous Jomsvikings and it was he who had led the Danish fleet on an abortive expedition to conquer Norway early in Swein Forkbeard's reign over Denmark. His brother, Heming Strut-Haroldsson, was one of the leaders of the great Scandinavian army which invaded England during the period 1006 to 1012. He was killed in 1010 or 1011, in England. A third brother, Thorkell inn Havi Strut-Haroldsson, became the leader of King Æthelred's mercenary army in 1012 but defected to join King Cnut's invasion of England in 1015. Thereafter, he was Cnut's leading earl and counsellor and was effectively regent of England during Cnut's absences in the early years of his reign. See Howard, *Swein Forkbeard's Invasions*, Chapters 5–7, pp. 72–143.

40 H. Pálsson and P. Edwards, *Knytlinga Saga, The History of the Kings of Denmark* (Odense, 1986), p. 24. The kings are historical figures and *Knytlinga saga* is derived from information collected by Snorri Sturluson, although it was not written by him.

41 John of Worcester, 1049: Darlington and McGurk, *John of Worcester*, pp. 548–9: *Beorn comes, filius . . . Vlfi filii Spraclingi filii Vrs*, 'Earl Björn, son of Ulf, son of [Thorgils] Sprakaleggr, son of Bear [=

doing, shows that the Anglo-Danish establishment in England knew that Eilaf, Ulf and Gytha were descended from King Harold Gormsson through their father's ancestry as well as that of their mother. It follows that the Anglo-Danish establishment in England were aware that Harold Godwinesson was of royal descent through his mother, Gytha.[42]

Eilaf Thorgilsson had come to England as one of the leaders of a great Scandinavian army in 1006 and he eventually became the friend and ally of King Cnut and one of his leading counsellors. Eilaf's sister, Gytha, was married to Earl Godwine and so was the mother of his sons, Swein, Harold and Tostig and his daughter Queen Edith. Eilaf's brother Ulf Thorgilsson was one of Cnut's earls and he was married to Cnut's sister, Estrith. They had a son, Swein Ulfsson (or Estrithsson). Swein Ulfsson's maternal grandfather was Swein Forkbeard, king of Denmark and England, and his paternal grandfather was Jarl Thorgils; he was the nephew of Cnut the Great and the cousin of Harthacnut, both kings of Denmark and England. Arguably, therefore, there was nobody more throne-worthy than Swein Ulfsson when King Harthacnut died. As events were to show, Swein Ulfsson believed that he had a better claim to the thrones of Denmark and England than anybody else and he was prepared to fight to obtain them. Unfortunately, he did not get off to a good start. Whatever the terms of the peace accord between Magnus the Good and Harthacnut may have been, as soon as Magnus became aware of Harthacnut's death, he invaded Denmark and took over the kingdom.[43] Swein Ulfsson was not there. His father, Ulf, had betrayed King Cnut's trust and had been killed on Cnut's orders. Swein Ulfsson had fled to Sweden and was still living there, in exile, when Harthacnut died. Snorri explains this in *Heimskringla*:

> There was a man named Swein, son of Jarl Ulf, [grand] son of Thorgils Sprakalegg. Swein's mother was Estrith, daughter of King Swein Forkbeard. She was a sister of Cnut the Great by the father's side, and of the Swedish King Olaf Ericsson by the mother's side; their mother was Queen Sigrid the Haughty, daughter of Skogul-Tosti. Swein Ulfsson had dwelt a long while with the Swedish kings, his kinsmen, ever since Jarl Ulf, his father had been killed [by King Cnut's orders] . . . at Roskilde; for which reason Swein had not since been in Denmark.[44]

Following the death of Harthacnut, Swein Ulfsson was to spend many years plotting and fighting to recover what he perceived to be his rightful inheritance. However, in 1042, Swein Ulfsson was in no position to assert his title to the throne of England and so there appears to have been little or no objection to the election of Harthacnut's brother, the Ætheling Edward, as king of all England.

Björn = Björn the Strong = Styrbjörn]'. See also Pálsson and Edwards, *Knytlinga Saga*, pp. 24, 26, 44. W. G. Searle, *Anglo-Saxon Bishops, Kings and Nobles: the Succession of the Bishops and the Pedigrees of the Kings and Nobles* (Cambridge, 1899), pp. 354–5.

42 As noted above, saga sources should be treated with caution. However, the *Chronicle* of John of Worcester (n. 41, above) provides the evidence that the English *believed* that Harold Godwinesson was of royal descent. How they derived that knowledge is not significant for the purposes of this paper.

43 *Magnús konungs góða*, XVIII–XXI: Jónsson, *Snorri Sturluson*, pp. 432–4. Snorri quotes supporting verses by Arnór jarlaskáld and Þjóðólf.

44 *Magnús konungs góða*, XXII: Jónsson, *Snorri Sturluson*, p. 434. My translation.

Edward the Confessor's Title to the English Throne

The *Encomium* is evidence that Edward became king because he was Harthacnut's brother, not because he was Æthelred's son. His mother was a Norman and Edward had spent many years in Normandy. There was no need for him to seek a restoration of West Saxon hegemony and the House of Cerdic and, given the proofs he had seen of violent antipathy to such a restoration, he was well advised to avoid this issue. He seems to have been more inclined to favour the development of Norman interests in England; a trait which did not please some of his subjects.

Once king, of course, Edward showed pride in his ancestry and reminded his subjects of his royal antecedents.[45] Although Archbishop Wulfstan and others had undermined King Æthelred's reputation to some degree, he had not been blamed personally for the disasters which befell England in the last decade of his reign. Indeed, since we are examining English history through the prism of Scandinavian sources such as *Heimskringla*, it should be recorded that these sources regarded King Æthelred with respect and expected King Edward to be proud to acknowledge him as his father.

King Edward the Confessor did have relatives who could have claimed a title to the throne because they were descended from King Æthelred. The most obvious such relative was Edward's nephew, his sister's son, Ralf, who was made earl of Hereford. Ralf's father was count of the French Vexin and so Ralf was three-quarters Franco-Norman by birth and, like his uncle Edward, had been brought up on the Continent.[46] Any favour which Edward showed to this nephew could be deemed to be because of his liking for things Norman and need not be taken as an interest in a restoration of the House of Cerdic.

Earl Björn Ulfsson

King Edward's authority as king was probably strengthened by the fact that there were several men who had claims to the English throne; a feature that reduced the potential for power and influence to gravitate towards an obvious successor as a king grew older. Another potential candidate for the throne, living in England during King Edward's reign, was Earl Björn Ulfsson, the brother of Swein Ulfsson. Whilst his brother continued to struggle to obtain the Danish throne, Björn lived in England and was advanced to an earldom. Not only was he the nephew of King Cnut, he was also

45 Snorri has Edward speak of Æthelred's 'royal dignity and authority' (*Magnús konungs góða*, XXXVII: Jónsson, *Snorri Sturluson*, p. 446). There are saga tales of how Edward loved to read aloud from the book which King Olaf Tryggvason had given to his father, King Æthelred (J. Sephton, *The Saga of King Olaf Tryggwason who reigned over Norway A. D. 995 to A. D. 1000* (London, 1895), p. 470). A version of this story is to be found in M. Ashdown, *English and Norse Documents relating to the Reign of Ethelred the Unready* (Cambridge, 1930), quoting from *Agrip: Epitome of the Sagas of the Kings of Norway*, CCLXXXVI).

46 Edward's sister, Goda (Godgifu), married Drogo, count of the Vexin. They had a son, Ralf the Timid, earl of Hereford, who died in 1057. After Drogo's death, Goda married Eustace I, count of Boulogne.

the nephew of Earl Godwine because his aunt, Gytha Thorgilsdaughter, had married Godwine. This meant that Earl Godwine's sons, Swein, Harold and Tostig, were his cousins. In terms of the Anglo-Danish hegemony, Earl Björn was the most throne-worthy man living in England at the time.[47] However, Earl Björn died before King Edward, in circumstances that shocked the Anglo-Danish establishment. Swein Godwinesson had committed many crimes, including seducing a nun, and he had been banished from England. In 1049, Swein sought reconciliation with King Edward and Earl Björn Ulfsson promised to help him. They were journeying to meet the king, when Swein treacherously killed Björn.[48] It ranked amongst the most heinous crimes of the eleventh century and Swein was condemned as a *nithing*:[49] a creature of no account who had forfeited the right to live with civilized people.

The death of Earl Björn removed a throne-worthy candidate who might have succeeded King Edward. Björn's death advanced the claims of his cousins, Earl Godwine's sons, to be considered candidates for the throne, but the thought of Swein Godwinesson benefiting from having murdered his cousin must have been insupportable.[50] In any case, Swein, who was outlawed twice and possibly three times,[51] can hardly have been regarded as a suitable candidate for kingship.

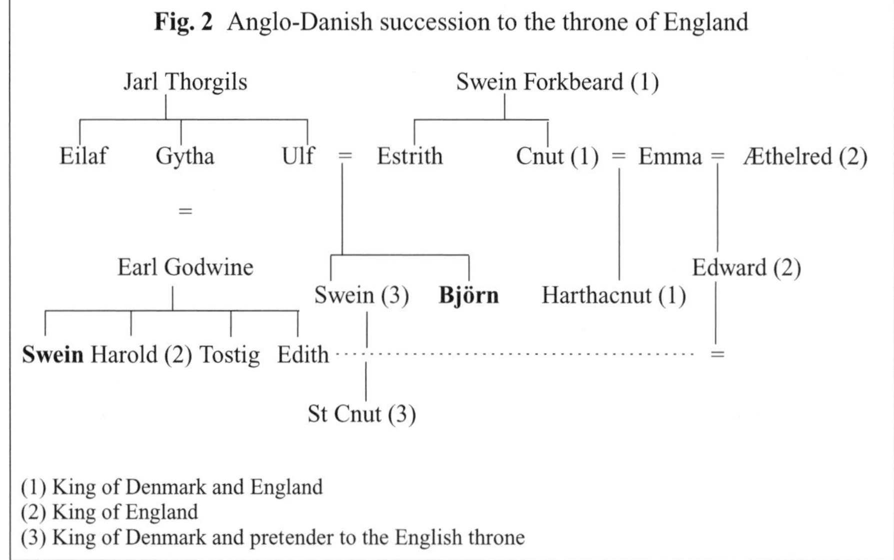

47 I have followed the conventional understanding that Swein Ulfsson was older that his brother, Björn. They are named in this order in *Knytlinga saga*.

48 *ASC* 1050 D (= 1049): Thorpe, *Chronicle*, pp. 308–10.

49 *ASC* 1049 C: G. N. Garmonsway, *The Anglo-Saxon Chronicle* (London (1st ed. 1953), 1972), p. 171, translates *nithing* as 'a man without honour'. Swanton, *Chronicle*, p. 171, n. 17, explains *nithing* as 'a Scandinavian legal term of abuse'.

50 See n. 49, above: *ASC* 1049 C. The reaction of the king and his army is evidence of the general abhorrence felt against Swein, which would have made any pretension to the throne insupportable at that time.

51 Swein was outlawed, and went to Denmark as a result of the incident with the abbess (*ASC* 1046 C (not in D)); again because he had murdered Björn, when he went to Bruges (*ASC* 1049 C: D includes the

The Ætheling Edward

It was probably at this time that a romantic notion gained ground that a nephew of King Edward might be brought to England from his exile in Hungary:[52] this nephew was the Ætheling Edward, the son of King Edward's elder half-brother, Edmund. One of the leaders of the party interested in this project was Ealdred, bishop of Worcester, who was to become Archbishop of York later in Edward's reign. King Edward does not appear to have discouraged this initiative, but, as will be seen, nor did he encourage it. In this King Edward was probably wise. In the middle of the century, when it was becoming increasingly clear that King Edward would not have a son to succeed him, Bishop Ealdred, or an associate, commissioned a political treatise extolling the virtues of King Edmund, the son of King Æthelred, who had died in November 1016. This *Life of Edmund Ironside* has not survived, but passages from it are quoted in the *Chronicle* of John of Worcester. The title of the *Life* is uncertain but Edmund is referred to as 'Ironside' throughout the passages in the *Chronicle* of John of Worcester and he is referred to as 'Ironside' in an annal in the *Anglo-Saxon Chronicle* which is associated with Bishop Ealdred.[53] The *Life* is a melodramatic story about a hero king who is constantly thwarted on the verge of victory through the machinations of his archenemy, Ealdorman Eadric of Mercia, who is referred to in the story as Eadric Streona, meaning 'the acquisitive'. At about this time, Bishop Ealdred went on a mission to Germany, which eventually resulted in Edmund's son, the Ætheling Edward, returning to England with his family. Again, King Edward gave no active support to the restoration of the House of Cerdic to the extent that he did not receive his nephew, the Ætheling Edward, at court. *The Anglo-Saxon Chronicle* says:

> Here [in this year] the Ætheling Edward came to England; he was son of King Edward's brother, King Edmund, called 'Ironside' for his boldness. King Cnut had sent this ætheling away into Hungary to betray, but he there grew to be a great man, as God granted him for he was well bred, so that he won the Emperor's [Caesar's] relation for [his] wife, and by her bred handsome offspring; she was called Agatha. We do not know for what cause it was arranged that he might not see his kinsman, King Edward.[54] Alas! that was a wretched fate, and grievous to

murder but does not say that he fled the country); again with his father after Earl Godwine had, unsuccessfully, raised an army against King Edward (*ASC* 1052 D (= 1051)): see Thorpe, *Chronicle*, pp. 302–21.

52 See Higham, 'Harold Godwinesson', in this volume, for the beginnings of this scheme.

53 Edmund is referred to as 'Ironside' (*Ferreum Latus*) several times in John of Worcester's annal for the year 1016 and again in his annal for 1057 (Darlington and McGurk, *John of Worcester*, pp. 480–97, 582–3). He is also referred to as 'Ironside' (*Irensid*) in *ASC* 1057 D (see Thorpe, *Chronicle*, p. 328). See also n. 7, above.

54 This is difficult to translate. It is possible that there is a word or phrase missing as Cubbin suggests, though there is no gap in the MS: see Cubbin, *MS D*, p. 75, n. 2. Swanton (*Chronicle*, p. 188) translates 'King Edward's [face]' apparently assuming a missing word. I have followed Garmonsway (Garmonsway, *Chronicle*, p. 188), where the passage is treated as verse, but see Cubbin, *MS D*, p. 75, n. 3.

> all this nation, that he so quickly ended his life after he came to England to the misfortune of this wretched nation. . . .[55]

As it happens, both King Edward's nephews, the Ætheling Edward and Ralf of Hereford, died before him.[56]

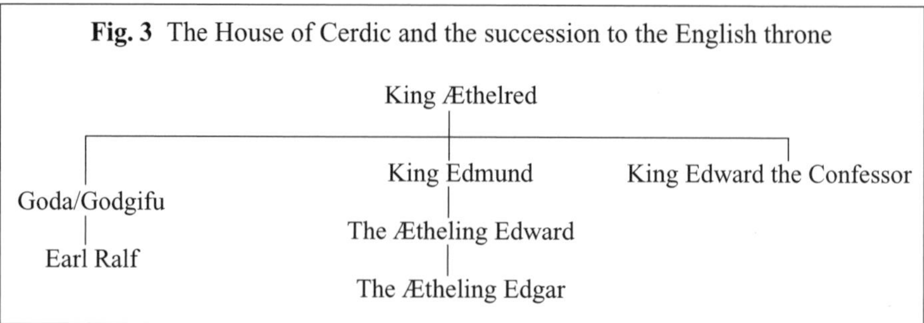

Fig. 3 The House of Cerdic and the succession to the English throne

Claimants to the Throne of England

Swein Godwinesson died, in exile, in 1052. The deaths of so many throne-worthy men meant that the candidates for the throne of England during the last period of King Edward's reign were Harold Hardrada, the king of Norway, who claimed that Magnus's agreement with Harthacnut should extend to include the throne of England; Swein Ulfsson; and Harold Godwinesson, who was in England. King Edward seems to have become increasingly reliant upon the very capable son of Earl Godwine, Harold, who took a leading role in political and military affairs during the closing period of Edward's reign.

During the intervening years, the pretender to the thrones of Denmark and England, Swein Ulfsson, had struggled against the Norwegians Magnus the Good and Harold Hardrada. Swein Ulfsson was an intelligent and personable man. As well as his claims to be king of Denmark, king of England, and ruler of Norway, he was also related to the ruling family in Sweden. Consequently, he had no difficulty in raising armies for repeated attempts to conquer Denmark. Magnus, who had strong support in parts of Denmark as well as the loyalty of his Norwegian kingdom, always proved the superior in the encounters between them. However, the problems caused by Swein Ulfsson's attacks on Denmark constitute one very good reason why Magnus did not

55 *ASC* 1057 D (see Thorpe, *Chronicle*, p. 328; my translation). The Ætheling Edward had a young son, Edgar, who featured briefly as a candidate for the throne in an unsuccessful attempt by Ealdred (then archbishop of York) and others to organize resistance against William of Normandy after the death of Harold and his brothers at the Battle of Hastings.

56 *ASC* 1057 D (Thorpe, *Chronicle*, p. 328): '. . . And in that year, Earl Ralf passed away on 21 December and lies in Peterborough.' *ASC* 1057 E confirms that the Ætheling Edward died in 1057 and says that 'his body is buried in St Paul's Minster in London': Thorpe, *Chronicle*, p. 329; my translation.

pursue his claims to the English throne by an invasion of this country.[57] When Magnus died, Swein was able to establish himself as king of Denmark,[58] but warfare continued in Scandinavia. Harold Hardrada had inherited the throne of Norway from his nephew,[59] Magnus, and declared that he had inherited Magnus's claims to the thrones of Denmark and England. This meant that Swein Ulfsson and Harold Hardrada were fully occupied fighting each other in Scandinavia and so the threat of an invasion of England was minimized. It was during this period that King Edward felt able to disband his fleet and abolish the tax known as *heregeld*.[60] Between 1062 and 1064, the political balance in Scandinavia swung significantly in Harold Hardrada's favour because he won a major sea-battle at Nissaa.[61] Swein was able to agree a peace accord with Harold Hardrada after the battle, from which he barely escaped with his life, but in 1065 and January 1066 he was in no position to assert his claim the English throne.[62] Harold Hardrada was a formidable warrior and was gathering a great fleet, so he remained a threat to Denmark.

It seems that, in the last years of his reign, Edward was favouring the succession of Harold Godwinesson. According to Snorri Sturluson's *Heimskringla*, Harold was leading an expedition by sea to Wales when contrary winds drove his ship onto the Norman coast. He stayed some time with Duke William and is said to have been betrothed to Duke William's daughter, who was then too young to marry immediately.[63] There is support for this betrothal story in William of Poitiers' *History of William the Conqueror* where it is stated that William had betrothed his daughter to Harold.[64] An enigmatic scene in the Bayeux Tapestry (**Plate 8**), which has the caption '*VBI VNUS CLERICVS ET ÆLFGYVA*', might also be interpreted as a reference to this betrothal.[65]

57 *ASC* 1046 and 1048 D: Cubbin, *MS D*, p. 67.

58 *Haraldz konungs harðràða*, XXVIII–XXXI: Jónsson, *Snorri Sturluson*, pp. 464–6.

59 Harold Hardrada was the (half-)brother of St Olaf. St Olaf was the father of King Magnus the Good.

60 *ASC* 1052 D (= 1051): Cubbin, *MS D*, pp. 69–70 and Thorpe, *Chronicle*, p. 328. The action may have been welcomed, but it was followed by Earl Godwine's uprising, when a fleet might have been very useful to the king. By 1058, the threat from Norway was growing again: *ASC* 1058 D: Cubbin, *MS D*, p. 76.

61 Probably off the coast of Halland (present-day Sweden): see *Haraldz konungs harðràða*, LX–LXIV: Jónsson, *Snorri Sturluson*, pp. 484–9.

62 *Haraldz konungs harðràða*, LXXVIII: Jónsson, *Snorri Sturluson*, pp. 498–9.

63 *Haraldz konungs harðràða*, LXXVI: Jónsson, *Snorri Sturluson*, p. 497.

64 See Brown, *Norman Conquest*, p. 38, section 53 and n. 66, where he quotes William of Poitiers: 'William had not sought the death of Harold but had wished to increase his power and had betrothed his daughter to him' (see William of Poitiers, XXXI–XXXII: Foreville, *Guillaume de Poitiers*, pp. 222–36).

65 This scene, which was no doubt readily understood by an Anglo-Norman audience, is not clear to a modern audience and it has been variously interpreted. I am grateful to Gale Owen-Crocker for providing information on the different interpretations. (See Gale Owen-Crocker 'Telling a tale: narrative techniques in the Bayeux Tapestry and the Old English epic *Beowulf*', in *Medieval Art: Recent Perspectives. A memorial tribute to C. R. Dodwell*, ed. Gale R. Owen-Crocker and Timothy Graham (Manchester, 1998), pp. 40–59, esp. p. 57, n. 15: also Catherine E. Karkov, 'Gendering the Battle? Male and Female in the Bayeux Tapestry', in this volume, esp. n. 13.) My attention was first drawn to the possibilities of the 'betrothal scene' in the Bayeux Tapestry in a paper delivered to the Manchester Centre for Anglo-Saxon Studies by Dr David Hill in October 1998. The name, Ælfgyva, in the Tapestry is a reminder of the custom for a change of name when a lady married into a different nationality. The choice of name is not a surprise in an English context, but inevitably it is a reminder of the

A marriage alliance between Harold and William would seem to guarantee that Norman interests in England would be safeguarded after King Edward's death. According to this version of the story, Harold betrayed his obligations when he married the sister of Earls Edwin and Morcar to secure their political support and it was this act, which threatened Norman interests in England, coupled with Harold's election to the English throne, which precipitated the Norman invasion in 1066.[66]

Harold II: King of England

In January 1066, King Edward died. Harold Godwinesson was then the most throne-worthy man in England. Because of the difficulties occasioned by his defeat at the Battle of Nissaa, Swein Ulfsson was in no position to assert his claim to the English throne. In these circumstances, Harold was elected king without opposition.

This analysis of the rejection of the House of Cerdic explains how Harold II Godwinesson was deemed throne-worthy in January 1066. If, as has been argued, King Edward the Confessor's reign represented a continuance of Anglo-Danish hegemony, then his successor should have been found from the family of Kings Cnut and Harthacnut. In fact, the most throne-worthy candidate to be king of England, Swein Ulfsson, was never available during Edward's reign, or in January 1066; but Harold Godwinesson, Swein Ulfsson's cousin, was available. Since all the other throne-worthy candidates who had been in England were now dead, Harold II was elected king, as the most throne-worthy candidate available in England in January 1066, not because he was the son of the great Earl Godwine but because he was the grandson of the Danish Jarl Thorgils and so was Swein Ulfsson's cousin and a descendent of the Gormsson kings of Denmark.

significant marriage of Emma of Normandy to King Æthelred in 1002 and the English name that she was given when she married.

66 *Haraldz konungs harðràða*, XCV: Jónsson, *Snorri Sturluson*, p. 509. The marriage also antagonized Harold's brother, Tostig, who had reason to hate Morcar and Edwin: see *ASC* 1065 D: Cubbin, *MS D*, pp. 77–9. See also Higham, 'Harold Godwinesson', in this volume, for the importance of Tostig.

4

The Myth of Harold II's Survival in the Scandinavian Sources

GILLIAN FELLOWS-JENSEN

I AM neither a historian nor a student of folklore but forty years ago I published what is still, I believe, the definitive edition of the Icelandic text known as *Hemings þáttr Áslákssonar*, a text which contains the most elaborate account of the survival of Harold to be found in the Scandinavian sources.[1] I shall therefore preface my discussion of the myth with a brief account of this text.

The word *þáttr* in the title of the text would originally seem to have meant 'part of a whole' but to have developed the meaning 'short, independent narrative' and to have been typically used of short, often amusing, narratives of encounters of Icelanders with a Norwegian king, particularly Harold Hardrada, and most of them have been preserved in the great thirteenth- and fourteenth-century Icelandic vellum codices containing collections of sagas of the Norwegian kings.[2] *Hemings þáttr* is typical in that it describes Heming's relationship with Harold Hardrada and has been transmitted to us in codices such as *Hrokkinskinna* and *Flateyjarbók* but it is longer and more leisurely in form than most *þættir*, almost a short saga, as well as being more serious in tone and, atypically, the hero is a Norwegian and not an Icelander. Heming, the son of a prosperous farmer called Áslák, is a legendary Norwegian athlete. He incurs the enmity of Harold Hardrada by proving himself superior to the king and the king's men in contests in archery, swimming and skiing. Harold, a notoriously bad loser, commands Heming to ski down from the top of a mountain and bring himself to a standstill at the brink of a precipice. The task is impossible and Heming plunges over to his death, or so the king believes. Heming, however, is saved by supernatural means, first by a relic of St Stephen, the piece of cloth with which the saint was blindfolded when he was stoned to death and which winds itself round a protruding crag and breaks Heming's fall, and subsequently by St Olaf, the half-brother of Harold Hardrada, who appears to Heming in a vision in answer to a vow and a prayer, hauls him to safety and enjoins him to fulfill the vow to go to Rome. St Olaf promises Heming that he will be present when King Harold dies but asks him not to be too

1 *Hemings þáttr Áslákssonar*, ed. Gillian Fellows Jensen, Editiones Arnamagnæanæ Series B3 (Copenhagen, 1962). Abbreviated below as *HÞ*.

2 John Lindow, 'Þáttr', in *Medieval Scandinavia. An Encyclopedia*, ed. Phillip Pulsiano, Kirsten Wolf, Paul Acker and Donald K. Fry (New York and London, 1993), pp. 661–2.

active in bringing about the king's death. Heming goes on the pilgrimage and on his return seeks refuge at the court of Edward the Confessor in England. He faithfully serves King Edward and then his successor, Harold II, and is present with Harold at the Battle of Stamfordbridge. In the heat of the battle Harold reproaches Heming for not killing the Norwegian king, since he is the only man in the English army who can recognize him. Heming says that he dare not do so because of his promise to St Olaf but he marks out the king by shooting a loose arrow into his cheek, a somewhat casuistical way of keeping his vow, since this action makes it an easy task for Harold II to kill his namesake. After Harold's subsequent defeat at the Battle of Hastings by William the Conqueror, he is left for dead among the fallen and rescued from the battlefield by a peasant couple and nursed back to health. Harold refuses Heming's offer to help him to try and recover his kingdom but determines instead to follow the example of Olaf Tryggvason and retire into a hermit's cell, where Heming keeps the king supplied with food for three years until his death. William the Conqueror then gives Harold an honourable burial in London and grants Heming permission to take Harold's place in the cell.

Hemings þáttr (*HÞ*) would seem to have been a popular tale, for it survives in over forty manuscripts, three of them vellum codices, but it has not survived in complete form in any of the early manuscripts. The first part of the tale, dealing with the athletic contests, is preserved in two slightly different versions in two vellum codices containing sagas of the Norwegian kings. The first version is found in a late-fifteenth-century hand, probably that of Þorleif Björnsson, the governor of western Iceland, the then owner of the large, stately and beautifully illustrated manuscript known as *Flateyjarbók* (Gammel Kongelig Samling 1005 fol., now in the Arnamagnæan Collection, Reykjavik),[3] in a later insertion which contains the text from the beginning to *HÞ* 28^{31} in the edition, where it breaks off after Heming has been rescued by St Olaf. The second version is somewhat abbreviated and is found in a sixteenth-century hand in *Hrokkinskinna* (Copenhagen, Royal Library, Gammel Kongelig Samling 1010 fol.), a manuscript the name of which, meaning 'the wrinkled vellum', is rather appropriate and which contains the text as far as *HÞ* 38^{6}, where it breaks off. The second part of the tale, including the myth of Harold's survival, is found written, probably in the period 1306–8, in the hand of Hauk Erlendsson, an Icelander who served as lawman in Norway, in manuscript AM 544 4to, now in the Arnamagnæan Collection, Copenhagen, part of a vellum codex that was split up by Árni Magnússon and which is known as *Hauksbók* because it might be described as Hauk's own private library.[4] This manuscript contains the end of the *þáttr* from *HÞ* 42^{21}. In spite of the disparity in the nature of their subject matter, it would indeed seem that the two parts of *Hemings þáttr* originally belonged together. A transcript made in Copenhagen in the winter of 1697–98 of a now-lost leaf of *Hauksbók*

3 Kolbrún Haraldsdóttir, 'Flateyjarbók', in *Medieval Scandinavia*, ed. Phillip Pulsiano *et al.*, pp. 197–8, and Jonna Louis-Jensen, 'Den yngre del af Flateyjarbók', *Afmælisrit Jóns Helgasonar 30. júní 1969* (Reykjavik, 1969), pp. 235–50. The Arnamagnæan Collections are now divided between both Copenhagen and Reykjavik.

4 Gunnar Harðarson and Stefán Karlsson, 'Hauksbók', in *Medieval Scandinavia*, ed. Phillip Pulsiano *et al.*, pp. 271–2.

contains text from the tale that overlaps with that surviving in *Hrokkinskinna*, showing that when the copy was made, one more leaf must have survived in *Hauksbók* of the gathering which proceeded what now survives of the tale in that manuscript. In addition, the author's fondness for drawing parallels provides several links between the two sections.[5]

The text of the latter part of *Hemings þáttr* is largely dependent for its content on *Haralds saga Sigurðarsonar* and includes much supernatural matter such as dreams and portents that is omitted from a rationalistic text such as that in *Heimskringla*. There is also much additional material, including the same kind of legendary and folklore motifs that are found in the first part of the tale. The existence of this text of *Hemings þáttr* in a version that was written down in the first decade of the fourteenth century is proof that the *þáttr* cannot have been compiled later than about 1300.

It is evident from both parts of the tale that the author had a great interest in all things supernatural, whether these were related to Christianity or to heathen beliefs and legends. The relic of St Stephen, for example, which is instrumental in saving Heming's life, is given prominence. This relic may well have been known to the author at first hand, for there is reliable information that it was kept in the church at Mel in Iceland, which is in fact dedicated to Stephen and where the relic was known to a disapproving, anti-papistical Arngrím Jónsson at the end of the sixteenth century and could still be seen as late as in 1712.[6]

St Olaf, king, missionary and martyr, who hovers over the whole of the tale, was never officially canonised but his cult spread swiftly even outside Norway and at least thirteen churches in England have medieval dedications to Olaf or Olave.[7] It is not surprising that his interventions play such a prominent role in this tale with a Norwegian hero. Occasionally the episodes would seem to have been invented by the author of the *þáttr*. It is only here, for example, that I have been able to find the account of Harold Hardrada's sending his accomplice Tostig, a brother of Harold II, to swear an oath of loyalty on the shrine of St Olaf (*HÞ* 39$^{14-15}$). St Olaf remains popular to this very day in Norway. He gave his name to a ship on the Oslo–Copenhagen route early in the last century and several Norwegian streets are now named after him. In present-day Oslo he has also given his name to a hairdresser and a pub. There have always, however, been those who have preferred to honour Olaf Tryggvason as the first missionary to Norway. Odd Snorrason, a monk at Þingeyrar in northern Iceland, states specifically in the prologue to the saga he composed in Latin about Olaf Tryggvason that the king deserved a saga of his own because he was the first to bring Christianity to Norway. Olaf Tryggvason was certainly a practising advocate of muscular Christianity and violent methods. In connection with the rivalry between advocates of the two Olafs, it is incidentally worth pointing out that the Norwegian professor Bjarne Fidjestøl drew attention at the end of the last century to the fact that Olaf Tryggvason and St Olaf are not the only candidates for the title of prime

5 *Hauksbók. The Arna-Magnæan Manuscripts 371, 4to, 544, 4to, and 675, 4to*, ed. Jón Helgason, Manuscripta Islandica 5 (Copenhagen, 1960), XXVIII, and *HÞ*, XCV–C.

6 *Arngrimi Jonae Opera Latine Conscripta* I–IV, ed. Jakob Benediktsson, Bibliotheca Arnamagnæana IX-XII (Copenhagen, 1950–57), at I. 295, IV. 213–14, and *HÞ*, XCV–C.

7 Francis Bond, *Dedications & Patron Saints of English Churches* (Oxford, 1914), pp. 78, 127.

christianiser of Norway, for there are those who prefer the claims of Hans Nielsen Hauge, a revivalist lay preacher who died in 1824.[8]

Omens and dreams play a significant role in the part of the tale that is concerned with Harold Hardrada's expedition to England and his attempt to win the English throne there. Many of these, but not all, are found in other versions of *Haralds saga Sigurðarson* but the author of the *þáttr* introduces episodes for which no immediate source has been identified. The fable of the greedy dog, for example, is one of those ascribed to Aesop but I have not been able to locate a Scandinavian model for the episode in which it occurs here, an encounter between Harold's rebellious brother Tostig and King Swein of Denmark. Their conversation is practically the same in the various recorded versions of *Haralds saga* but it is only *Hemings þáttr* that makes Swein employ the fable of the dog with a loaf of bread in its mouth that catches sight of its own reflection in the water while crossing a bridge and dives into the water to get the reflected loaf, losing in the process the one it already had, to warn Tostig off the vainglorious pursuit of idle dreams.[9]

The various versions of *Haralds saga* all agree with the English historical sources that Harold II died at the Battle of Hastings so it cannot be these which are the source for the version of the survival story recorded in the *þáttr*. This is briefly as follows:[10]

> On the night after the battle a peasant (*kotkarl*) and his wife go to the battlefield in search of anything of value and see a bright light shining. They agree that it must be a holy man and begin to clear away the bodies near the light. A man's arm bearing a great gold ring emerges. The peasant takes hold of it and asks if the man is alive. The reply is positive and the woman says she thinks it is the king. They place him on their cart and take him home with them. The woman instructs her husband to kill the draught-horse, tear out its muscles and cut off its ears and says that if anyone should come looking for the body of the king, he was to say that she had gone mad and that the horse had been attacked by wolves. They cleanse the king's wounds and conceal him in their dwelling. Shortly afterwards William's men arrive and ask the peasant why he had carried away the king, alive or dead. The man denies that he has done so and bemoans the loss of his horse and his wife's madness. They insist on going inside and find the woman eating coal. She leaps up, seizes a *skálm* (the weapon characteristically borne by troll-women), curses and says that she will kill them. The ruse works and William's men leave. The couple nurse the king until he has recovered from his wounds and sends for Heming. Heming offers to travel round the country gathering support to help Harold regain his kingdom but the king replies that although this might be possible, too many would then be oath-breakers and he did not want to be responsible for that. He would rather follow the example of Olaf Tryggvason who after his defeat off Wendland did not wish to return to his kingdom but went to Greece and there served God for the rest of his life. 'I shall have a hermit's cell (*ermita*

8 Bjarne Fidjestol, 'Óláfr Tryggvason the missionary – a literary portrait from the Middle Ages', in *Selected Papers*, ed. Odd Einar Haugen and Else Mundal, trans. Peter Foote (Odense, 1997), pp. 201–27, at p. 201.

9 Cf. *HÞ*, CXXXIII.

10 An English translation is contained in Margaret Ashdown's article 'An Icelandic account of the survival of Harold Godwinson', in *The Anglo-Saxons. Studies in some Aspects of their History and Culture Presented to Bruce Dickins*, ed. Peter Clemoes (London, 1959), pp. 122–36.

kofa) built for me in Canterbury, where I can see King William as often as possible and I shall eat no food other than what you bring me'. Heming agrees to this. Harold rewards the couple who have saved his life and enters the cell. He stays there for three years and no-one knows who he is except Heming and the priest who hears his confession. One day he tells Heming that he has been stricken by an illness that will lead to his death. And one day, while King William is dining, he hears the bells ringing all over the town and asks why. 'I think a monk has died who is called Harold', replies Heming. 'What Harold is that?', asks the king. 'Godwine's son', replies Heming. 'Who has been looking after him?', says the king. 'I have', answers Heming. 'If that is true', says the king, 'it shall be your death but we want to see the body'. He enters the cell where the body was lying naked. It was so beautiful to look at and there was such a sweet smell that everyone recognized that Harold had indeed been a holy man. The king asked Heming what he was willing to do in return for his life. Heming asked, 'What do you demand, sire?' 'That you shall swear to be just as faithful to me as to King Harold and that you shall serve me as you have served him'. Heming says, 'I would rather die with him than live with you but I could have betrayed you long ago if I had wanted to do so'. 'It is true', said the king, 'that there will be one less most valiant man in England if you are killed'. 'I will now offer to make you the most eminent baron in England and you shall remain with me and be in control of my court or if you do not wish to do this I will give you an income of £300 per annum and you may live wherever you want in England'. Heming thanked the king for his offer and said, 'I will agree to remain in England but I have no wish for wealth from now on. I would ask you to grant me this same cell and here shall I live to the end of my life'. The king was silent for a long time but then he said, 'Since you ask this of a pure heart, it shall be granted to you'. Then William had Harold's body clothed in royal raiment and his obsequies performed most fittingly and he was buried with great honour. Shortly afterwards Heming entered the above-mentioned cell and served God there to the end of his days, eventually becoming blind and dying in his cell.

The fact that Harold II elects to follow the example of King Olaf Tryggvason in entering a hermit's cell gives a clue as to where we should look for the inspiration for this episode and it is true that the only two other Icelandic sources to mention the survival of Harold II are both associated with Olaf Tryggvason.

The closer parallel is found in a chapter that was added to an Icelandic translation of a saga of Olaf that was originally written in Latin by Odd Snorrason, a monk in the monastery of Þingeyrar in the north of Iceland, in about 1190.[11] Odd collected his material from many different sources, some of which are now lost, and his chief aim was to glorify Olaf as the first missionary king of Norway, whom he thought deserved a saga of his own, as mentioned above. Odd's Latin text has been lost and only survives in three different redactions of an Icelandic translation, each represented by a single manuscript: AM 310 4to in the Arnamagnæan Collection, Copenhagen, written between 1250 and 1275 and now incomplete, Perg. 4to no. 18 in the Royal Library Stockholm, written about 1300 and also incomplete and a fragment also in the Royal Library Stockholm containing two folios, De la Gardie 4–7, written in about 1270. It

11 Ólafur Halldórsson, 'Óláfs saga Tryggvasonar', in *Medieval Scandinavia*, ed. Phillip Pulsiano *et al.*, pp. 448–9, and *Saga Óláfs Tryggvasonar af Oddr Snorrason munk*, ed. Finnur Jónsson (Copenhagen, 1932), pp. 118–19, 245–6.

would seem that Odd's work ended with chapter 78 in AM 310. This is followed in this manuscript by four chapters containing material loosely related to Olaf Tryggvason, including a description in chapter 79 of the reverence shown by King Edward the Confessor towards King Olaf Tryggvason, Edward's knowledge of Olaf's doings after his apparent death at Svold and his announcement of the news from Syria that Olaf is dead. Chapter 80 deals with the survival myth of Harold II, a subject that was presumably thought relevant because Harold's decision not to attempt to regain his kingdom is motivated by his desire to follow the example of Olaf Tryggvason. The source for this chapter has not been identified.[12] It is a good deal shorter than the text in *HÞ* and no mention is made, of course, of the legendary Heming's part in the story. It begins very similarly to the account in the *þáttr*:

> A peasant (*þorpkarl*) arrives at the battlefield in pursuit of booty but without his wife. Harold hails the peasant, who runs home to his wife for advice. She reacts quickly and tells him to harness the horse to the cart and accompany her to the battlefield. Here she asks if there is any man present who can answer her. Harold draws attention to himself and the couple clear away the dead bodies round about him. They ask him his name and family but he refuses to answer. They consider that he must be a man of rank, however, from his equipment and bearing. The author explains that it was Harold II, who had collapsed from exhaustion and loss of blood and his many but small wounds. He was also incapacitated by the layer of dead bodies on top of him. Afterwards the peasants take him home to themselves in the wagon and nurse him back to health. The day after the battle Harold's enemies go to the battlefield to take away his body but they cannot find it and are amazed. After he is restored to health, Harold considers what he should do and thinks of the example of Olaf Tryggvason and decides not to return to his kingdom but is filled with the Holy Spirit and yearns for heavenly joy. He chooses to live in a cell and stays there for a long time. King William has Harold's body taken to London and buries it honourably beside the other kings.

The third account of the survival of Harold II to be found in the Icelandic sources is much briefer than the two that have been discussed so far. It is found in the text known as *Játvarðar saga*, the saga of Edward the Confessor. This survives in two vellum codices. The manuscript known as Stockholm Perg. fol. no. 5 was written between about 1350 and 1365, probably at Þingeyrar, and the part of the manuscript containing the saga can be dated to the early 1360s.[13] The other codex to contain the saga is Gks 1005 fol. or *Flateyjarbók*, which was written not far away from Þingeyrar and has been described above. *Játvarðar saga*, however, is found in the original part of the manuscript, written in the hand of Magnús Þórhallsson between 1387 and 1394. It is

[12] It has been assumed by Finnur Jónsson and Bjarni Aðalbjarnarson that chapters LXXVIII–LXXX in AM 310 4to derive from Gunnlaugr Leifsson's *Óláfs saga Tryggvasonar*, which was also written in Latin in Þingeyrar and is also lost except for some passages that would seem to be found in other sagas (cf. Bjarni Aðalbjarnarson, *Om De Norske Kongers Sagaer* (Oslo, 1937), p. 63, and Óláfur Halldórsson, 'Óláfs saga Tryggvasonar', in *Medieval Scandinavia*, ed. Phillip Pulsiano *et al.*, p. 449.

[13] *Byskupa Sǫgur. MS Perg. fol. No. 5 in the Royal Library of Stockholm*, ed. Jón Helgason, Corpus Codicum Islandicorum Medii Aevi 19 (Copenhagen, 1950), p. 21; *Sagas of Icelandic Bishops: Fragments of Eight Manuscripts*, ed. Stefán Karlsson, Early Icelandic Manuscripts in Facsimile 7 (Copenhagen, 1967), p. 46.

specifically stated in both manuscripts that the authority for the account is a narrative recorded by Englishmen. The text in Perg. fol. no. 5 gives only the very bare bones of the narrative:

> On the night after the battle some of Harold's friends went to the battlefield and searched for his body and found him alive and carried him off to be cared for. He was healed in secret. And when he was restored to health, he refused to fight with William for his kingdom. And many men say that he lived on into the days of Henry the Old (presumably Henry I [reigned 1100–1135]).

There is a little more flesh on the bones of the narrative in *Flateyjarbók*:

> On the night after the battle some friends of King Harold went to the battlefield to look for his body and found him alive and carried him off to be cared for and he was afterwards healed in secret. When King Harold was restored to health, his friends offered to fight against William so that his land might be restored to him, cost what it might. But King Harold did not wish this to happen and said that he understood that God in heaven begrudged him the kingdom and that was perhaps for the best. The king then made the desirable decision to forsake worldly glory and entered a hermit's cell [*gekk i stein*] and remained a hermit for the rest of his days, serving almighty God incessantly both night and day. And many men say that King Harold lived on into the days of Henry the Old.

Since the appearance of my edition of *Hemings þáttr* the source for much of the material in *Játvarðar saga* has been identified by Christine Fell.[14] It is an unpublished world chronicle up to the year 1219, known as the *Chronicon universale anonymi Laudunensis*, which was written in Latin, probably by an English monk of the Premonstratensian order at Laon in north-eastern France. It only survives in two thirteenth-century manuscripts, one now in Paris, the other in Berlin, but Christine Fell was convinced that there must have been another manuscript which found its way to northern Iceland and that the remark about Harold's surviving into the reign of Henry the Old in *Játvarðar saga* must be derived from the statement in the *Chronicon* to the effect that Harold had lived as a hermit until the twenty-third year of the reign of Henry II of England, that is 1177.

It should not be forgotten, however, that an English source, the *Chronicon Anglicanum* of Ralph of Coggeshall, written in Latin in the third decade of the thirteenth century, also records that Harold survived until the last years of Henry II, when Harold would have been about 168.[15] Lars Lönnroth noted this parallel and assumed that the *Chronicon* and *Játvarðar saga* must at this point go back to a common source but that this source must have referred to the time of Henry I, since it was absurd to suggest that Harold could have lived until the end of the reign of Henry II.[16] Jonna Louis-Jensen has rightly objected to this comment, however, that it is exactly the

14 Christine Fell, 'The Icelandic version of the Anglo-Saxon emigration to Byzantium', *Anglo-Saxon England* 3 (1974), 179–96, and 'English history and Norman legend in the Icelandic saga of Edward the Confessor', *Anglo-Saxon England* 6 (1977), 223–36.

15 *Radulphi de Coggeshall Chronicon Anglicanum*, ed. Joseph Stevenson, Rolls Series 66 (London, 1875), p. 1.

16 Lars Lönnroth, 'Studier i Olaf Tryggvasons saga', *Samlaren* 84 (1963), 54–94, at 78.

absurdity that shows that there must be a literary link between the two texts.[17] There would also seem to be a similar link with another English text from the beginning of the thirteenth century, namely the *Vita Haroldi*, although here it is Harold's younger brother Gyrth who makes an appearance in the days of King Henry II.[18] As noted by Marc Cohen, irrespective of whether the author of *Játvarðar saga* adopted the claim about Harold's longevity from Ralph's chronicle or the Laon chronicle or some other source, it would seem that it was he who was responsible for having replaced Henry II by Henry I on his own initiative to make Harold's longevity seem slightly less improbable.[19] In connection with the obvious relationship between *Játvarðar saga* and the English chronicles, it is interesting to note that other works associated with England are known to have found their way to the monastery at Þingeyrar.[20]

It is difficult to know whether it is the skeleton version of the survival myth in Perg. fol. no. 5 or the longer one in *Flateyjarbók* that is closer to the source for this part of *Játvarðar saga*. It seems unlikely, however, that either of the versions can have been a source for the longer versions of the survival myth in *Hemings þáttr* and *Óláfs saga*.

Let us return to these versions. They have sufficient similarities for it to seem likely that they share a common source, although I have been unable to identify this. Among the features they have in common are the peasant couple who are responsible for removing Harold from the battlefield, hiding him from his enemies and nursing him back to health, although the detailed accounts of these events are not in fact very similar. Some of the differences, of course, merely reflect the need for the author of *Hemings þáttr* to give Heming a significant role to play at the end of his tale. Both accounts record Harold's decision to follow the example of Olaf Tryggvason and to renounce worldly power in favour of life in a hermit's cell and joy in heaven and they also agree that Harold, unlike Olaf, instead of leaving his kingdom in the sense of travelling abroad, desires to remain in England, in *Hemings þáttr* specifically to be able to see William as frequently as possible in the church in Canterbury, presumably as a kind of expiation. The omission of the pilgrimage motif is striking in the light of the fact that the Icelandic versions of the survival of Olaf tell of a pilgrimage to Byzantium, Syria and Jerusalem and that *Hemings þáttr* notes that Olaf would not return to his kingdom after his defeat but journeyed instead to Greece, while in the appended chapter to *Óláfs saga Tryggvasonar* in the manuscript AM 310 4to, Harold decides that he would not turn back to his kingdom (*villdi eigi snuaz til rikis sins*). In the context in which it stands this expression is rather inappropriate, for Harold is actually still in the kingdom which was his, although it is so no longer. The

17 Jonna Louis-Jensen, *Kongesagastudier. Kompilationen Hulda-Hrokkinskinna*, Bibliotheca Arnamagnæana 32 (Copenhagen, 1977), 134 and n. 26.

18 For the *Vita Haroldi* cf. the paper by Stephen Matthews in this volume and the comments by Lilla Kopár, 'Leben und Taten verstorbener Könige. Entstehung literarischer Zeugnisse über das Leben von Óláfr Tryggvason und König Harold II von England nach ihrem (angeblichen) Tod', in *Arbeiten zur Skandinavistik*, ed. Fritz Paul, Joachim Grage and Wilhelm Heizmann, Texte und Untersuchungen zur Germanistik und Skandinavistik 45 (Frankfurt am Main, 2000), 181–7, at 182.

19 Marc Cohen, 'From Throndheim to Waltham to Chester: Viking and post-Viking attitudes in the survival legends of Óláfr Tryggvason and Harold Godwinson', in *The Middle Ages in the North-West*, ed. Tom Scott and Pat Starkey (Oxford, 1995), pp. 143–53, at p. 149.

20 Helgason, *Byskupa Sǫgur*, pp. 21–2.

pilgrimage motif obviously belonged originally to the Olaf myth rather than to the one about Harold. I find it rather surprising, however, that the author of *Hemings þáttr* decided not to exploit it, since he had earlier sent Heming on a pilgrimage to Rome after his miraculous escape from death (*HÞ* 29[6]) and pilgrimages of various kinds are associated with the thirteenth-century English versions of the survival myth of Harold.[21] Both the *þáttr* and the saga let Harold enter a monastic cell. The fact that the author of *Hemings þáttr* locates the cell, and presumably also William's court, in Canterbury reflects his general ignorance of the geography of England. *Óláfs saga* wisely makes no mention of the location of the cell. The accounts of Harold's time spent in the cell, 'three years' in the *þáttr*, 'a long time' in the saga, also differ greatly. That in the *þáttr* is by far the more expansive, mainly because there are several loose ends still to be tied up by the author of *Hemings þáttr* in his reasonably successful attempt to make a unity out of a conglomeration of motifs. It would thus seem that the account in the addition to *Óláfs saga Tryggvasonar* is the more reliable representative of the original version of the myth in the Icelandic sources.

Appendix

The three versions of the survival legend in the Icelandic sources are as follows:

I. According to the text in *Hemings þáttr Áslákssonar* as recorded in the manuscript known as *Hauksbók* (AM 544 4to), written by Hauk Erlendsson within the period 1306–08, printed here from the edition of the *þáttr* edited by Gillian Fellows Jensen and published as Editiones Arnamagnæanæ Series B3 (Copenhagen, 1962), pp. 56–9.

(71v–72v) *Græddr Haralldr konvngr G(vðina) s(vn)*

Nott þa eftir er Haralldr konvngr G(vðina) svn var fallin þa ok til valsins kotkarl ein ok kona hans at fletta valin ok fa ser fiar. þav sia þar stora valkostu. þav sia þar biart lios. þav talaz við ok segia at þar man vera heilagr maðr i valnvm. Taka þav nv at ryðia [72r] valin þar er þav sa liosit. þav sia at manz hond kom vpp or valnvm ok var a gvllringr mikill. bondin tok til handarinar ok spvrði hvart sa maðr lifði. sa svarar lifi ek. kerling mællti ryð af likvnvm. ek hyG þetta konvngen vera. þav setia vpp manin og spyria ef hann er grœðandi. konvngr s(egir) eigi syn ek at mik mætti grœða en ecki geti þit þat gort. kerling mællti a þat skal hætta. þav tokv hann vpp ok logþv i vagnin og aka heim með hann. kerlling mællti þv skallt skera or voðvana or eyknvm ok af eyrun ok ef menn koma at leita liks konvungs til þin þa skalltu segia at ek em œr en ross þitt hafa rifit vargar. þav fœgia sar konvngs ok binda ok leyna hanvm með ser.

[21] Alan Thacker, 'The cult of King Harold at Chester', in Scott and Starkey, *The Middle Ages in the North-West*, pp. 155–76.

litlv siþaR koma þar menn Vilialms konvngs ok spyria hvi hann hefir flvtt til sin Haralld konvng lifanda eða davðan. kall svarar þat hefir ek eigi gort. þeir svorvðv ecki er at dylia þvi at til þinna hvsa liGr bloðdreifin. karl s(egir) vm konvng yðarn þicki mer engi skaði. meiri skaði þicki <mer> at eyk minvm er vargar rifv fyRi nott er bardagin hafþi verið. þeir svorvðv satt man þetta vera þvi at ver sam her eykin rifinn en þo viliv ver her inn ganga ok ransaka hvat her er tiðs. karl mællti mer þrytr eigi illa at ganga. kona min varð œr af þvi at hon <heyrði> lvðra ok heropit. þeir vilia þo ganga in at einv en er þeir koma in þa sat kerling við arin og att kol og er hon ser mennina leypr hon vpp ok þrifr skalm eina ok bannaz vm ok segir at hon skal drepa þa. þeir ganga vt ok læia at henni ok fara heim við sva buið ok segia konvngi at þeir fina eigi lik H(aralldz) konvngs. En þav kerling grœða konvng a lavn þar til er hann var heill. þa sendir konvngr kerlingv til Hemings ok segir hon hanvm hvar konvngr var. Hemingr s(egir) þyrfti nv fostra at þv vissir nockot. kerling svarar ecki var ek œr. Annan dag eftir kemr Hemingr til konvngs ok verðr þar mikill fagna fvndr. tala þeir þann dag allan. Hemingr byðr konvngi at fara vm allt land ok draga her saman ok megv þer skiott fa landit vndan Vilialmi. konvngr mællti se ek at þetta ma fram ganga en of margr verðr þa eiðrofi ok vil ek eigi at sva illt leiði af mer. nv vil ek gera eftir dœmvm Olafs konvngs TryGva s(vnar) at siþan er hann for vsigr fyri Vinlandi þa villdi hann eigi fara aftr til rikis sins helldr for hannv́t <i> Grecia ok þionaði þar gvði meðan hann lifði. nv vil ek lata gera mer ein ermita kofa i Kantara byrgi þar sem ek mega sem oftaz sia Vilialm konvng i kirkivnni en þann ein skal ek mat hafa er þv fœrir mer. þersv iattar Hemingr. konvngr gefr þeim karli noga penninga en gengr siþan i einsetv. hann er þar sva .iíj. vetr at engi maðr veit hvat manna hann er vtan Hemingr ok prestr sa er hanvm skriftaði ok ein dag er Hemingr kom til Haralldz þa segir hann hanvm at hann hefir sott fengit þa er hann man til bana leiða ok ein dag <er> Vilialmr konvngr sat yfir borði þa heyrðuz hringingar vm allan staðin. konvngr spyR hvi sva fag<r>t ringi. Hemingr svarar ek get at mvnkr ein se andaðr sa er Haralldr het. hverr Haralldr er sa segir konvngr. Gvðina s(vn) segir Hemingr. hverr hefir hann varðveitt segir konvngr. Hemingr svarar ek hefir þat gert. ef þat er satt segir konvngr þa skal þat vera þin davði en sia viliv ver lik hans. gengr hann siþan i kofan þar er likit la. var þat þa berað. kendv þa allir Haralld konvng. likit var fagrt ok þeckileg<t> ok kendv menn þar sœtan ilm sva at allir vndir stoðv þeir er hia varv at hann var sanheilagr maðr. konvngr spvrði þa Heming hvat hann villdi ser til lifs vinna. Hemingr spvrði hvers beiðiz þer konvngr. at þv sverir mer þers at þv skallt vera mer iamtrvr vm alla lvti sem Haralldi konvngi ok fylgia mer sva sem hanvm. Hemingr s(egir) helldr vil ek deyia með hanvm en lifa með þer en longv matta ek þig svikit hafa ef ek hefða viliað. þat er sannaz sagþi konvngr at er einvm vaskazta manne færa i Engl<an>di ef þv ert drepin. vil ek nv bioða þer at [72v] gera þig framaztan barvn i Englandi ok vera i minni hirð ok stiorna henni allri ella. vil ek gefa þer ef þv villt eigi þetta .ccc. pvnda ingialld a hverivm .xij. manvðvm ok ver hvar i Englandi er þer gott þickir. Hemingr þackaði konvngi boð sin ok mællti þat vil ek þiGia at vera i Englandi en goðs lystir mik eigi að eiga heðan af en þers vil er biðia yðr at þer lofið mer ok gefið þenna sama kofa ok vil ek her min alldr i enda. konvngr þegir langa stvnd ok mællti af þvi at þersa <er beðit> af reinv briosti þa skal þetta veita þer. siþan let Vilialmr klæða lik Haralldz konvngs med konvngs skrvða ok let gera hans vtferð sem sœmelexta ok var hann iardaðr með enne merstv sœmð. litlv siþaR geck Hemingr i fyrir nefndan kofa ok þionaði þar gvði til ellidaga ok varð vm siþir sionlavs ok andaðiz i þeiri einsetv ok lykr þar nv fra Hemingi at segia.

II. From an addition made to an Icelandic translation of a saga of Olaf Tryggvason written in Latin by Odd Snorrason in about 1190. The text here is taken from the manuscript AM 310 4to which was written between 1250 and 1275, as printed in the edition *Saga Óláfs Tryggvasonar munk*, ed. Finnur Jónsson (Copenhagen, 1932), pp. 245–6.

(fols 118–19) En um nottina eptir bardagann þa com þorpkarl einn i valinn oc villdi fletta mennina. Oc þat sa einn maðr er var ivalnum og avitaði hann um þat hit illa verk. oc hit suivirðlega. þorpkarliN liop þa heim oc segir þetta conu sinni. En hon bra við skiott oc bio ser vagn og beitti hest firir. oc bað hann fara með ser til valsins. Oc er þau comu þar þa spyrr hon ef nocquorr se sa maðr ivalnum er henni megi þa suara. Oc þa suaraði maðr. Er sa maðr ivalnum er þer ma suara. hon geck þa til hans. oc uelltu þau fra fotum ser dauðum mannum. Oc er hon sa þenna mann. Þa letu þau hann i slæðann. Þau spurðu hann at nafni oc at ætt. en hann uilldi huarki segia. Þau þottuz þo skilia at hann myndi vera gofugr maðr. bæði firir sakir umbuðar oc yfirbragðz. Þessi maðr var Harallðr Guðina son oc hafði fallit firir mœþi oc bloðrás. oc morg hafði hann sár. oc engi miok stór En þat þrœngði honum mioc oc angraði. er sua þyct lagu hinir dauðu menninir a honum. at firir þeim matti hann eigi hrœraz. Siþan flutte þau hann heim ivagninum. oc grœddu hann En annan dag eptir orrostu comu uvinir hans. oc villdu taca liket ibrot oc fundu eigi oc undruðuz miok. Oc eptir þat er hann var grœddr. þa ihugaði hann sitt rað. oc hugði at dœmum. Olafs konungs Tryggua sonar oc tok hann þat rað at hann villdi eigi snuaz til rikis sins. helldr varð hann ablasiN af helgum anda. oc leitaði af allri girnd himinrikis fagnaðar. oc valði ser til bygþar æinn stein. oc var þar lengi. Vilhialmr konungr let fœra lik hans iLundunir oc grava uegliga hia aðrum konungum.

III.A. According to *Játvarðar saga* in Stockholm Perg. fol. no. 5 written between 1350 and 1365.

(70v) þat er sogn enskra manna at um nottina eptir orrostu þeirra Vilhialms ok Haraldz hafe nokkurir vinir Haraldz konungs farit til ualsins ok leitad eptir like hans ok fundu hann lifanda ok fluttu til lækningar uar hann græddr aa laun. Ok er hann uar heill uilldi hann eigi strida med Vilhialmi til Rikis. Ok er þat margra manna sogn at hann hafe lifat a<ll>t a daga fram Heinreks hins gamla.

III.B. From *Játvarðar saga* in Gks 1005 fol. (*Flateyjarbok*), where it is found in the hand of Magnús Þórhallsson, written between 1387 and 1394. Printed here from *Flateyjarbók. En Samling af Norske Konge-Sagaer* I–III, eds. Guðbrandur Vigfússon and C. R. Unger (Christiania, 1868), III, 469.

(213v) þat er sogn enskra manna sannordra at a næstu nott eftir bardagann hafi nockurir vinir Halldz konungs farit til valsins ok leitat eftir liki hans ok fundu hann lifanda ok fluttu til lækningar ok var sidan græddr aa laun. Enn er Haralldr konungr var heill vordinn þa var honum bodit af sinum vinum at strida aa Vilhialm ok faa landit huat er kostadi. Enn Haralldr konungr villdi þat eigi ok kuaz vndirstanda at gud i himinriki vnti honum eigi rikisins enda ma vera af sua se betr. Tok konugrinn þaa vpp æskiligt raad at fyrirlaata þessa heims metnat ok geck i stein ok var einsetumadr medan hann lifdi þionandi sua almaattigum gudi vaflaatiga bædi naatt ok dag. ok er þat margra manna sogn at Haralldr konungr hafi lifat allt fram aa daga Heinriks gamla.

5

The Content and Construction of the *Vita Haroldi*

STEPHEN MATTHEWS

THIS article addresses some features of an early-thirteenth-century Latin account of the life of King Harold II, the *Vita Haroldi*, which survives in a unique later copy from Waltham Abbey, of which Harold was the distinguished early patron.[1] It speculates upon the construction and to a limited extent, the purpose of the *Vita*. The text has been described as 'little else than an historical romance'[2] and so it is, considered as conventional history, but that is not an appropriate way of regarding it. It is secular hagiography and should be read in that light. As hagiography, the story makes perfect sense, even though it does not quite reach to the full stature of a saint's *Life*, for as Marc Cohen observed, it lacks two essentials, a list of miracles (although there is a reference to their happening) and a final resting place for the saintly body.[3] These two features apart, it has all the other necessary hagiographical elements, and even the lack of miracles is remedied in the *Waltham Chronicle*.[4] It is the life of a saint (or near saint) who was destined to be a king, rather than the life of a king whose virtues were sufficient to make him a saint. Read this way, its purpose is clear and achieved.

Contact with Reality

The work falls into two parts. First, there is Harold's life before the Battle of Hastings, as the trusted minister of Edward the Confessor, and then as king, through the Battle of Stamfordbridge, through to Hastings. He lost the battle and the crown passed to William, but Harold himself was not killed, only severely wounded. After a long period of recuperation, he became a hermit and a wanderer before settling finally at

1 London, BL, Harley 3776, 1r–25v; 4°, vellum and bearing the rubric *Incipit prologus in vita venerabilis Haroldi, quondam Anglorum Regis*. Harley 3776 also contains the later of the two versions of the *Waltham Chronicle (De Inventione Sanctae Crucis)*, referred to in n. 4 below. The *Vita* has been printed in *Vita Haroldi: the Romance of the Life of Harold, King of England*, ed. and trans. Walter de Gray Birch (London, 1885), pp. 3–203 and translated in M. Swanton, *Three Lives of the Last Englishmen* (London, 1984), pp. 3–40.

2 Thomas Duffus Hardy, *Descriptive Catalogue of Materials relating to the History of Great Britain*, 3 vols (London, 1862–71), I (1862). No. 1267, 668–71, at 668.

3 Marc Cohen, 'From Throndheim to Waltham to Chester: Viking and post-Viking attitudes in the survival legends of Olaf Tryggvason and Harold Godwinson', in *The Middle Ages in the North West*, ed. Tom Scott and Pat Starkey (Oxford, 1995), p. 150.

St John's Church in Chester where he died. The whole work is largely fanciful, the second part almost entirely so, but throughout it there are occasional glimpses of the real world and these give it enough credibility to place it in an historical setting, however improbable.[5] If we look first at Harold's life before death, if I may put it that way, the narrative does contain real facts. His parentage is given correctly and whilst one may doubt the degree of affection and admiration with which he was held in Edward's court, there is no doubt that he became a central figure in it.[6] He did conduct a successful military operation against the Welsh King Gruffydd, though he did not reduce that country to the point of extermination. It is quite possible that Harold did go to Rome in 1056 or 1058[7] and that this journey is reflected in the *Vita*, although the details of his return journey were borrowed from the journey of 1061 undertaken by Tostig and his large party who were robbed a few days out of Rome and had to return.[8] The imported detail, though erroneous, gives credibility to what was in reality an ill-documented journey. There certainly was a Norwegian invasion in 1066 and it is fairly described although there is no contemporary record of Harold's illness and the vision of Abbot Ælfwine, which is discussed below. Harold's defeat at Hastings (p. 14)[9] is another undeniable fact, though the compiler had difficulty with his death, as we shall see.

Whilst the events that, according to the *Vita*, took place after the Battle of Hastings have no historical reality, it is worth looking at two of them in relation to the contemporary world. After his alleged 'death', Harold did not immediately adopt the pilgrim role for which he was destined. He first travelled to Saxony to try to enlist military support from his historic kin, but was rebuffed both there and later in Denmark, because of the network of alliances which William had created and which he was unable to break. This could be an echo of the diplomatic support that William had been careful to gain before his invasion. This failure led to further wanderings and Harold finally returned to England, disguised as a pilgrim, and settled in a cave near Dover for ten years before moving further west to Wales and Chester.

The second posthumous quasi-historical feature is the compiler's attitude to the Welsh, whom the disguised Harold tried to convert and improve, and I include it as historical because it must reflect English attitudes to that race, or at least attitudes of those living in the borders. They were 'treacherous and savage little men' (p. 30) who were violent, stole Harold's belongings and extorted money from him. Gradually, by patience, gifts of food and drink, and kindness, Harold softened their hearts. It may be

4 *The Waltham Chronicle*, ed. and trans. L. Watkiss and M. C. Chibnall (Oxford, 1994). There is a full description of the manuscript collections at pp. xlviii–liii.

5 A mixture recognized by Hardy: 'There is probably some truth in this curious narrative, but its errors are great and numerous' (*Descriptive Catalogue*, I. 670).

6 For details of Harold Godwinesson's career, see N. J. Higham, 'Harold Godwinesson: the construction of kingship' in this volume.

7 *Vita Ædwardi*, I. v: Barlow, *Vita Ædwardi*, pp. 52–3. See also P. Grierson, 'A visit of Earl Harold to Flanders in 1056', *English Historical Review* 40 (1936), 90–7; Ian W. Walker, *Harold, the last Anglo-Saxon King* (Stroud, 1997), p. 82.

8 Tostig's journey is recorded in *Vita Ædwardi*, I. v: Barlow, *Vita Ædwardi*, pp. 52–7.

9 Bracketed page references in the text are to Michael Swanton's translation of the *Vita* in *Three Lives of the Last Englishmen.*

that the Welsh were as barbaric as they were described, but whether they were or not, the purpose of their villainy was, by a contrast, to enhance the virtue of the exiled king. Our hero had to suffer the indignities borne by Christ himself, to be mocked, injured, even whipped, by lesser people, so that he could pass to spiritual triumph and his final home.

Problems

The cycle of fate

The compiler had to address three serious problems in composing his *Vita*. The first is Harold's own nature and his failure to keep his kingdom, which is tackled in a way which gives a spiritual tone to the whole work, by a series of twists of fate. It is not the story of a whole-life wheel of fortune but a succession of shorter revolutions of fate, juxtapositions of good and bad, luck and ill fortune, without a life-long pattern of origin, rise and fall. There is neither space nor need to consider each of these twists in turn, and I will mention enough to give the pattern. Because of his virtues rather than his victories Edward 'admitted as a brother one whom previously he had found useful only as a soldier' (p. 4). Harold consolidated his position by conquering Wales

> reducing it nearly to the point of extermination. These victories made him a shining example even during the lifetime of the saintly King Edward; and through his bravery in the field he gained a peace and tranquillity of advantage to both king and country. (p. 5)

Then came the first turn of fate that wiped away all the worldly good fortune that Harold had enjoyed. Like Alfred some two hundred years before, Harold was struck by a devastating illness, in this case by a paralysis 'by which one's body when affected forgets its normal functions and refuses one its customary obedience' (p. 5).[10] This was of course a bodily affliction that was designed simply to improve the soul and Harold rose to the challenge. At first he sought human assistance but neither the king's own special doctors nor the learned Master Ailard, who was sent by the Emperor of Germany, could bring about a cure. Ailard, who was to become Abbot of Waltham, realised that it was foolish to struggle against the powers of Heaven and turned Harold towards the stone cross, 'a statue of our crucified King', which had only recently been discovered, but was already working miracles of healing at Waltham (p. 6). Harold asked for the prayers of the clergy there, and as a result was very soon restored to complete health. Later, as Harold, by now king, was hurrying to meet the Norwegian invasion in the north he was seized by a most violent pain in the leg. He spent the whole night in pain and prayer, fearful for the fate of his people if he could not fight. He turned again to the 'familiar aid of the Holy Cross' (p. 21). Another miracle restored his strength: an apparition of Abbot Ælfwine of Ramsey assured him in the name of King Edward that his present pain was a portent of victory by divine aid. Again he triumphed and again fortune turned, for William landed in the

10 Asser's *Life of Alfred*, lxxiv: S. Keynes and M. Lapidge, *Alfred the Great* (Harmondsworth, 1997), pp. 88–9.

south. Despite his haste to meet the Norman duke in battle, Harold could not pass the church at Waltham without turning aside and praying for another victory. Here Harold had perhaps his greatest spiritual triumph, for, when he bowed to the cross as he left the church, the cross itself bowed back to him. This was a sign of both disaster and triumph. It presaged earthly defeat, for Harold was to lose his battle, but it also presaged spiritual victory for 'in bending His head to the king, the King had shown that he would grant him a better victory than others looked for or understood' (p. 24). Harold therefore went on from an earthly triumph over the Norwegians and the spiritual triumph of future acceptance into Heaven, to defeat at the hands of the Normans. It was the culmination of the fluctuation between greatness and defeat. Harold travelled, in the words of the narrator, 'first to the country of the Angles and then that of the Angels'.

The compiler wanted to compare Harold's character favourably with that of his evil father, Godwine, and in doing so, drew upon two familiar medieval literary images, the rose/thorn and the lily, symbols especially of love and of the Virgin Mary. This device provides one of the many contrasts in the text, for God had made Harold of finer clay and this redounded to his honour, strengthening his virtues so that 'Thus the thorn will, as it were, produce bright red roses and bring forth snow-white lilies whose natural virtue is not diminished by the meaner character of the thorn, but rather enhanced by the association in an additional beauty' (p. 5). Despite its botanical improbability, the image sums up the extreme manner in which the compiler regarded Harold, and how, despite the adversity of his birth, he was destined to have the stature of a saint.

Did Harold die at Hastings or not?

The narrator had next to face his most difficult biographical problem. The words just quoted suggest that the king did die at Hastings, for no living man can inhabit the world of the angels; but this was an untenable position since the compiler had already given details of Harold's acts after Hastings and was about to give more. The difficulty was solved by ignoring it or by treating acceptance into Heaven as a future guarantee rather than an immediate event. In Swanton's modern edition the short space of six printed lines separates Harold's hurrying to the land of the angels before Hastings, from his return after 'many years in the saintly sweat of religious pilgrimage'. The stage was set long before in the repetition of the story told by Saebeorht, Harold's servant, when it was claimed that the king had been wounded not killed, rescued, cured and launched on his life of sanctity:

> When the English army was overcome and beaten by this initial Norman onslaught, King Harold was thrown to the ground amongst the slain, pierced through with innumerable blows. But his wounds, although many and deadly could not entirely deprive of life one of whom the goodness of the Saviour had happily destined to restore to life and victory. So as the hosts of the enemy left the field of slaughter, he who just the day before was so powerful, was found stunned and scarcely breathing by certain women whose pity and a desire to bind up the wounds of the injured had led there. Acting as Samaritans towards him and binding up his wounds, they carried him to a nearby cottage. From thence, it is reported, unrecognised and cunningly hidden, he was brought by two peasants to

> the city of Winchester. Here, keeping to a secret hiding place in a certain cellar for two years, he was healed by an Arab woman who was particularly skilled in the art of surgery; and with the co-operation of the medicine of the Most High, he was restored to undiminished health. (p. 13)

As his people had by now 'submitted their necks to the yoke of the Conqueror' and all the leading men were annihilated or driven from their homeland, Harold departed for Germany and Denmark to seek help, which was refused. He then decided to become a pilgrim, returned to England and in another contrast, this time of place, settled for ten years in a cave near to Dover, not far, the narrator stressed, from the place where he had lost his kingdom and nearly met his death. Here he could meditate upon 'his own and his nation's past misfortunes and the present arrogance of the enemy' (p. 29). This is a remarkable phrase for a work written in the first decade of the thirteenth century and we will return to it. We do not need to retell how Harold eventually left his cave for Wales and his final resting place in Chester but turn instead to the compiler's obvious awareness of the improbabilities in his account. He told the story, which appears also in the *Waltham Chronicle* (quoted below), that the Canons of Waltham asked Edith Swan-Neck, Harold's mistress, to make a search for the body and that she came back with the wrong one, their claim being denied in the reign of Henry II by Harold's younger brother Gyrth, testing his memory, as Thacker calculated, at the minimum age of 130![11] The mystery thus set, the compiler embarked upon an essay on the writing of history, pointing out that things are seen and told differently by different people. His difficulty was to reconcile what he knew with what he wanted to believe, a common enough problem for historians, but having presented and perhaps thoroughly muddled both sides of the question, the compiler concluded that he had simply set down the story as he learned it: 'I do not discuss all these matters here [he said] but the Lord will give anyone who walks honestly the ability to understand what I write, and feel what I feel' (p. 33).

Breaking the oath

The compiler's next problem was that it is difficult for a perjurer to be a saint. To his credit he tackled the issue head on. He accepted that Harold had sworn an oath to William to support the Norman's claim to the throne. He also accepted that Harold broke it. Once more, he gave both sides of the question. The perjury was so serious that the oak tree near Rouen under which the oath was given had since withered, turned white and died, as the author had himself seen (p. 20). God punished the perjury, not by Harold's defeat at Hastings, but by the 'most violent pain in the leg' which he suffered before the battle at Stamfordbridge. In justification of the perjury, the compiler pointed out that an oath made under duress was illegal and had no force. Giving it was Harold's only means of escape. Moreover the English were outraged, then as now, by the prospect of being ruled by a foreigner. 'Heaven forbid that the

11 A. Thacker, 'The cult of King Harold at Chester', in Scott and Starkie, *The Middle Ages*, pp. 155–76, at p. 157, n. 20; Watkiss and Chibnall, *Waltham Chronicle*, p. 55. The Bayeux Tapestry depicts the death of Gyrth at the Battle of Hastings with the explicit caption *HIC CECIDERVNT LEVVINE ET GYRÐ FRATRES HAROLDI* ('here Leofwin and Gyrth, Harold's brothers, were killed'; Scene 52, Wilson, *BT*, Plates 63–4).

liberty of our city and of our English nobility should ever be subject to the barbarian yoke of Norman arrogance!' (p. 21). Harold was then raised to the throne by unanimous acclamation, an act which led to the Norwegian invasion and defeat. The biographer had no doubt that Harold was justified in breaking his oath and taking the throne, shameful though any act of perjury must be.

The Composition of the Vita

It is unfortunate that we have only a copied text, for at certain points we must distinguish between the first edition (*c*. 1206) and its copying and inclusion in the Waltham collection up to a century later. This becomes material particularly when we turn to the Prologue and chapter headings (*capitula*). Its ethos is distinctly anti-Norman and its opening words are combative in the extreme: 'To recount the deeds of Harold, a most famous and lawful king – rightfully and lawfully crowned – is no less than to display to pious minds the most brilliant reflection of godly serenity and humility.' That is extraordinary for a work compiled about 1206, being totally opposed to the whole basis of the Conqueror's regime. It goes beyond the cautious approval of Harold's breaking of his oath already considered. The antagonism towards the Normans is reinforced by the criticism of William for despoiling the treasures of Waltham Abbey, carefully listed by the compiler (p. 8) and by the remark about Norman arrogance quoted above. This is not the place to explore lingering opposition to the Norman (and by now Angevin) rulers, sufficient to say that whether the sentiments spring from the compiler himself or were just copied from the sources which he inherited, they must have been views with which he agreed or at least sympathised, for otherwise he would surely have omitted them. Such words remind us of the dangers of seeing past events only through the eyes of the victors. They are echoed by the opening words of the *Waltham Chronicle* itself, to which the *Vita* has been linked, for its author identified himself as English. When describing the finding of the Cross, he began: '. . . there lived in a place called Montacute, which my fellow-countrymen called Ludgersbury, a man who was a smith by trade'.[12]

The compiler strung together a number of traditions, written or oral, in a manner which is really quite clumsy. Of these sources, some are easily identified. The first is the account of Saebeorht, Harold's servant in life, a resident of Chester, who emulated his master by making a tour of all the Holy Places and then finally, on his return to England, settling as a hermit at Stanton Harcourt (Oxfordshire). The second is the Waltham-inspired *Waltham Chronicle (De Inventione Sanctae Crucis*), written about twenty years before, which described the finding of the stone cross which Harold venerated so deeply. Last, there is another Chester account, that of Moses, Harold's servant after death, who guided his master to St John's Church in Chester and his final home. In places the compiler referred to other accounts and opinions, including William of Malmesbury's *History of the Kings*. Other sources are harder to identify, though we may guess at some, like Gerald of Wales and Osbert of Clare's *Life of*

12 Watkiss and Chibnall, *Waltham Chronicle*, p. 2.

Edward the Confessor, from which he may have obtained the vision of Abbot Ælfwine.[13] The compiler also introduces elements from other writings, such as the illness, which recalls that of Alfred, and the word-play on angels and Angles, which is a well-known pun attributed to Pope Gregory.[14] Further, although much of the setting is Chester, other indications are that the work was connected with Waltham, and editors have assumed that it was written by someone who had been a resident there. The two locations create a tension, for although the compiler was prepared to follow the *Chronicle* in places, in others he contradicted it. Crucially, he did so in the question of Harold's final resting place, for although he was not prepared to say explicitly that the king was buried at Chester, he argued against Waltham's claim that his body was there. The *Chronicle* stated quite explicitly:

> When Osgod had brought [Edith] she pointed out the king's body amongst the heaps of dead from several identifying marks . . . they brought the body to Waltham and buried it with great honour, where, without any doubt, he has lain at rest until the present day, whatever stories men may invent that Harold dwelt in a cave at Canterbury and that later, when he died, was buried at Chester. I can now in my old age remember that I was present when his body was translated for the third time, occasioned either by the state of building work in the church, or because the brethren out of devotion were showing reverence for the body.[15]

In retelling the story of the king's last years in St John's Church, the compiler of the *Vita* ignored this account completely and, whilst not saying explicitly that the king was buried in Chester, he left the reader with the inevitable conclusion that it was so. He also introduced the story of Gyrth's denial that Waltham had the body. Another difference in emphasis is that the compiler of the *Vita* explicitly regarded Harold as a saint, whilst at Waltham he was regarded as no more than a Christian hero and benefactor of the house. These differences make it hard to envisage that a work so critical of the Abbey's claims would have been written within the Waltham tradition, yet its unique manuscript is bound with the other accounts of the house. Unfortunately, of the various authorities only Birch addressed the question of when the manuscripts within the codex were first associated. In his opinion, the same scribe copied both works in the late thirteenth century, and if he is right we have to accept that even though it diverged greatly from the Waltham orthodoxy, the *Vita* was known and copied there.[16]

Given the disagreements between the two works, we may wonder why it was included in the collection. The question was raised indirectly by Hardy when speculating upon the identity of the author. His opinion was dismissed by Birch and although the issue has been reconsidered by Thacker,[17] it has not been satisfactorily

13 'La Vie de Edouard le Confesseur par Osbert de Clare', ed. Marc Bloch, *Analecta Bollandiana* 41 (1923), 5–131, at 114.

14 *The Earliest Life of Gregory the Great*, ed. B. Colgrave (Laurence, KS, 1968), p. 90. Bede, *Ecclesiastical History*, II. i: *Bede's Ecclesiastical History of the English People*, ed. and trans. B. Colgrave and R. A. B. Mynors (Oxford, 1969), pp. 132–5.

15 Watkiss and Chibnall, *Waltham Chronicle*, p. 55.

16 Birch, *Vita Haroldi*, p. vi.

17 Hardy, *Descriptive Catalogue*, I. 668: Birch, *Vita Haroldi*, pp. xi–xii: Thacker, 'The cult of King Harold', pp.159–60.

resolved. Hardy was puzzled by the inclusion of a document so critical of Waltham's claims and advanced the solution of authorship by an embittered ex-canon, displaced by the reforms. This is far from impossible, though one would expect his grudge to be against those who ousted him rather than against the spiritual treasure of the House, and it does not explain his knowledge and promotion of the Chester stories. When we compare the two works we note that the hero of the *Chronicle* is the Holy Cross whereas the hero of the *Vita* is clearly Harold. The tone of the latter is not strikingly laudatory of Waltham and in so far as Waltham is involved, its theme is the relationship between Harold and the Abbey and their mutual benevolence. The insertion of the Chester elements may suggest that the compiler of the *Vita* had St John's interests at heart. The appearance of Waltham does not detract from Harold's virtues nor from the place of his death. Such a bias would explain the composition of the *Vita*, but it does not address the two questions of its copying into the Waltham collection and the Prologue to the whole work. Included also in the original Waltham collection is an account of miracles which had been performed at St John's by the fragment of the True Cross which was in the church from at least the middle of the thirteenth century. It is worth noting here a spiritual link between the churches in that both became centres of the cult of the Holy Cross, a fragment of which was first mentioned at St John's in the middle of the thirteenth century.[18]

The Prologue is puzzling and it is unfortunate that we have to consider a copied rather than an original text. We do not know if the Prologue originally prefaced the *Vita* or whether it was created when the collection was assembled and copied afresh. Its author could be the unskilled scribe, suggested by Birch,[19] who was trying to show off his skills for his superiors. Both the Prologue and *capitula* may have been composed for the rewritten collection and we might not reach the start of the original *Vita* until fol. 3, where, perhaps for this reason, Swanton begins his translation. If this were so, the Prologue might be an attempt to marry the diverse elements of the collection, for, despite the rubric, its terms are general enough to apply to the whole work rather than just the *Vita*. The solution is beyond the scope of this paper and this author, and the questions must be left unanswered as they were by Hardy so long ago. The only fact to add is that unlike the *Chronicle*, the *Vita* was never copied again, but remained a unique document, presumably because it was out of favour with the Waltham establishment.

Within the text of the *Vita*, another remarkable thing is that the compiler claimed to have heard the Chester stories at first hand. He heard Saebeorht's story when the latter was a hermit in his old age in Oxfordshire, when he, the compiler, 'being still of a tender age' was 'bound to him by a bond of affection'. The compiler had Moses' account from the man himself when Moses, who had been Harold's 'posthumous' servant, served him (the compiler) for two years, while he lived in the same cell that Harold had occupied. Although he did not explicitly say so, the compiler wanted us to understand that he had read the *Waltham Chronicle*. We may believe that he had read the *Chronicle*, but in claiming first hand contact with either of Harold's associates,

18 Thacker, 'The cult of King Harold', p. 160 and n. 36, p. 161.

19 Birch, *Vita Haroldi*, p. vi.

before or after death, the compiler was plainly copying blindly what was written in his original sources, without realising its absurdity. In doing so, he confirmed that there was a number of accounts in circulation and that Chester played an important part in them, playing host as well to another posthumous monarch, the Emperor Henry V.[20] As the background detail of Chester is realistic in, for example, the reference to the city walls and the existence of an actual church (St John's), we may disregard the possibility that the tale was set in the city by chance. Whilst it is tempting to see the *Vita* as a lingering element of Mercian nationalism, though by 1206 surely rather anachronistic, there is little in its content to support this, for its tone is wistful and mystic, with nothing of Drake's Drum about it. The dead Harold is not cast as a hero ready to lead his people again in war or insurrection. That also undermines any argument that the text might have been a work intended to bolster the independent attitude of the Norman earls of Chester. Although I cannot resolve these questions, I would offer one small contribution. Until the early years of the twelfth century, St John's had always been the senior church of Chester. Whatever happened, tended to happen there. It was reckoned to be the older foundation and in 973 for example it was there and not at St Werburgh's that Edgar held his ceremony of submission after being rowed down the Dee. This primacy culminated in the establishment of the see at St John's in 1075 following the Synod of London in that year and the consequential rebuilding of the cathedral on a site outside the city walls. The site must have had great significance, for it scarcely accorded with Lanfranc's intention that cathedrals should be built inside the walled circuit of their cities.[21] The extra-mural site must be unique. In the early twelfth century the influence of St John's was soon lost with the removal of the see to Coventry and the church then seems to have declined in relation to St Werburgh's, which had been refounded on a regular footing in 1092, and in 1541 after the Reformation was chosen as the site of the new cathedral. Leaving aside how they came to be included in the Waltham collection, is it possible that the genesis of the Chester stories is an attempt by St John's to keep its end up both spiritually and financially, against declining fortunes? There was no point in doing more than try to undermine Waltham's claim to have Harold's body, hence presumably the comments attributed to Gyrth. St John's could not claim possession of the body itself and therefore had to settle for second best, and claim him as a former member of the community. If this is right, then the compiler of the first edition of the *Vita* must have been associated more with Chester than Waltham.

20 The various legends are summarized by E. A. Freeman, *The History of the Norman Conquest of England*, 6 vols (Oxford, 1st ed., 1867–79), III (1869). 758–63. The story of the ex-Emperor Henry living in Chester appears first in Gerald of Wales (*Giraldus Cambrensis Opera*, Rolls Series, 8 vols (1861–91), I (1861), ed. J. S. Brewer, 186; VI (1868), ed. J. P. Dimock, 139) and was repeated with variations in *Polychronicon Ranulphi Higden, monachi cestrensis*, ed. Joseph Rawson Lumby, Rolls Series, 9 vols (London, 1865–86), VI (1865), 138.

21 Freeman, *History of the Norman Conquest* IV (1877). 414–18 esp. 415, n. 3; *The Victoria County History of Cheshire* III, ed. B. E. Harris (Oxford, 1980), 5, follows A. J. MacDonald, *Lanfranc* (Oxford, 1926), p. 101. For a recent study of early Chester see S. Matthews, 'St John's Church and the Early History of Chester', *Journal of the Chester Archaeological Society* 76 (2002), 63–80.

Plate 1 Scene 2: Harold rides to Bosham, goes to church and feasts

Plate 2 Scene 7: Guy arrests Harold

Plate 3 Scene 8: Harold rides to Beaurain with Guy

Plate 4 Scene 10: William's messengers and their horses

Plate 7 Scene 13: Meeting of Harold, Guy and William; border nudes

Plate 5 Scene 11: William's messengers

Plate 6 Scene 11 border: Detail of chained bear

Plate 8 Scenes 14–15: Approach to palace; William and Harold; Ælfgiva; border nudes

Plate 9 Scenes 16–17: William's army rides to Mont-Saint-Michel; Harold rescues Normans from quick

VBI·VNVS: CLERICVS: ET· HIC·V
ÆLFGY VA

ELIS
ET HIC: TRANSIERVNT: FLVMEN: COSNON
HIC: HAROLD: DVX: TRAHEB
DEARENA

Plate 10 Scene 21: William arms Harold

Plate 12 Scenes 24–5: Harold's return to England

Plate 11 Scene 23: Harold swears oath, watched by William

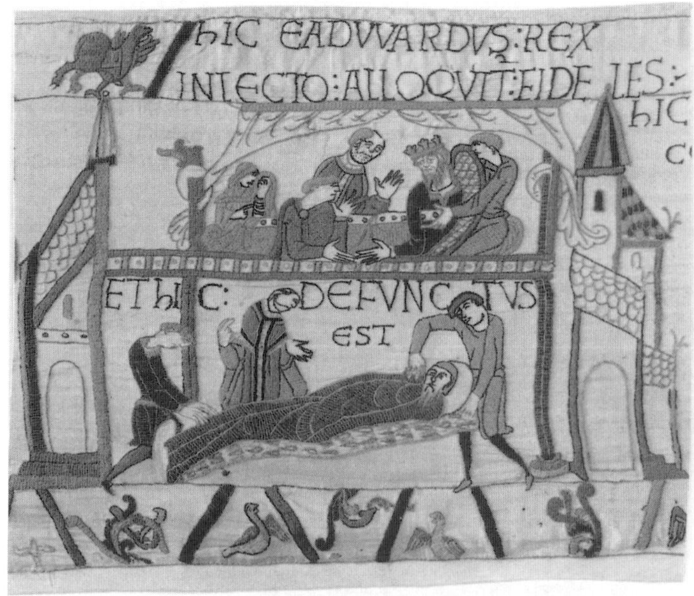

Plate 13 Scenes 27–8: Death and shrouding of Edward

Plate 15 Scene 35 – beginning of 36: Ordering the fleet to be built; construction and launch of ships

Plate 14 Scenes 29–30: Harold is offered the kingdom and crowned

Plate 16 Scenes 43–4: Feast at Hastings; Odo, William and 'Rotbert'

Plate 18 Scene 47: William's horse standing at Hastings

Plate 17 Scene 47: Woman and child flee burning house

Plate 19 Scene 48 border: Detail of nudes

Plate 20 Scenes 49 – beginning of 51: Reporting about Harold; Norman attack

ISTE
NVNTIAT:HAROLDVM
REGĒ
DEEXER
CITV
VVILLELMI
DVCIS
VIRILITER
ETSAPIENTER:
ADPRELIUM:

Plate 21 Scene 53: Horses falling in battle

Plate 23 Scene 57: Harold's death; border nudes

te 22 Scenes 54–5: Odo in battle; William raising visor

Plate 24 Scene 58: The last stallion in the Tapestry; border nudes

Part II

The Bayeux Tapestry

6

Body Language: a Graphic Commentary by the Horses of the Bayeux Tapestry

SARAH LARRATT KEEFER

THE *galop volant* ('flying gallop') is a posture in art for a horse moving at top speed, long known to the Western eye.[1] It dates back to the Mediterranean and Near East where it was widely used on metal, ceramic and stone in the Graeco-Roman world,[2] and mosaics depicting the *galop volant* are preserved from Roman-British villas of the fourth century AD.[3] It was not however an attempt at realism:[4] despite the visual impression of thrust forward with forelegs and push backward with hind-legs that a horse's gallop-stride provides, it is not representative of a genuine moment in the gallop sequence at any time.[5] In today's society where the horse is associated with

1 For further study in this singular posture, see Paul Vigneron, *Le Cheval dans l'antiquité Gréco-Romaine*, 2 vols (Nancy, 1968), II. Figs d, e, Plate III; M. Rostovtzeff, *Parthian Art and the Motive of the Flying Gallop*, Harvard Tercentenary Conference of Arts and Science 1936 (Cambridge, 1937), pp. 44–56; S. Reinach, *La Représentation du galop dans l'art ancien et moderne* (Paris, 1925), *passim*.

2 It also appears in Assyrian lion-hunt sculptures of the seventh century BC: see R. D. Barnett and Amleto Lorenzini, *Assyrian Sculpture in the British Museum* (Toronto, 1975), Plates 115, 117. Very early (fourteenth century BC) images on a wooden chest and a gold-covered wooden fan from King Tutankhamun's burial chamber show a pair of horses pulling a chariot: they are in a 'proto-*galop volant*', with hind feet still on the ground: David P. Silverman, *Wonders of Tutankhamun* (New York, 1978), pp. 38 and 42.

3 A good example comes from the Low Ham villa in Somerset from most probably the mid-fourth century: K. M. D. Dunbabin, *Mosaics of the Greek and Roman World* (Cambridge, 1999), p. 97, Fig. 96.

4 I am grateful to Dr J. P. Moore for her suggestion that the earliest *galop volant* images may have had their genesis in realism, indicating the 'starting position' moment, and thus perhaps originating with competitions, at which chariot horses spring forward from a halt into a gallop to begin a race. This indeed seems likely from some Roman-British images of chariot racing where the *galop volant* is like the pose, with both hind feet on the ground and forehand launched forward, that Vigneron terms *le cabré allongé* (*Le Cheval dans l'antiquité*, II. Fig. a); but see the Horkstow mosaic, where this *cabré allongé* has already become emblematic, as it is here interpreted as 'proceed[ing] at a gallop' and either 'mak[ing] a turn' or 'hav[ing] completed the race': J. H. Humphrey, *Roman Circuses: Arenas for Chariot Racing* (London, 1989), p. 432 and p. 434, Fig. 202.

5 As Eadweard Muybridge's 1878 photo-panel of Leland Stanford's racing mare *Sallie Gardner* was to demonstrate, at no time does a horse ever extend fore- and hind-legs in this fashion during the gallop: while all four of a horse's feet do leave the ground simultaneously, at least one fore-leg is moving back under the body or one hind-leg is moving forward to support it, at all times throughout the gallop sequence. See Eadweard Muybridge's *Attitudes of Animals in Motion* (1881) (cited on www.kingston.ac.uk/Muybridge/muytext4.html).

sports almost exclusively, it is important to remember that it was an intrinsic part of European and Asian culture up until at least the early 1800s. The vast majority of people were therefore as familiar then with equine movement as we are today with the turning radius of an automobile, and would have known without having to be told that a real horse's gallop did not resemble a 'rocking-horse' configuration in any way. The universal adoption of this pose within the visual arts of the antique and medieval cultures therefore is indicative of a cultural topos, emblematic rather than actual.

The Bayeux Tapestry borrows not only the *galop volant* but the self-referentiality of that *topos*'s formulaic nature in order to create a graphic commentary for those paying attention to detail. The woven narrative is filled with equine images, and it soon becomes clear to the discerning eye that impossibilities, of which the enormous *galop volant* of Odo of Bayeux's warhorse (**Plate 22**) is only one instance, are everywhere to be seen. Other horse images in the Tapestry are found to be echoes of originals preserved in Anglo-Saxon manuscripts of Prudentius and the illustrated *Hexateuch*, suggesting startling thematic equivalents. Although Odo is generally believed to have commissioned the Bayeux Tapestry, its principal designer may have been 'a monk or dependent' of St Augustine's, Canterbury, and the Tapestry itself produced by English workmen.[6] Given the overwhelmingly military theme, so pithily described by Menéndez Pidal of *chansons de geste* as 'les monotones combats',[7] we must wonder what interest a monastic craftsman would have in reproducing nearly two hundred horses and their riders in advance, skirmish and slaughter over and over again.[8] It is therefore not implausible to suggest, as earlier critics have done, that a commentary of sorts was constructed within these images of war, 'a double meaning', 'messages that are at odds with one another', or 'one message for its Norman audience, but also . . . [an English] version [as well]'.[9] However my assumption is that the commentary discernible in the Tapestry horses privileges neither Norman nor English, but is equally critical of both.

Indeed, if Dodwell is correct in connecting border narrative with main narrative to create 'editorial asides' in the manner of the *chansons de geste*,[10] then the Tapestry designer was more than equal to the task of building a graphic commentary into his depictions of the English and Norman warriors. And if the *terminus ad quem* for the Tapestry's completion is more likely to have been the early 1080s than the death of

6 See R. Gameson, 'The Origin, Art and Message of the Bayeux Tapestry', in Gameson, *Study*, pp. 157–211, at p. 161; Brooks and Walker, 'Authority and Interpretation', p. 77; J. Bard McNulty, *The Narrative Art of the Bayeux Tapestry Master* (New York, 1989), quoting Wormald ('Style and design'), p. 12.

7 R. Menéndez Pidal, *La Chanson de Roland et la tradition épique des Francs* (Paris, 1960), quoted by Dodwell, 'BT and the French secular epic', p. 51, n. 21.

8 C. H. Gibbs-Smith, *The Bayeux Tapestry* (London, 1973), p. 6, counts 190 horses; by my count there are 177 full or partial horses (suggested by heads etc.) in the central Tapestry register, with eight in the borders, totalling 185. It is generally assumed to be monastic, despite Dodwell's ingenious proposal that a French *chanson* tradition lay behind the master plan of the Tapestry (see note 7 above).

9 Wilson, *BT*, p. 61; Bernstein, *Mystery*, p. 59, and see also pp. 111–12; Brooks and Walker, 'Authority and interpretation', p. 72.

10 Dodwell, 'BT and the French secular epic', pp. 59–60.

Odo in 1097,[11] its design, prior to the beginning of stitching, might have been drawn up within a decade of the Conquest itself, a very short time indeed within the memories of the conquered English who would still probably have retained an abiding horror of war and its aftermath. I suggest that the horses of the Bayeux Tapestry as a group are intended to be formulaic, and indicative of a subtext that was apparently deliberate on the part of the principal designer, and quite possibly at odds with the overt intention of the work as a whole. Most of the horses in the Tapestry have riders who are either unnamed subjects of an overlord, or depictions of those overlords themselves. Power politics run through the narrative of Harold's imprisonment by Guy, his association with William and his return to England, and through the ensuing preparation for and engagement in war. The carnage of the final scenes is thus the result of a lust for power which informs the principal named actors of the Tapestry – Harold, Guy, William and Odo – and I suggest that the Tapestry's horses comment mutely on the ambitions of Normans and English alike. This subtext of equine body language is conveyed for those who can read the code and pay attention to graphic detail, and runs parallel to the main narrative of the Tapestry while offering a counterpoint commentary on it, much as the upper and lower borders comment on the narrative unfolding between them.

'Gender-shifting' Horses

When the Tapestry's horse images are regarded as a whole and 'read' as a commentary, a number of anomalies present themselves for further investigation. To begin with, both Norman and English figures of importance to the narrative start out riding one gender of horse, but then have a gender shift occur underneath them, sometimes in the very next scene. Guy de Ponthieu's case comes to mind here: when he captures Harold (**Plate 2**), he is on a stallion which is *equus caballus*, a horse, but when he must hand Harold over to William (**Plate 7**), he is depicted as riding a mare, the head and neck of which can only be that of a mule.[12] If this shift is formulaic rather than representational, then it indicates ranked status within the Norman hierarchy, with Guy's mount inferior by both breed and gender to William's great stallion which prances under the words *NORMANNORVM DVCEM.* The Bayeux Tapestry designer may have known Bede's story of the conversion of the North, where the priest Coifi

[11] Dodwell, 'BT and the French secular epic', p. 62. Gameson, 'Origin, Art and Message', p. 161 would narrow these dates further to 1072–7.

[12] C. H. Gibbs-Smith, 'Notes on the plates', in Stenton, *BT*, pp. 174–88, at p. 177, assumes it is 'a mare with her ears pricked' although this in itself does not explain the mule's head. Unlike Gibbs-Smith, I consider manes important pieces of information, and have argued elsewhere ('Hwær cwom mearh? The horse in Anglo-Saxon England', *Journal of Medieval History* 22.2 (1996), 115–34, at 130–2), against the assumption that the English horses in the Tapestry demonstrate 'hogged' manes (for which see Eric Maclagan, *The Bayeux Tapestry* (Harmondsworth, 1949), p. 23). The mane on Guy's mare here is singular and suggests a different kind of equine from those preceding or following her in the Tapestry. For the suggestion that Guy's mount is created to make its rider look inept in relation to William, see Gale R. Owen-Crocker, 'Telling a tale: narrative structures in the Bayeux Tapestry and the Old English epic *Beowulf*', in *Medieval Art: Recent Perspectives. A Memorial Volume for C. R. Dodwell*, ed. Gale R. Owen-Crocker and Timothy Graham (Manchester, 1998), pp. 40–59, at pp. 54–5.

abandons his mare and his paganism simultaneously, mounting the *stodhors* of the king to cast his spear at the pagan sanctuary. Where before *non enim licuerat pontificem sacrorum uel arma ferre uel praeter in equa equitare* ('he wasn't allowed to bear arms or ride on anything but a mare'),[13] Coifi adopts a new horse when he accepts the Christian God. Bede's Latin terms this steed *emissariu(s)*[14] which is a breeding stallion, accurately rendered by the Old English ***stodhors***[15] – but whether there is any suggestion in the Tapestry of only righteous Christians riding well-endowed studs, remains to be seen.

I suggest that we can locate Harold's own status at any given time during the narrative leading up to his coronation if we follow his accoutrements and the gendering of his mount. At Bosham (**Plate 1**), Harold wears spurs, holds a hawk and rides a stallion, the only one in the group. When conveyed to Beaurain by Guy (**Plate 3**), he again holds a hawk but is mounted on a gelding and has no spurs. Spurs are added once more to the picture when he is conveyed to William (**Plate 7**) but he remains on a gelding. To pause here and translate the graphic commentary, we see the hawk as a constant symbol of Harold's social rank as a noble, as we find it at the beginning of *The Battle of Maldon*.[16] His spurs may be an indication of whether he is 'free to gallop away', whether he is an independent warrior or a political prisoner; however spurs are also one of Prudentius's details about the vice *Superbia* in the poem *Psychomachia*, to whose depictions on horseback we shall presently turn, and their presence may well carry a semantic of 'warrior's pride' that is once again part of the Tapestry's subtext. So Harold is reduced in political status below Guy when he first appears on a gelding while Guy rides a stallion who tends towards the priapic (**Plate 3**), but political status is re-established with Harold-on-a-gelding but Guy-on-a-mule-mare (**Plate 7**), the former again more important than the latter to the narrative, and both inferior to William while in France.

Harold approaches William's palace (**Plate 8**) wearing spurs (his freedom has been 'acquired' by William and perhaps his hopes – and ambitions – have again been raised) but with no hawk (a detail perhaps no longer needed),[17] and his chestnut gelding is now a chestnut mare which Gibbs-Smith calls 'one of the Tapestry's most delightful horses'.[18] William's stallion, right behind her, has the makings of a sizeable erection: this in and of itself is quite possible but as a detail it should be suspect in light of the gender-bending that Harold's horse has just effected. Attention is drawn to

13 Bede, *Historia Ecclesia*, II. xiii; *Bede's Ecclesiastical History of the English People*, ed. B. Colgrave and R. A. B. Mynors (Oxford, 1969, reprint 1998), p. 184, translation mine.

14 Bede, *Historia Ecclesia*, II. xiii: '*ascendens emissarium regis*'; Colgrave and Mynors, *Bede's Ecclesiastical History*, p. 184.

15 Bede, *Historia Ecclesia*, II. xiii: Thomas Miller, *The Old English Version of Bede's Ecclesiastical History of the English People*, Early English Text Society, original series 95 (London, 1890, repr. 1989), p. 138, emphasis mine.

16 So noted by Gale Owen-Crocker in 'Hawks and horse-trappings: the insignia of rank', in *The Battle of Maldon, A.D. 991*, ed. D. G. Scragg (Oxford, 1991), pp. 220–337 and quoted by Gameson, 'Origin, art and message', p. 197. It is discussed by Bernstein, *Mystery*, pp. 124–5, as a 'narrative technique' regarding Harold's changing status that is not unlike the kind of graphic commentary that I am proposing here.

17 The hawk now appears on William's fist: see Bernstein, *Mystery*, p. 124.

18 Gibbs-Smith, 'Plates', in Stenton, *BT*, p. 178.

this gender-shift by a foreshadowing in the bottom border, as we see elsewhere:[19] below the image of Harold riding the gelding soon to turn into a mare (**Plate 7**), we find one of the 'obscenities'.[20] A nude priapic man crouches with open arms inviting a naked woman into his embrace. She appears to be reluctant, for her legs are closed together with her left wrist covering her crotch and her right hand is held to her head; however she is bending slightly towards the right, thus is inclined towards the man, and her long hair trails down her back rather than modestly covering her bare breasts, so there is evident ambiguity in her stance.[21] I suggest that this border scene prefigures the gender-shift of Harold's horse from impotent male to female in the next scene, together with the body language commentary on ambition that is to be deduced from William's priapic stallion close behind her. Thus I would translate the Harold configuration in **Plate 8** as meaning 'free after a fashion but the inevitable loser in the game of power being played.' He is here decidedly inferior to William, with his status to be compared to that of the naked woman in **Plate 7**, half-unwilling but nevertheless flirting with danger that can only resolve itself one way.[22]

Falling horses

The quicksand that awaits William's retinue at the Couesnon river only three scenes later may reflect something of Harold's ambiguous situation. Under the first depiction of William in the Tapestry, learning of Harold's capture by Guy, we see a horse, one of only six in the bottom border, dragging a plough at seedtime; here, in the Couesnon quicksands, we read that Harold is dragging out the Norman soldiers who have fallen in, *TRAHEBAT*[23] *EOS*. He is depicted on foot, carrying one soldier on his back and pulling a second, right hand to right hand, from the sand, *DE ARENA*. His role can thus be likened to that of a horse who both carries and pulls; perhaps here, Harold, like the lower border horse shown earlier, is sowing the seeds of the relationship with William that will lead to a gift of arms after the siege of Dinan, and a related oath of fealty (*SACRAMENTVM FECIT VVILLELMO DVCI*) on their return to Bayeux. A horse falls into the Couesnon river as well (**Plate 9**), pitching her rider forward over her head: while colour consistency cannot be regarded as significant,[24] this is another chestnut mare whose fall into an awkward situation might possibly refer back to Harold's gender-shifting mount of a few scenes earlier. This mare serves to foreshadow the Battle of Hastings proper, the ultimately awkward – and fatal –

19 See H. E. J. Cowdrey, 'Towards an interpretation of the Bayeux Tapestry', in Gameson, *Study*, pp. 93–110, at p. 103.

20 I must disagree with Gibbs-Smith who (in 'Plates', in Stenton, *BT*, p. 177) describes this as 'the first of the groups of nude figures, which appear to have no special significance'.

21 R. Choulakian, *The Bayeux Tapestry and the Ethos of War* (New York, 1998), p. 86 mentions, but does not attempt to interpret, this scene.

22 For a discussion of 'gendering' in the Tapestry, see Catherine Karkov, 'Gendering the Battle? Male and Female in the Bayeux Tapestry' in this volume.

23 The only imperfect verb in the extant Tapestry narrative; for another discussion of it, indicating the rescue was 'performed several times in succession', see Gameson, 'Origin, art and message', pp. 189–90.

24 Brooks and Walker, 'Authority and interpretation', p. 64.

Fig. 4 *Superbia* with spur, from *Psychomachia*, London, BL, MS Cotton Cleopatra C. viii, fol. 15v

situation into which Harold's ambition both for the throne and for William's approval here in France serves to precipitate him. In the battle, three horses fall in spectacular succession (**Plate 21**), two of them stallions and the gender of the other hidden by its rider's spurred leg. Brooks and Walker comment on the Tapestry designer's ability to 'portray . . . strained, tumbling and terrified horses . . . so assuredly and vividly',[25] but I suggest that these falling horses at the Couesnon river and in the battle proper furnish a fascinating graphic prediction of the uncertainty in the vicissitudes of war, into which men spur their mounts where angels fear to tread.

Three manuscripts from Anglo-Saxon England[26] present graphic images to accompany Prudentius's celebrated *Psychomachia* poem: in each case, the vice *Superbia* rides for a fall, spurring her horse on to ruin when she tumbles into the inevitable pit:

> Talia uociferans rapidum calcaribus urget
> Cornipedem laxisque uolat temeraria frenis

[25] Brooks and Walker, 'Authority and interpretation', p. 66.

[26] CCCC 23, 12r–16v and esp. 14v and 15r (Canterbury, Christ Church, or Malmesbury, s. x^{ex}, see Thomas H. Ohlgren, *Insular and Anglo-Saxon Illuminated Manuscripts: an Iconographic Catalogue c. A.D. 625 to 1100* (New York, 1986), items 153: 21–28, pp. 115–16; and Mildred Budny, *Insular, Anglo-Saxon and Early Anglo-Norman Manuscript Art at Corpus Christi College, Cambridge*, 2 vols (Kalamazoo, MI, 1997), I. 275–437; II. Plates 242–247, esp. Plate 245); London, BL, Cotton Cleopatra C. viii, 13v–16r and esp. 15v (Canterbury, Christ Church, s. x/xi, see Ohlgren, *Illuminated Manuscripts: Catalogue*, items 154: 18–21, pp. 122–3 and Thomas H. Ohlgren, *Anglo-Saxon Textual Illustration* (Kalamazoo, 1992), 9–10); and London, BL, Additional 24199, 12r–15v, and esp. 14r (?Bury St Edmund's, s. x^{ex}); see Ohlgren, *Illuminated Manuscripts: Catalogue*, items 156: 20–5, pp. 129–30.

Hostem humilem cupiens inpulsu umbonis equini
Sternere deiectamque supercalcare ruinam.[27]

(Thus exclaiming she spurs on her swift charger and flies wildly along with loose rein, eager to upset her lowly enemy with the shock of her horse-hide shield and trample her fallen body.[28])

In each manuscript illustration, *Superbia* charges towards *Humilitas* and *Spes*. Her horse is generally positioned in what seems to be a modified *cabré allongé*,[29] with arched neck and flowing tail. The image in London, BL, Cotton Cleopatra C. viii appears on folio 15v above the text *calcaribus urget* ('with spurs she drives forward'), and there may well be a spur sketched onto her bare heel in this one image (**Fig. 4**).[30] Beneath the same verse of text we see horse and rider toppling into a pit, below *supercalcare ruinam* and just before the opening words of the next line on folio 16r, *sed cadit in foueam*, spurred on to ruin by her arrogance (**Fig. 5**).[31] The horse's composition, in particular that of its hindquarters, with airborne tail and a somersault-like energy to the hindlegs, is very similar to the hindquarters, tail and legs of the third falling horse on the extreme right in the Battle of Hastings, and in its posture (head down, falling to the right in a diving motion) it is to some degree also reminiscent of the falling horse at the quicksands of Couesnon. In the light of other associations of Tapestry images with those Prudentius *Psychomachia* manuscripts from eleventh-century Canterbury,[32] it is plausible that the Bayeux Tapestry designer knew this falling horse image, and included it as part of the subtextual graphic commentary on the fall of pride into the quicksand of war and a lust for power.

27 *Psychomachia*, lines 253–6, here transcribed from London, BL, Cotton Cleopatra C. viii, 15v, in Ohlgren, *Illustration*, p. 492, Plate 15.20.

28 H. J. Thomson, *Prudentius*, Loeb Classical Library, 2 vols (London, 1949–53), I (1949). 297.

29 See note 4, above.

30 Ohlgren, *Illustration*, p. 492, Plate 15.20; *Superbia* is barefoot and without spurs in the other plates from the manuscript that precede her fall, Ohlgren, *Illlustration*, pp. 490–1, nos 15.18–19, pp. 490–1. Spurs were certainly not unknown in Anglo-Saxon England: the Viking burial at Balladoole on the Isle of Man contained 'spurs [that] recall those from early 10th century burials in north-western England' (M. Redknap, 'Great sites: Balladoole' in the online text of *British Archaeology* 59 (June 2001), www.britarch.ac.uk/ba/ba59/feat4.shtml, although whether these are in fact Saxon requires further investigation), and we see spurs on many of the horse images of Cotton Claudius B. iv: while Esau's mounted retinue of 51r and the king's messengers of 141v wear spurs but ride without stirrups (an impractical combination), the mounted troops on 25rv wear spurs but are stabilized in their saddles by using stirrups as well. The lack of stirrups in 51r and 141v may be an attempt at 'accurate historical detail', see note 44 below, which nevertheless forgot to leave off the spurs, suggesting that the wearing of spurs was a common detail to the eleventh-century Anglo-Saxon imagination, with perhaps a wider early use of the stirrup than has otherwise been thought.

31 Bernstein, *Mystery*, pp. 51–2, deals with other falling horses, here in connection with a *vita* of Saint Caesarius, but the image is in a manuscript of 1110 which postdates the Bayeux Tapestry.

32 For a discussion of images in the Bayeux Tapestry that derive from the Prudentius illustration cycle, see Wormald, 'Style and design', p. 32; Brooks and Walker, 'Authority and interpretation', p. 74; Gameson, 'Origin, art and message', p. 166; and Bernstein, *Mystery*, pp. 39–40, but see Bernstein, p. 51, n. 1, querying the St Augustine's provenance for the Cleopatra *Psychomachia*, preferring a Christ Church origin, also Ohlgren, *Illuminated Manuscripts*, p. 120.

Fig. 5 *Superbia* in pit, from *Psychomachia*, London, BL, MS Cotton Cleopatra C. viii, fol. 16r

Priapic Horses

The falling stallion on the left in the Hastings battle scene (**Plate 21**) is (to a lesser extent) priapic as well: an ungelded horse will, in fact, 'drop' at the moment of death so this is perhaps not impossible. However, it is impossible for a stallion to gallop with a full erection: nature does not permit this to happen in the equine world, or in the human world either. A stallion engaged in any activity other than breeding is generally as circumspect as a gelding, and the great war-horses, the glory days of which only passed with the advent of armoured vehicles, were trained to much the same degree as modern Olympic horses: a well-schooled stallion, past or present, always knows where his immediate priorities lie. Yet if we consider one of the last horses of the Tapestry (**Plate 24**), we see the English running in disarray, with the battle-drunk Normans pursuing them on galloping horses with fully erect phalluses: the impossibility of this phenomenon would strike any horseman as significant.

Bernstein notes that 'many of the horses, particularly those used by the Normans, were extremely virile',[33] but this is only a passing observation rather than an attempt

33 Bernstein, *Mystery*, p. 71. Choulakian, *The Bayeux Tapestry and the Ethos of War*, p. 65 also misses the clue for commentary when he would have the Tapestry horses with 'muscles stretched, genitalia oversized . . . defin[ing] the ideals of the military establishment'. His statement that 'the horse's . . . giant genitals give proof of strength in warfare', p. 69, is particularly short-sighted, especially since it is made with reference to what he calls a 'massive workhorse' pulling the plough in the lower border: scale in comparison to the workman leading it would have it standing around 14.2 hands (that is, cob-sized, 1.47m or 4ft 10in to the back) and detail indicates that, unlike the priapic steed which

at reading the commentary that equine priapism presents for us here. It is not only the Norman horses which demonstrate this lust, but since there are a lot more Norman than English horses, let us begin with them. While horses in art may be emblematic of men, the intercourse of horses seems more like rape than passion to the untrained eye, and this apparent aggression driven by lust may have served the Tapestry designer well as a metaphor for power driven by ambition. In the Tapestry programmes to which the priapic Norman stallions belong, there is invariably a desired objective (the capture of a city, the co-opting of Harold to a Norman agenda, the engagement with the English at Hastings) to be read. William's messengers convey his demands to Guy while a small bearded figure under the name *TVROLD* holds their horses, the outer one in a state of erectile agitation (**Plate 4**). William's stallion is fully aroused behind Harold's mare (**Plate 8**) as they near William's palace and the inevitable negotiations about authority to be conducted between the two. And William and his retinue ride stallions in various stages of priapism on the advances to Dol, to Rennes and to Dinan, on receipt of the keys from the duke of Brittanny, and of course on approaching the fleet bound for England. But lest we be seduced by the notion of Normans as rapists with the English their maidenly victims, I would hasten to point out the stallion upon which Harold reappears when he has returned to England (**Plate 12**). Like William's stallion on the approach to the palace earlier on, this horse is giving us body language clues about Harold's own lust for power. The Anglo-Saxons have returned from France safe and sound and perhaps with their own agenda, and here we see Harold on the road back to Edward – and the English throne.

The most extreme priapic stallion in the Tapestry is that generally believed by most art historians to be William's own mount (**Plate 18**).[34] This horse appears, oddly enough, facing left rather than right under the heading *HIC MILITES EXIERVNT DE HESTENGA* ('here the soldiers go out from Hastings') with the last two words directly over him. Design of the Tapestry seems to have a sense of 'journey towards', to be read from left to right, as the western reading eye is trained: thus, Harold journeys to the right to get to France and Ponthieu (roughly south-east on a compass), the Norman retinue journeys right to get to Brittanny (roughly south-west), and William journeys right to get to England (roughly due north). Ultimately, the Norman invasion cavalry gallops right to the battlefield (north-east from Pevensey and a little north of Hastings) to meet the English whom they chase off the Tapestry in an undetermined compass direction but again to the right, at the end of the concluding fragment remaining to us; but here William's stallion faces left, towards the town of Hastings and not the battlefield. Possibly this offers an invitation to read deeper than the linen and the wool.

While *DE HESTENGA* clearly means 'from [the town of] Hastings', perhaps a metathetic pun on several levels might also have been intended by this word.

precedes the nude male and female 'obscenity' described on p. 97, above, this 'workhorse' is a gelding and not a stallion.

34 Cowdrey, 'Towards an interpretation', p.105 and n. 41, refers to William's 'magnificent warhorse with its prodigious masculinity', and suggests a connection between this graphic image, the later exhortation by William that his men fight *viriliter* and the nude scenes in the upper border that follow William's priapic stallion.

Fig. 6 Esau's horse, from *Hexateuch*, London, BL, MS Cotton Claudius B. iv, fol. 51r

Hestenga, metathesized, would read *hengesta*. *Hengest* can mean 'stallion', the image below the lexeme; and Hengist was of course the leader of the last continental invasion of England.[35] This stallion, standing in the Tapestry in full erectile splendour, was described in the *Roman de Rou* as a gift from Alfonso of Castille, and elsewhere I have discussed the likelihood that the horse was probably of Iberian bloodstock, a valuable kingpin for any breeding programme.[36] We cannot know for certain whether William would have risked such an asset in battle, but the horse is generally agreed to be a noteworthy emblem for William himself,[37] occupying a substantial space of his own.

Parallels between the Bayeux Tapestry's ships, its household accoutrements and some of its battle artefacts, and those to be found in the Old English *Hexateuch* illustrations of London, BL, Cotton Claudius B. iv, were drawn by Wormald, and developed by Dodwell and Clemoes, the latter concluding that the *Hexateuch* paintings are 'far from being a mere copy of something dead and distant'.[38] Since this manuscript has been associated with St Augustine's, Canterbury,[39] it is possible that the Tapestry

35 This was perhaps a nickname, meaning something like 'Hoss'.

36 Keefer, 'Hwær cwom Mearh?', pp. 130–2.

37 If so, could William have worn that nickname 'Hoss' or something akin to it himself?

38 Wormald, 'Style and design', p. 32; Dodwell and Clemoes, *Hexateuch*, pp. 71–3 and Plates X–XIII. Borrowings from the *Hexateuch* are further discussed in Bernstein, *Mystery*, pp. 40–2; C. R. Hart, 'The Canterbury contribution to the Bayeux Tapestry', in *Art and Symbolism in Medieval Europe – Papers of the 'Medieval Europe Brugge 1997' Conference* V (Zellik, Belgium, 1997), ed. Guy de Boe and Frans Verhaeghe, pp. 7–15; and Gale R. Owen-Crocker, 'Reading the Bayeux Tapestry through Canterbury eyes', in *Festschrift for C. R. Hart*, ed. Simon Keynes and Alfred P. Smyth, forthcoming.

39 See Dodwell and Clemoes, *Hexateuch*, pp. 15–16; Brooks and Walker, 'Authority and interpretation', pp. 74–7; Gameson, 'Origin, art and message', pp. 171–2.

designer appropriated some of its configurations as well as drawing from life. To the increasing list of parallels between manuscript and Tapestry should be added William's stallion, not for his priapism but for his position in the scene that he commands. Horses are rare in the *Hexateuch*: animals that are identifiably horses (rather than asses or mules) appear on only twelve pages of the entire manuscript.[40] It is perhaps noteworthy that no horses appear on the Ark, and that Pharaoh, pursuing the Israelities in Exodus, has his battle wagons pulled by oxen, with no evidence of cavalry.[41] Yet a portrait which could well be the model for William's horse does appear on folio 51r (**Fig. 6**), ungendered as horses in this manuscript are, at the reconciliation of Esau and Jacob, and like William's stallion, it is facing to the left.

There are a number of similarities in the positions of these two horses: both stand in their own space, so that the appropriation of the *Hexateuch* horse by the Tapestry artist for a specific scene would not have required any deletion of detail. The major differences lie in the tack, rather than the steeds: William's horse wears a war saddle[42] while the *Hexateuch* horse's saddle, the only one evident in the manuscript, is a curved affair with smaller pommel and cantle and a fringed saddle-pad; it lacks stirrups and is clearly not designed for cavalry charges, so while it may reflect contemporary custom, it may also be an attempt on the part of the *Hexateuch* artist to recreate something that resembles an artefact from the antique world.[43] Both horses have their legs in the same configuration, not a square halt but an attempt to show all four feet, here planted in identical sequence. Perhaps it is a rudimentary attempt at perspective or an effort to preserve the notion of movement within stasis. William's stallion stands obediently with his head lowered, but he clearly has ambition built into his body language that mirrors that of his owner. He prefers to be in motion, *doing* something, fulfilling the compelling desire evident in his priapism, but it is a desire that is arguably power-lust and not sexual lust. This *Hexateuch* horse also stands with all four legs visible, its head again obediently bent. It is desirable to identify its owner and question what can be learned of him through his horse. From this point we are confronted with a potential equation deliberately created between the owner of this *Hexateuch* horse and the owner of the Tapestry stallion standing in a similar space and positioned just like it. As will be demonstrated, the *Hexateuch* horse is Esau's, not Jacob's.

It is important to remember that William's stallion is facing left, towards the town of Hastings, despite the fact that the battlefield is manifestly intended to lie to the right in the Tapestry. Esau's horse is the only unmounted yet tacked-up single horse

40 These being 4r, 6r, 25r, 25v, 37r and 51r where we find the horse that I am concerned with in this study, 69r, 71v, 72r, 84v, 141v and 154r.

41 See 91v.

42 Identified by James Mann, 'Arms and armour', in Stenton, *BT*, pp. 56–69, at p. 68 as having 'an upright bow in front and cantle behind, both abruptly curled outwards'. Mann compares these Norman war-saddles with tack on the pony being led by Wadard's axe-carrying servant: here he notes that we see 'a saddle extending in a rounded shape, covering most of the horse's belly. From the context it is probably not a war horse', a valid deduction considering the scale that would make this animal no more than eleven or twelve hands high (1.12–1.22m, 44–48in), roughly the size of a New Forest pony.

43 It is not unlike the saddles evident in the mid-fourth-century Low Ham mosaic from Roman Britain (see Dunbabin, *Mosaics*, p. 97, Fig. 96) but may have closer parallels in Byzantine or Syrian manuscript art of a later period.

with evident space around it available from this manuscript to the Tapestry designer, but he was not so feeble in his capabilities as to have chosen Esau's horse for that reason alone. A good candidate for a right-facing horse appears on folio 69r of the *Hexateuch*, where the Egyptians come to Joseph to buy bread and he requisitions their goods, including horses, as payment. The front horse is well detailed and, while lacking a saddle, is more filled in than Esau's horse, and could easily have a saddle added and been isolated from its companion, which is a mere shadow-outline behind it. It is standing as still as Esau's horse, and although it is not surrounded with quite as much space (the muzzles of the beasts behind are touching its tail), this again would hardly have been a deterrent to the Tapestry designer. It seems likely that those of the audience who had seen the *Hexateuch* art were being invited to draw a parallel between the owner of the priapic stallion and the owner of the *Hexateuch* horse on folio 51r.

This section of the *Hexateuch* deals with the story of Jacob and Esau's reconciliation. Earlier illustrations clearly show that Jacob has camels, sheep, oxen and goats but not horses,[44] as stated in the Genesis XXXII account of the gifts he prepared for his brother.[45] It is Jacob who is clad in the light gown, Esau in the dark: we can see multiple images of this light-clad figure on the previous page, 50v, illustrating the seven prostrations that Jacob makes to Esau in Genesis XXXIII. 3.[46] In the Vulgate text Esau approaches Jacob with a company of four hundred men,[47] but is described in XXXIII. 4 as *currens* ('running'), which suggests that he was on foot; for the *Hexateuch* artist, this retinue was instead a mounted army and so Esau himself must be depicted as having been mounted as well. This horse stands out from the cavalry that accompany Esau, and is to his right, looking on, as it were, when Esau embraces his brother Jacob, to his left. It is therefore without dispute Esau's horse as far as the *Hexateuch* artist is concerned.

If the Tapestry designer did borrow Esau's horse from the *Hexateuch* as the model for William's stallion, just as other drawings from the *Hexateuch* seem to serve as models for Tapestry images, the corollary may be that William is being cast as an Esau. If so, this suggests that Harold, who is his brother noble and indeed his Anglo-Saxon double in the desire for the English throne,[48] is to be seen as a Jacob. The implication of such a parallelism is that the privileged viewer is led to understand Harold as stealing William's inheritance by ingratiating himself with Edward and the West Saxon council, and ascending the throne on Edward's death, just as Jacob stole Esau's inheritance by ingratiating himself with their father Isaac and extracting Esau's complicity for a cauldron of soup. We must work through the interpretation that these two very similar horses present, all the time bearing in mind the assumption that,

44 Dodwell and Clemoes, *Hexateuch*, 48v–49v.

45 See *Biblia Sacra iuxta Vulgatam Versionem* , ed. R. Weber, 2 vols (Stuttgart, 1985), I. 48–9.

46 Brooks and Walker, 'Authority and interpretation', p. 88, make reference to these very folios in their discussion of 'duplication' as 'a standard technique of the artists at St Augustine's who illustrated the . . . Hexateuch', but they fail to recognize William's stallion in Esau's horse.

47 Genesis XXXIII. 1 *levans autem Iacob oculos suos vidit venientem Esau et cum eo quadringentos viros*; Weber, *Biblia Sacra*, I. 49.

48 This and other doubling is discussed in Gale R. Owen-Crocker, 'Brothers, rivals and the geometry of the Bayeux Tapestry' in this volume.

while the Tapestry was commissioned by one of the conquerors, it was designed and constructed *in situ* in the land that was conquered, and by craftsmen whose lives were affected by that act of conquest.

Ambitious riders

The Tapestry commentary may also treat issues of kinship – blood-kin and claim-kin – within its subtext. Harold and William are a kind of claim-kin, brother claimants to the English throne and, in respect of their lineage in relation to Edward, neither one with a sizeable advantage of claim over the other.[49] William is illegitimate but he is descended through that bastardy from the brother of Edward's mother. Harold is legitimate and he is the choice of the people, but he is linked to the king only through marriage. If Edward had had a male heir, Harold would have been that child's uncle; but if Edward had had an heir, there would have been no need for Hastings. It has already been suggested that the priapism of the stallions ridden both by Harold and William points to an opinion held by the Tapestry designer about nobles whose object of desire is a throne. However, there is a blood-kin relationship in this Tapestry as well: Harold is accompanied by his two brothers who perish in the battle and appear only on foot, but William is also flanked by two brothers, and one of these occupies a very large space in a panel, on horseback, in a singular configuration. Odo of Bayeux, the likely commissioner of the Tapestry, is the first impossible horseman mentioned in this study (**Plate 22**). He is William's half-brother, he rides in the army, but he is a bishop, a consecrated man. His horse is a stallion but without evident priapism, and it is constructed to demonstrate the largest example of the *galop volant* in the Tapestry.[50] Odo himself sits bolt upright and brandishes his *baculus* with which he is said to be exhorting the young men[51] of the Norman army.

Art historians have worried about this *baculus* for decades, and they have done so with justification. Dodwell associates Odo with Bishop Turpin of the *chansons de geste*, 'weapon in hand', and makes the *baculus* into a mace or cudgel, while Brooks and Walker would have 'Odo, carrying a mace, who is shown rallying the lads'. Maclagan and Wormald also render *baculus* as 'mace', and Bernstein translates it as 'baton'.[52] Wilson comes closer to the mark by noting that, while in classical Latin *baculus* means 'stick' or 'cudgel', it has a special significance for a bishop and he

49 See N. J. Higham, 'Harold Godwinesson: the construction of kingship' and Ian Howard, 'Harold II: a throne-worthy king' in this volume.

50 See Owen-Crocker in this volume.

51 *HIC ODO EP[ISCOPV]S BACVLV[M] TENENS CONFORTAT PUEROS.* See Stenton, 'Historical background', p. 22, for the suggestion that *pueri* is 'a simple Latin rendering of the Old English word *cnihtas* . . . the young household retainers who had not yet completed their apprenticeship to arms'. However, for the unreliability of the inscription see Owen-Crocker, in this volume, n. 10.

52 Dodwell, 'BT and the French secular epic', p. 57. Gibbs-Smith translates *baculum* as 'club' and describes the object as a 'mace': see Gibbs-Smith, 'Plates', in Stenton, *BT*, p. 187. See also Brooks and Walker, 'Authority and interpretation', p. 68; Maclagan, *The Bayeux Tapestry*, p.14; Francis Wormald, 'The inscriptions with a translation', in Stenton, *BT*, pp.189–92, at p. 192; and Bernstein, *Mystery*, p. 142.

suggests that it is another word for 'crozier'.[53] Musset gives the issue some attention by noting that it is *not* an episcopal cross which, like Wilson, he (wrongly) assumes can also be designated *baculus*. He considers it likely to signify either a mace or simply a baton of authority.[54] Cowdrey, and Lewis after him, both associate it with what they consider another *baculus*, carried by William (Scene 49, Wilson, *BT*, Plate 54), although the Tapestry contains no textual reference to the item in his hand. Cowdrey prefers the term 'staff' over 'mace' or 'club' as we find in both Stenton himself and McNulty, and notes that 'the use of baculum for a bishop's pastoral staff should be remembered'.[55] Gameson terms the *baculus* a 'staff' as well, and associates it with the miracles of St Benedict, but forgets that a *baculus* has a specific meaning for a bishop and that Benedict never underwent episcopal ordination.[56]

The function of the *baculus* is indicated in the extant pontificals from Anglo-Saxon England.[57] The Anderson, Sampson and Corpus-Canterbury pontificals from the eleventh century all preserve a *benedictio baculi siue cambuttae* suggesting alternatives in the item to be blessed.[58] A *cambutta* is a curved stick and more properly a crozier by shape, while a *baculus* is instead a simplified symbol or formulaic image of that which the crook stands for, 'the staff of pastoral office' which is presented to the new bishop in the prayer *Accipe baculum pastoralis officii* in the *ordinatio episcopi* synaxes contained in the Anderson, Sampson and Lanalet Pontificals.[59] The object in Odo's hand in the Bayeux Tapestry has no crook and is specifically called a *baculus*: it is therefore a formulaic image of his episopal status, with all which that implies. Indeed, in Psalm XXIII, God's rod and staff of consolation are *virga et baculus*, used for comfort and not for war. In the *benedictio baculi uel cambuttae* mentioned above, God is addressed as *tu baculus nostrae et rector per saecula uitae* ('thou the staff and ruler of our life throughout eternity'), and He is asked to sanctify 'this little staff', *bacillum*, by which evil may be levelled and the righteous are ever governed, *istum sanctifica pietatis iure bacillum quo mala*

53 Wilson, *BT*, p. 225.

54 Lucien Musset, *La Tapisserie de Bayeux: oeuvre d'art et document historique* (Paris, 1989), pp. 294–5.

55 Cowdrey, 'Towards an interpretation', p. 95 and n. 6; see also Suzanne Lewis, *The Rhetoric of Power in the Bayeux Tapestry* (Cambridge, 1999), p. 12, where it is referred to as 'a clublike symbol of command'; Frank Stenton, 'The historical background', in Stenton, *BT*, pp. 9–24, at p. 22; and McNulty, *Narrative Art*, p. 64.

56 Gameson, 'Origin, art and message', pp. 179–80 and nn. 116, 177.

57 The very close relationship of late Anglo-Saxon and Norman service-books should not be forgotten; since the 970s, liturgical practice to be found in England and in Norman churches was exceedingly similar, and influence in both directions across the Channel was common. Therefore these contemporary English pontificals would well reflect the kind of synactic language in the *ordinatio episcopi* synaxis that raised Odo to the position of bishop.

58 London, BL, Additional 57337, s. xi^{in}, Canterbury; CCCC 146, s. xi^{in}, Winchester or Canterbury, later at Worcester; CCCC 44, s. xi^{med}, Canterbury.

59 Rouen, Bibliothèque Municipale A. 27, s. xi^{in}, used in Cornwall; *Pontificale Lanaletense*, ed. G. H. Doble (London, 1937), here p. 58, and in CCCC 146, p. 134. An expanded version of this sentence from the same prayer, adding *idem potestatem ligandi atque soluendi*, is preserved in CCCC 163, p. 166, a mid-eleventh-century Romano-Germanic pontifical the text of which derives from the liturgical developments of *Ordo Romanus L* and the Romano-Germanic pontifical design from Mainz in the mid-tenth century. It is not impossible that Odo might have heard this version of the prayer, with its Petrine echoes, instead of the simpler version recorded in the body of my study.

sternantur quo semper recta regantur. If Odo is carrying his consecrated *baculus* into battle as a symbolic weapon in a political cause, he would seem to be taking this injunction rather too literally.

On ordination, an eleventh-century Anglo-Saxon bishop invested with the *baculus* was adjured to be 'ardent in the correction of vice but holding justice without ire yet when angered' – presumably by that vice – 'being mindful of mercy', *sis in corrigendis uitiis seuiens, in ira iudicium sine ira tenens cum iratus fueris misericordie reminiscens*.[60] An alternate adjuration enjoins the bishop to accept the *baculus* as a sign of sacred guidance, *sacri regiminis signum*, by which those who are weak are to be strengthened, those staggering supported, the perverse corrected, the upright directed to the path of eternal salvation, and by this same sign the new bishop is to be given the power to encourage the worthy and correct the unworthy:

> accipe baculus sacri regiminis signum ut inbecilles consolides titubantes confirmes prauos corrigas rectas dirigas in uiam salutis eterne habeasque potestatem erigendi dignos et corrigendi indignos cooperante domino nostro IHU XPO qui cum patre.[61]

Gameson's contention that 'nothing [Odo] is shown doing in the Bayeux Tapestry is inconsistent with the dictates of eleventh-century Christianity'[62] must come under question when we compare the synactic injunctions of the pontifical *ordinatio episcopi* evidence with the Tapestry's image of Odo in the thick of the fray. Here he is apparently 'encouraging the young men' but is doing so from a political motive, that is, employing his episcopal *potestatem erigendi dignos* ('power to encourage the worthy') by equating *dignos* with *milites Normannos* and using his *baculus* to do so. Regardless of the tone – ironic or idealistic – of this image by which we are to infer that God was indeed Norman that day at Hastings, we remain faced with the anomaly of a *signum* ***sacri*** *regiminis* ('a sign of *sacred* guidance') being appropriated for a very secular end. Just as the phalluses of the stallions are not sexual, it is arguable that the *baculus* in Odo's hand is not spiritual: both emblematize an *auctoritas* that is either out of control or being misused for a self-driven goal instead of its appropriate one. A bishop in mail[63] on a galloping horse who uses the consecrated symbol of spiritual authority to further political ends through slaughter and invasion should again cause those who view the Tapestry and read the code aright, to reassess its narrative.

An argument can be made for the Tapestry's graphic commentary being one that cries out against the ambition that breeds civil unrest and disaster for the common man. If Odo were the inspiration behind it, then the depiction of him as a warrior misusing his episcopal directives is not inconceivable, even if the Tapestry designer were a St Augustine's dependant, Norman or English. That three of Odo's Norman tenants in Kent are presented by name (Turold, Wadard and Vital) may indicate, not 'fond memory' but more examples of this misuse of power by Odo: as with the

60 From Lanalet (86r); Doble, *Pontificale Lanaletense*, p. 58.

61 From CCCC 146, p. 134.

62 Gameson, 'Origin, art and message', p. 178.

63 Conventional mail is visible at Odo's neck and wrists although his 'battle-suit' is depicted differently, see Owen-Crocker in this volume.

master, so with his men.[64] Even if a case may be made for St Augustine's, which remembered Odo with gratitude, as a provenance for the Tapestry, the act of war which devastated England (and especially the south in the months leading up to, and then following William's coronation), would have been hard to celebrate without considerable reservation.[65]

While the overall design of the Bayeux Tapestry presents exalted deeds done by glorious heroes riding what at first glance seem to be canonically valorized *equi emissarii*, the subtle interplay of horse gendering, graphic quotations from other illustrated texts, and impossible equine physiognomy tells another story. The Normans are priapic with lust for the English throne, but so again is Harold. This kind of lust ends only one way, in acts of violence that are as brief, brutal and lacking in dignity as the intercourse of horses. Neither Harold nor William are entirely admirable when we look at them on this level: Jacob was a trickster and a thief while Esau was a hunter. William has slightly more claim to rule than Harold, but the struggle was perhaps as inevitable as sibling rivalry, each side driven by pride or *superbia*, and each side doomed to fall, either into the quicksand of ambition or into the arms of death. The Bayeux Tapestry tells the story of the successful invasion of England and the defeat of the Anglo-Saxons by the Normans. The Bayeux Tapestry horses propose the counter-text: war is appalling, for men die like beasts and change comes invariably for the worse. The craftsmen who are charged with creating a bright and colourful 'history', be it in words or in wool when any war is over, may well have their own views about that 'history' which suggest a different tale.

64 See Cowdrey, 'Towards an interpretation', p. 94; and Brooks and Walker, 'Authority and interpretation', p. 68, n. 22 for an excellent summary of the historical evidence pertinent to these three men. Indeed, on p. 69, n. 23, they observe that 'Vital . . . was charged with plundering the urban gild of its lands around Canterbury', hardly the stuff of which fond memories are made.

65 Brooks and Walker, 'Authority and interpretation', p. 77, but also *The Anglo-Saxon Chronicle*, ed. G. N. Garmonsway (London, 1972), pp. 198–204. Both the Worcester Chronicle (D) (London, BL, Cotton Tiberius B. iv), its original from the North (pp. xxxvii–xxxix), and the Peterborough Chronicle (E) (Oxford, Bodleian, Laud 636) attest to punitive devastation in both the north and the south of England by William's forces that echoes phrasing used earlier of the Vikings (1066 D, 'Nevertheless, in the meantime, they [the Normans] harried everywhere they came', p. 200, and again, 'In this year [1067], the king imposed a heavy tax on the unhappy people of the country, yet notwithstanding he allowed his men to harry wherever they came. He marched to Devonshire, and besieged the borough of Exeter for eighteen days. Although a great part of his host was destroyed there, he made favourable promises to the citizens which were badly kept', pp. 200–1).

7

Brothers, Rivals and the Geometry of the Bayeux Tapestry

GALE R. OWEN-CROCKER

The Graphic Prominence of Odo of Bayeux

BISHOP ODO riding his horse at *galop volant*[1] (**Plate 22**) captioned *HIC ODO EP[ISCOPV]S BACVLV[M] TENENS CONFORTAT PVEROS* ('Here Bishop Odo, holding his *baculus*, encourages the boys'), is the widest single figure in the Tapestry, measuring, from the edge of the back hoof to the muzzle of the horse, about 53.27cm (20.97in).[2] The horse is larger than any other in the battle scene, or in other scenes of the Tapestry, but it is not only its relative size that conveys the impression of width. Unlike other horses in the crowded scene of conflict, this one is entirely foregrounded, not overlapped at any point of its body by animals or riders; and other horses at the Battle of Hastings, even when depicted at a gallop, lack the forward thrust of the head which contributes to the impact of Odo's horse. The stretched effect of the mounted rider is enhanced by the borders at this point. In the upper border, the right hand lion, above the abbreviation *BACVLV̄*, stretches its rear legs[3] while beneath, a horse has died with one limb extended.

There are of course wider images in the Tapestry: ships full of men and horses; buildings containing people; and clusters of figures, on horseback and foot, which generally overlap one another to form dense groups, particularly in the battle sequences. Throughout the Tapestry this overlapping technique ensures that although one rider may be in advance of the others in terms of linear progression, he is not necessarily the most prominent in his group because some part of the following horse and rider overlaps him and establishes that he is behind in terms of distance from the viewer (**Plate 9**). Even the first horse and rider seen in a left-to-right progression, which by definition are not overlapped, lose something of their individuality by being doubled, or multiplied: the addition of another horse's head behind the first horse, or

1 See Sarah Keefer, 'Body language: a graphic commentary by the horses of the Bayeux Tapestry' in this volume.

2 Measurements taken at different times are inconsistent because of variation in the tension of the cloth; and even different photographic facsimiles give slightly different distances.

3 The lion occupies a proportionately wider space than that of its partner. The same is true of the birds which precede the lions in the upper border. There is an obvious attempt here to fill space: some plant ornament shares the wide space of the second bird, which has a wing extended. Perhaps some adjustment of the upper border was needed to catch up with the extensive battle scene, and the usual 'pairing' of creatures was slightly modified.

another two or three men with spears and shields in the same position, give the impression of massed riders. Odo and his horse are not multiplied. Instead, two other riders, behind them, highlight Odo's resolution by galloping in the opposite direction. Odo's body stands out clearly against the plain background, with his *baculus* penetrating the identifying caption *ODO EP̄S*. His costume is distinctive. Fully coloured, alternating triangles distinguish him from other men in their open rings of mail[4] and a knob surmounts his helmet, a detail unique in the Tapestry. In contrast, William, the future conqueror, is depicted later in the same scene in the crush of battle, overlapped and awkwardly twisted in the saddle as he tips back his helmet to reveal his face, showing the men behind him that he is still alive.

Odo's prominence in this scene is indisputable but the reason for and the manner of his inclusion in the battle depiction must be questioned. The equestrian image itself and its relation to the text above are ambiguous. As a cleric, Bishop Odo should not have borne arms, and indeed he is not pictured carrying the conventional spear or sword but a wooden club. He is depicted in an individual costume which was perhaps meant to be leather[5] but he has defensive armour beneath it and wears a helmet. While one should recognize that the concept of a bishop on the battlefield was not unacceptable in the Middle Ages,[6] there is no reliable independent evidence that Odo took part in the Battle of Hastings[7] though he may have helped finance and man the fleet and army and probably accompanied the invasion force.[8] William of Poitiers' account of

4 Conventional mail is visible at his forearms and beneath his helmet.

5 Gale R. Owen-Crocker, 'The search for Anglo-Saxon skin garments and the documentary evidence', in *Leather and Fur: Aspects of Early Medieval Trade and Technology*, ed. E. A. Cameron (London, 1998), pp. 27–43. It is possible that the suit of triangles not meant to be realistic and was simply a distinguishing mark, as Harold's striped skirt when he is arrested by Guy of Ponthieu distinguishes him from other English and Norman men (**Plate 2**).

6 Strongly argued by Richard Gameson, 'The origin, art and message of the Bayeux Tapestry', in Gameson, *Study*, pp. 157–211, at pp. 179–81. In practice, however, a bishop would not take to battle without conventional weapons. Gameson (p. 179 and n. 113) cites Bishop Leofgar of Hereford, who 'gave up spiritual weapons . . . and took up sword and spear' according to *ASC* 1056 CD, and the wargear bequeathed by Ælfwold, bishop of Crediton (997–1016). Only the ghost of St Benedict uses a *baculus* for mayhem which is more miraculous than combative; Gameson, pp. 179–80 citing the *Miracula Sancti Benedicti*.

7 The twelfth-century historian Wace describes an episode in which panicking *Vaslez* ('young noblemen'), who should have been guarding the *harneis*, are reassured by Odo to 'fear nothing, if God pleases we will be alright' (my translation). Odo then goes on to the thick of battle where he makes the *chevaliers* turn, stop and attack. This latter activity bears more resemblance to the Tapestry graphics than the Tapestry caption does, which corresponds to the *Vaslez* episode (*Roman de Rou*, iii, lines 8097–28, Wace, *Le Roman de Rou*, ed. A. J. Holden, 3 vols (Paris, 1970–3), II. 186–7). However, Wace may not be independent of the Tapestry: as a prebendary and canon of Bayeux 'it is inconceivable that Wace should have been unaware of it' (Matthew Bennett, 'Poetry as history? The Roman de Rou of Wace as a source for the Norman Conquest', *Anglo-Norman Studies* 5 (1983), 21–39, at 23; see also Martin K. Foys, *The Bayeux Tapestry Digital Edition* (Leicester, 2003)), though he used other sources, at least six identifiable written works as well as oral material. Wace's picture of Odo on a white horse, wearing a short mailcoat (*haubergol*) over a white *chemise* does not correspond with the Tapestry, though he has Odo carrying *un baston*.

8 Wace, *Roman de Rou*, iii, lines 5989 (consultation with the barons), 6163–8 (supply of mariners and pilots), 7356–60 (soldiers, gold and silver): Holden, *Wace*, II. 108, 114, 157. Marjorie Chibnall reflected the prevailing distrust of Wace in stating that he 'included in the participants of the battle of Hastings men who did not come to England until later' (Marjorie Chibnall, *The Debate on the Norman*

the battle, composed in the 1070s, mentions Odo's presence before the battle,[9] but attributes the dramatic turning of the conflict in the Normans' favour entirely to William,[10] though his statement that Odo had such affection for his brother that he refused to be far from him, even in battle, may imply his unarmed presence nearby.[11] Baudri de Bourgueil's roughly contemporary poetic description of the battle focuses on William's dramatic removal of his helmet to prove his survival, but omits Odo entirely.[12]

The accompanying text *HIC ODO EP[ISCOPV]S BACVLV[M] TENENS CONFORTAT PVEROS* does not tell us how Odo utilized his *baculus* and, since *pueros* is a reconstruction,[13] we cannot be sure whom he encouraged or comforted (*confortat*). As Sarah Keefer has shown,[14] the *baculus* was a bishop's staff of pastoral office, and there is nothing in the Tapestry inscription to suggest that Odo rode on to the battlefield brandishing a club of the kind carried elsewhere by his secular brother,[15] rather than, for example, that he blessed the warriors while holding an episcopal staff. In Psalm XXIII, the *virga et baculus* are God's rod and staff of consolation, and in the Harley Psalter (London, BL, Harley 603, 13r) a Canterbury manuscript, the illustration of this text shows the psalmist holding a slender stick as he is anointed with oil.[16]

Odo was half-brother to Duke William of Normandy. After the conquest he was made earl of Kent,[17] and ruled as William's regent. He was the most powerful man in England after the king and was awarded lands that had belonged to Harold

Conquest (Manchester, 1999), p. 17), but his reputation for reliability, particularly on the matter of the Conqueror's companions, is defended in Elisabeth van Houts, 'Wace as historian', in *Family Trees and the Roots of Politics*, ed. K. S. B. Keats-Rohan (Woodbridge, 1997), pp. 103–32, where, from the evidence of charters, it is argued that Wace used oral and family history derived from his contemporaries in Normandy. However, his attestation of the presence of Odo and Geoffrey of Coutances corresponds with William of Poitiers (see next note) and seems uncontentious.

9 William of Poitiers (II. xiv) mentions the presence of *duo pontifices*, Odo and Geoffrey of Coutances, together with numerous clergy and a few monks, and that the assembly prepared for the combat by prayer: *The Gesta Guillelmi of William of Poitiers*, ed. and trans. R. H. C. Davis and Marjorie Chibnall (Oxford, 1998), pp. 124–5.

10 William of Poitiers (II. xvii–xviii) attributes the Norman retreat to the supposition that William had been killed and relates how the duke cried out that he was alive and rallied them: Davis and Chibnall, *Gesta Guillelmi*, pp. 128–31.

11 William of Poitiers (II. xxxvii). William's panegyric says Odo never took arms, and never wished to: Davis and Chibnall, *Gesta Guillelmi*, pp. 166–7.

12 The poem, *Adelae Comitissae*, is translated by Michael W. Herren as Appendix III in S. A. Brown, *The Bayeux Tapestry: History and Bibliography* (Woodbridge, 1988), pp. 167–77.

13 Gameson tells us both the *tat* of *confortat* and *pueros* are reconstructions: Gameson, 'Origin, art and message', p. 177, n. 102. Note, however, Wace's *Vaslez* in the *Roman de Rou*, which was written by *c.* 1174: see n. 7, above

14 Keefer, 'Body language', in this volume.

15 Wilson, *BT*, Plates 54, 57.

16 Ohlgren, *Illustration*, p. 168. The manuscript is attributed to Christ Church, Canterbury: Ohlgren, *Illustration*, pp. 1–2.

17 David C. Douglas, *William the Conqueror: the Norman Impact upon England* (London, 1964, new edition 1999), p. 295 describes William's bestowal of the earldom of Kent as one of William's characteristic 'defensive measures', breaking the tradition of the English earldoms and creating smaller units, modelled on the Norman *comtés*, in the hands of men closely connected with the monarch.

Godwinesson when he occupied a similar position.[18] It is generally supposed by modern historians that Odo is featured in the Tapestry because he commissioned it,[19] but if we look at the discrepancies between what is said in the captions and what is actually illustrated, I suggest we have a more complex textual history: Odo is featured less in the inscriptions than in the illustrations. It is possible that the words which establish the sequence and general theme of the scenes were created first. This text, as I shall demonstrate below, reflects a William-centred orthodoxy. The graphic design of the Tapestry, which extracts and recycles images from manuscripts known to have been in the possession of Christ Church and St Augustine's, Canterbury, almost certainly originates from St Augustine's monastery, which came under the jurisdiction of Odo as earl of Kent.[20] It seems probable that Odo was able to influence the illustration in his own favour, or perhaps that the artist(s) chose to flatter him.

Twice elsewhere the Tapestry graphics give a role to Odo when the bishop is not mentioned in the caption. No commentators seem to doubt that the tonsured figure who advises William to build a fleet is Odo (**Plate 15**), and that the third man in the scene is William's other brother Robert,[21] but in fact the caption only gives credit to William: *HIC WILLEM DVX IVSSIT NAVES EDIFICARE* ('here Duke William ordered ships to be built'). It is only in a similar council scene after the landing in England, that the three figures are identified as *ODO EP[ISCOPV]S*, *WILLELM* and *ROTBERT* (**Plate 16**). There is nothing in the caption to the fleet-planning scene to hint that the strategy was Odo's, rather than William's, but the visual message is clear. The decision is not depicted as William's alone, nor attributed to the larger body of advisers William of Poitiers and Wace record.[22] This is a family council. Robert

18 Harold, the eldest surviving son of Godwine, had inherited the earldom of Kent on his father's death in 1053.

19 The cumulative evidence, including the focus on Bayeux and the naming of men who may have been Odo's tenants, is discussed in Bernstein, *Mystery*, p. 30. Bernstein (p. 29) attributes the association of Odo with the Tapestry to H. F. Delauney, *Origins de la Tapisserie de Bayeux. Prouvée par Elle-Même* (Caen, 1824), which I have not seen, saying that Delauney deduced it on the grounds of Odo's notorious lack of morality, his power in England, and the costumes and hairstyles of the Tapestry. The attribution was undoubtedly publicized by Francis Wormald's influential essay which appeared in the first (1957) facsimile edition of the Tapestry, and was repeated in the second edition (Wormald, 'Style and design', in Stenton *BT*, at pp. 33–4), where it was evidently taken from Frank Rede Fowke, *The Bayeux Tapestry: a History and Description* (London, 1898), pp. 22–3. Fowke had absorbed recent scholarship on the identification of Vital and Wadard (see also Fowke, pp. 103, 117–18), and Wormald repeated the probable association of the Tapestry with Odo on sober historical grounds, including the dedication of the new cathedral in Bayeux in 1077, which ignored, and so effectively suppressed, other, socio-cultural arguments. Wormald, convinced by the evidence of borrowing from Canterbury manuscripts, did not repeat Fowke's arguments for local, Bayeux, origin either.

20 The designer was familiar with manuscripts from both St Augustine's and Christ Church, but the latter, which was under the rule of Lanfranc, archbishop of Canterbury, an opponent of Odo's on several issues, is a less likely provenance than St Augustine's: see Bernstein, *Mystery*, pp. 51–4.

21 The scene is a borrowing from the Old English illustrated *Hexateuch* (Dodwell and Clemoes, *Hexateuch*, 31v), where the standing figure on the left is Lot, urging his (seated) sons-in-law-elect to leave Sodom. He is saying 'Leave this place': see Gale R. Owen-Crocker, 'Reading the Bayeux Tapestry through Canterbury eyes', in *Festschrift for C. R. Hart*, ed. Simon Keynes and Alfred P. Smyth, forthcoming.

22 William of Poitiers (II. i) mentions bishops and abbots and names seven laymen including Robert. Odo is not individualized: Davis and Chibnall, *Gesta Guillelmi*, pp. 100–3. Wace (*Roman de Rou*, III, lines 5979–6008) lists secular counsellors, including Robert, and also Bishop Odo: Holden, *Wace*, II. 107–8.

points to William and William points inward to himself. Odo, looking directly at William, points onward and upward. Like William he is seated. He is overlapped by the Duke, but rises higher. The steep incline in the positions of the men's heads takes the viewer's eye from Robert, through William, to Odo and hence to the carpenter who will build the fleet. Although William occupies the foreground, it is the figure of Odo who gives the scene (and hence the plan) its forward thrust.

Earlier in the narrative Harold Godwinesson had saved several men from the quicksands near Mont-Saint-Michel (**Plate 9**). The scene of Harold's triumph is, I believe, witnessed by Odo, among others, though he is not individualized in the caption, which says *HIC VVILLEM DVX ET EXERCITVS EIVS VENERVNT AD MONTE[M] MICHAELIS* ('here Duke William and his army came to Mont[-Saint]-Michel'). It has been assumed that the man in the distinctive costume is Duke William,[23] but his suit of coloured triangles (and rhomboids) and the club he carries surely anticipate Odo's appearance at Hastings. The figure lacks a tonsure, but this is not a major objection to identifying him as Odo because the two-tiered hair and profile cap depicted here are unique in the Tapestry, suggesting that an original drawing of a tonsure may have been misunderstood; the embroiderers make the mistake of overstitching Odo's tonsure twice elsewhere.[24] This man's horse is overlapped by the following horse, a position in which William is never placed, except at Hastings when he is forced to identify himself in the press of battle. William could be either the man on the aroused stallion[25] who rides directly beneath the words *DVX WILLEM*, or the lavishly armed figure in the centre of the scene on a (less priapic) stallion, neither of whom are overlapped; but the figure closely witnessing Harold's triumph is surely Odo.

Odo and Harold as Rival Heroes

The most obvious rivalry in the Tapestry is that between William and Harold for the English throne, but there is another rivalry here too – that of Odo and Harold. They share the curious position of the privileged brother who is outside the royal line. Though William had already greatly favoured his brothers, making Odo bishop of Bayeux and Robert count of Mortain, these younger siblings were the children born of the marriage of their mother, Herleve, to Herluin of Conteville. Only the bastard William was the son of the duke of Normandy. Harold belonged to one of England's most powerful families through his ambitious and successful father, Earl Godwine. Harold's sister Edith married King Edward. Harold was brother-in-law to the king, not brother. Though Edward and William were royal cousins, Harold was not descended from the Anglo-Saxon kings nor Odo from the dukes of Normandy.[26]

23 Thus Wilson, *BT*, p. 179.

24 At the Hastings feast and the subsequent council scene. It is the convention of the Tapestry to depict bare flesh by leaving it unstitched, as plain linen. Odo's tonsure is unstitched in the council scene in Normandy (**Plate 15**) and so is that of Archbishop Stigand (**Plate 14**).

25 Cf. Keefer, 'Body language', in this volume.

26 For the view that Harold had a legitimate claim as a member of the Anglo-Danish royal line see Ian Howard, 'Harold II: a throne-worthy king', in this volume.

Odo saw Harold win a place of favour at William's court, through heroism at Mont-Saint-Michel, in siege and in battle. As the Tapestry suggests, William discussed dynastic matters with the newcomer (**Plate 8**) and presented arms to him after the Brittany campaign (**Plate 10**). That in the Tapestry Harold is shown to swear his allegiance to William on the relics of Bayeux (**Plate 11**)[27] suggests an attempt by Odo, the bishop of Bayeux, to muscle in on the act. Perhaps he had seen Harold as a rival for his brother's attention and favour, occupying a position which he, because an ecclesiastic was forbidden to bear arms, could not fully share. Having inherited Harold's secular position in England, he may have felt it desirable to demonstrate that he too was a hero and wise counsellor, as well as an important churchman.

There is little doubt that Odo is being pictured as a hero in the Battle of Hastings scene (**Plate 22**). This may be designed to match the extraordinary heroism of Harold earlier, in the Brittany campaign. Subtle graphic echoes encourage us to relate the two scenes. At Mont-Saint-Michel the treacherous sands cause a horse to pitch on its nose, upside down (**Plate 9**). The rider, a man in a tunic, falls over its head with both arms stretched out. Harold, on foot, rescues one man by carrying him on his back and pulls another by the hand. This man clutches at Harold with his other hand. Odo's appearance at Hastings is preceded by violence (**Plate 21**) including a horse on its head at the same angle as the Mont-Saint-Michel horse, which has also tumbled because of treacherous ground;[28] the clutching gesture of a man on foot, as he grabs at the girth of the falling horse; and the motif of man-in-tunic-falling-with-hands-stretched-out, repeated as Englishmen tumble, wounded, from high ground.

Very often when studying the Tapestry, we may find the recurrence of a seemingly trivial detail draws attention to a thematic relationship.[29] As we have seen, Odo's appearance in the Battle of Hastings is notable for the abnormal width of the figure on horseback. Interestingly, this characteristic of appearing stretched out is shared by Harold, swearing his oath at Bayeux (**Plate 11**). The space occupied by this image, from the tip of the shaft of the portable reliquary which Harold touches with his right hand, to the farthest step of the altar on his left, is almost exactly the same as Odo on horseback. Just as the *galop volant* of Odo's horse is unnatural and impossible,[30] so is the depiction of Harold's body: his arms are disproportionately long; if they were perpendicular they would reach down to his knees. His position is exposed and probably humiliating. Figures in Anglo-Saxon art do not as a general rule stretch out their arms like this unless they are being crucified.

27 Not attested anywhere else except by Wace (*Roman de Rou*, III, line 5683: Holder, *Wace*, II. 97) for whom see note 7.

28 Identified as a ditch (later known as *Malfosse*) in the twelfth-century *Chronicle of Battle Abbey* (*Chronicle*, V: translated in Foys, *Digital Edition*, excerpted from Eleanor Searl, *The Chronicle of Battle Abbey* (Oxford, 1980)). The Tapestry shows that there is water in the ditch and it appears to have been fortified with spikes.

29 The recurrence, for example, of horns and walking sticks: see, respectively, Gale R. Owen-Crocker, 'Telling a tale: narrative techniques in the Bayeux Tapestry and the Old English epic *Beowulf*', in *Medieval Art: Recent Perspectives. A Memorial Tribute to C. R. Dodwell*, ed. Gale R. Owen-Crocker and Timothy Graham (Manchester, 1998), pp. 40–59, at p. 53; and 'The Bayeux "Tapestry": invisible seams and visible boundaries', *ASE* 31 (2002), 257–73.

30 Keefer, 'Body language', in this volume.

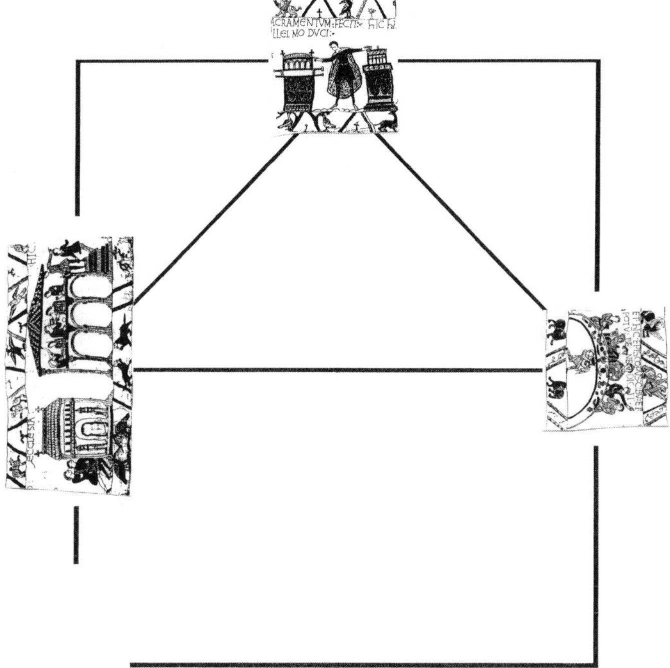

Fig. 7 Geometrical relationship of the Bosham and Hastings feasts with Harold's oath (details enlarged)

The Geometry of the Tapestry's Design

Harold's oath-swearing occupies a geometrically central position between two other scenes[31] which can be set out as a triangle **(Fig. 7)**.[32] The first point of the triangle is the double image[33] of Harold's attendance at church at Bosham and his feast (**Plate 1**), which precede his voyage from England. The banquet, which, like the biblical Last Supper (Mark XII. 15; Luke XXII. 12) takes place in an upper room, seems fairly lavish, if we are to judge by the decorated drinking horns, surely luxury items.[34] The third point of the triangle depicts a cleric blessing the food for a feast at

31 This point was established in Owen-Crocker, 'Telling a tale', pp. 52–4.

32 The effect can be recreated using a one-seventh size pull-out reproduction of the Tapestry, such as *La Tapisserie de Bayeux*, Dessin de Roland Lefranc (Ville de Bayeux, undated) and *La Tapisserie de Bayeux*, Réalisation Édition Artaud Frères (Ville de Bayeux, undated). Reproductions are available from the Centre Guillaume le Conquérant, Bayeux.

33 By 'double image' I mean that there is nothing between the two buildings and no separate captions for the two events. Surtitles explain the scene of men riding *VBI HAROLD DVX ANGLORVM ET SVI MILITES EQVITANT AD BOSHAM* ('where Harold duke of the English and his soldiers ride to Bosham'), and the caption *ECCLESIA* appears over the church; but there is no text relating to the feast. The church and feast are numbered as a single scene in an early-modern hand on the sixteenth-century backcloth of the Tapestry and are generally classified as such by modern art historians.

34 I am grateful to my former MA student, Joanna Clatworthy, for her unpublished research on drinking vessels depicted in selected Canterbury manuscripts.

Hastings after the Normans' voyage to England. The image is copied from a Last Supper illustration, probably from the St Augustine Gospels (CCCC 286, 125r)[35] which belonged to the Canterbury house. The cleric is assumed to be Odo, firstly since the caption identifies him as a bishop (*ET HIC EPISCOPVS CIBV[M] ET POTV[M] BENEDICIT*, 'and here [the] bishop blesses the food and drink') and secondly as one of the diners points at the abbreviated words *ODO EPS̄* which caption the following scene (**Plate 16**)[36] while gazing at the cleric who presides at the feast. The iconographic link of religion and feast in the two geometrically related scenes makes us aware of thematic links between them and the oath-taking scene at the central point of the triangle: that Harold's journey to the Continent culminated in his swearing an oath of allegiance to William and that the arrival of the Normans in England is justifiable, from their point of view, because of Harold's perjury in accepting the throne of England in contravention of that oath. If, as has been suggested, the Eucharist is displayed on the altar upon which Harold swears his oath,[37] the link between religion and feast is made at all three points.

The images of Harold stretched out ignominiously in Odo's cathedral and Odo stretched heroically in Harold's territory, which are, as I have demonstrated above, related thematically, may also have been spatially related in the design of the Tapestry. If, in addition to the 'religion and feasts' triangle we place these two images opposite one another, each at the centre point of parallel sides, the result (**Fig. 8**) is a cross composed of four religious episodes: Harold going to church and eating a 'Last Supper' before his voyage, Harold swearing an oath in Bayeux Cathedral, the bishop blessing the food and, though depicted in a secular manner, Bishop Odo described as holding his staff and giving comfort.

As an unexpected consequence of laying out the Tapestry in relation to these four points, it became clear that it had been designed as a square. The discovery was surprising because scholars, whether arguing that the intended location of the Tapestry was the nave of a cathedral or a medieval secular hall, have supposed that it was hung in a rectangle.[38] They have assumed the beginning of the Tapestry was located either beside a set of central doors or at the end of a wall, on pragmatic or subjective grounds[39] whereas my own reconstruction based on the geometry of design

35 Laura Hibbard Loomis, 'The table of the Last Supper in religious and secular iconography', *Art Studies (American Journal of Archaeology)* 5 (1927), 71–90; Brooks and Walker, 'Authority and interpretation', 74–6.

36 All three brothers are named but the names are separated by the roof of the building they occupy.

37 Brooks and Walker, 'Authority and interpretation', p. 66.

38 I initially tried to make a rectangular shape, but in order to place Odo facing Harold in the middle of a side, I had to slope the second long side inwards so very drastically it seemed improbable. An acute angled corner was not a problem in itself since in medieval buildings 'Most corners were not square, the walls were rarely straight . . .' (R. J. Darrah, 'Timber buildings', in Michael Lapidge, John Blair, Simon Keynes and Donald Scragg, *The Blackwell Encyclopaedia of Anglo-Saxon England* (Blackwell, 1999), p. 449). However, the wall would have been about 2.13m (7ft) out of alignment, which seemed too much. I also considered shortening two of the sides by assuming there were bays in the hall, but no parts of the Tapestry stood out as obvious candidates for lining alcoves.

39 Brilliant, for example, describes 'Placing . . . the beginning . . . at a corner, because that seemed to make the most sense, visually and conceptually': Brilliant, 'Stripped narrative', p. 114.

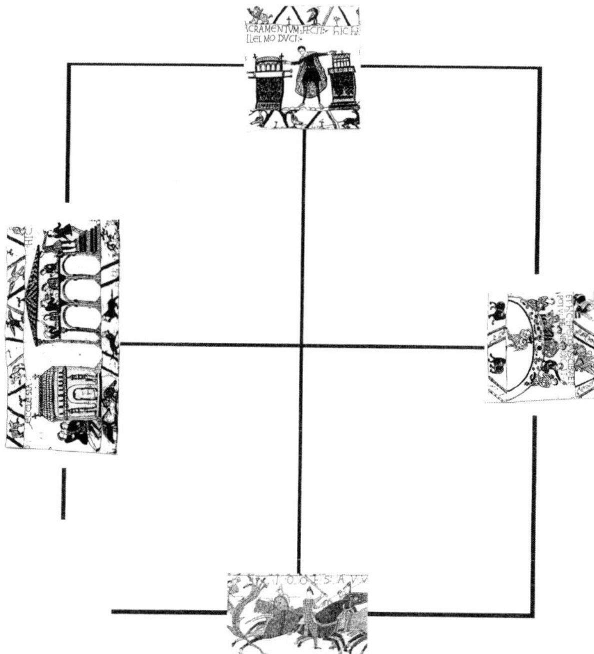

Fig. 8 A square design based on the relationships of Bosham/Hastings and Harold's oath/Odo on horseback (details enlarged)

placed the beginning of the Tapestry neither centrally nor at one end.[40] However, the square design was clearly correct because once the Tapestry was laid out this way, it was confirmed by the position of the first seam and the structure of the entire narrative.

The Geometry of Design and the Structure of the Narrative

It is clearly naive to suppose that the creator of any long work, verbal or graphic, would work purely on the principle that you 'Begin at the beginning . . . and go on till you come to the end; then stop.'[41] Yet in practice modern readers/viewers seem to

40 This placing, which initially puzzled me, elicited an immediate response by experts in Norman architecture when an early version of this paper was read at the Medieval Congress at Kalamazoo. My diagram suggested to them a square keep with a corner staircase. Professor Malcolm Thurlby, York University, Ontario, referred me to Castle Hedingham, Essex, in Malcolm Thurlby, 'The roles of the patron and master mason in the first design of the Romanesque cathedral of Durham', *Anglo-Norman Durham 1093–1193*, ed. David Rollason, Margaret Hervey and Michael Prestwich (Woodbridge, 1994), pp. 161–84, at p. 174, Plate 23; Chris Henige's response forms the next paper in the present volume.

41 Lewis Carroll, *Alice's Adventures in Wonderland*, Chapter 12; quoted from *The Complete Illustrated Works of Lewis Carroll* (London, 1982), p. 109.

assume it until the design structure is pointed out to them,[42] and the Tapestry narrative is no exception. I suggest that, as part of the design process of the Bayeux Tapestry, a square was marked out and the positions of what I have called 'the four religious episodes' were established as a cross within that square.[43] Not only is the cross significant as a Christian symbol; the quartered square was a basic device of design which had been used in Anglo-Saxon book art for centuries.[44]

Proceeding by the geometry of linked themes we may see that the Tapestry begins with an introductory stretch of narrative along one side, covering Harold's journey to the Continent and his capture by Guy of Pontieu, ending with the resolution of that situation with William's removal of him from Guy (**Plate 7**). This brings us to the first seam, which differs in several respects from the other eight which join the pieces of linen into its present 68.38m (224ft 4in) length.[45] The first seam is the only one that is not embroidered over to some extent. At this meeting of the first and second pieces of the Tapestry there is dislocation in the upper border and a gap in the main register which suggest that the sections were only brought together after they were completed, unlike the others. This is the only stretch of textile in the Tapestry in which a seam coincides so closely with a scene end. Although one man's finger points forward to the next episode, the group of men on horseback faces the other way, towards a focal point of the scene where William and Guy come face to face. The overall effect of this inward-turning by men and horses makes for a sense of closure. Although the opening border and scene of the Tapestry may no longer be quite complete,[46] it seems probable that the first piece of linen, which, at 13.70m (44ft 11in), is one of the longest of the nine pieces of cloth making up the hanging,[47] was specifically made to contain this introductory narration, and the first side of the design. Without any contrivance

42 See, for example, the history of *Beowulf* criticism, which has moved from seeing this Old English poem as 'curiously weak' in structure, manifesting 'lack of steady advance' to interpretations which see it as carefully shaped, variously binary, triple, cyclic or chiastic: Gale R. Owen-Crocker, *The Four Funerals in Beowulf: and the Structure of the Poem* (Manchester, 2000), pp. 133–5.

43 These are not of course the only religious episodes in the frieze. Edward's deathbed and funeral and Harold's coronation involve church buildings and clerics.

44 See Robert D. Stevick, *The Earliest Irish and English Bookarts: Visual and Poetic Forms before A.D. 1000* (Philadelphia, 1994). Stevick excludes the Benedictine Reform period from this method of composition (p. 12 and p. 244 n. 15) but it is a basic way of setting out a design which must have been practised by Anglo-Saxon carvers and metalworkers as well as illuminators.

45 See Owen-Crocker, 'The Bayeux "Tapestry": invisible seams and visible boundaries', pp. 161–2. An eighth seam, invisible to the naked eye, has recently been identified: Isabelle Bédat and Béatrice Girault-Kurtzeman, 'The technical study of the Bayeux embroidery', in *The Bayeux tapestry: embroidering the Facts of History*, ed. P. Bouet, B. J. Levy and F. Neveux (Caen, 2004), pp. 83–109, at p. 86, and Gabriel Vial, 'The Bayeux Tapestry embroidery and its backing strip', in Bouet, Levy and Neveux, *The Bayeux Tapestry*, pp. 111–16, at p. 111. I am grateful to the late Dr Levy for his kindness in allowing me to see these articles in advance of publication.

46 The present opening border is restoration: S. Bertrand, *La Tapisserie de Bayeux et la manière de vivre au onzième siecle* (La Pierre-qui-Vire, 1996), p. 46. Bertrand considers but rejects the possibility that the opening is an addition since it does not correspond with the Tapestry described by Baudri de Bourgueil. There could be some part of the Tapestry missing at the beginning but the fact that Harold is identified as *Dux Anglorum* in the second scene (the only time the full title is used) suggests that he has only recently been introduced.

47 Bédat and Girault-Kurtzeman, 'Technical study', p. 84. The second piece of linen is slightly longer, the rest considerably shorter.

on my part, once the 'four religious scenes' were aligned, the first seam came at the first corner.

There is nothing inevitable about the selection of events in the opening stretch of linen. The designer could have chosen to begin the story elsewhere, such as in the distant past with Edward's childhood exile and close relationship to William which, in Norman eyes, justified the invasion; or, if Harold went to Normandy deliberately to negotiate with William over a hostage or hostages, as has been suggested,[48] the Tapestry might have begun with the giving of the hostage. The visit of Harold to Normandy which is the designer's chosen starting point is, however, more than what Simone Bertrand calls *une sorte de long prologue.*[49]

The drawing of parallels between events from the distant past and the more recent past was a habit of mind which had been natural to the Anglo-Saxons since the seventh century when Benedict Biscop returned from the Continent bringing for his monastery at Jarrow pairs of pictures demonstrating that Old Testament events could be seen to prefigured New.[50] The device is used throughout *Beowulf* which begins with the funeral of Scyld Scefing and ends with the funeral of the hero, and we even find it in details of the *Anglo-Saxon Chronicle* story of Cynewulf and Cyneheard where men unjustly kill a king in a skirmish round a door then get their requital in a skirmish round gates. The well-established practice of prefiguring is the rationale for the Tapestry designer's choice of opening events. When the whole is placed as a square, Harold's landfall in France comes opposite the landing of William's fleet in England.

The second side is occupied with events leading up to the Norman invasion. It opens with riders approaching William's palace where William and Harold confer, apparently (to judge by the appearance of the woman Ælfgiva and the sexual suggestions in the lower border) discussing dynastic matters (**Plate 8**). It continues with the campaign against Conan, duke of Brittany, which begins with Harold's heroic rescue of men from the quicksands and continues via Dol and Rennes, culminating in a successful siege of Dinan, after which William presents Harold with arms and they go to Bayeux where, at the central point in the second side, Harold swears his oath to William (**Plate 11**). Harold's return to England and audience with Edward the Confessor are followed by Edward's death, Harold's acclamation as king, his coronation (of dubious authority from a Norman point of view since the presiding archbishop is depicted as the excommunicated Stigand), and Harold's rapid realization of

[48] Thus Eadmer (see *Eadmeri Historia Novorum in Anglia: et Opuscula Duo De Vita Sancti Anselmi et Quibusdam Miraculis Ejus*, ed. Martin Rule, Rolls Series 81 (London, 1884), pp. 6–8). Eadmer states that Harold went to Normandy because his brother Wulnoth and nephew Hacun were there as hostages, and that he returned with his nephew. William of Poitiers also mentions the hostages (I. xiv, I. xli): Davis and Chibnall, *Gesta Guillelmi*, pp. 20–2, 68–9.

[49] Bertrand, *La Tapisserie*, p. 61.

[50] After Biscop's fifth visit to Rome he brought back 'paintings shewing the agreement of the Old and New Testaments, most cunningly ordered; for example, a picture of Isaac carrying the wood on which he was to be slain, was joined (in the next space answerable above) to one of the Lord carrying the cross on which He likewise was to suffer. He also set together the Son of Man lifted up on the cross with the serpent lifted up by Moses in the wilderness.' See Bede, *Vita Sanctorum Abbatum Monasterii in Uyramutha et Gyruum, Benedicti, Ceolfridi, Eosteruini, Sigfridi atque Huaetbercti*: J. E. King, *Bedae Opera Historica*, Loeb Classical Library, 2 vols (London, 1954), II. 415.

imminent peril, manifested by a comet overhead and the outline of ships in the lower border. A messenger takes the news to Normandy, where another conference on dynastic matters is held, this time the brothers plotting the invasion as discussed above (**Plate 15**) and the side is completed with the preparation of the fleet.[51] Interestingly this arrangement of the images limits Harold's coronation to just one of a series of events, not the climactic point. It was certainly never the physically central point of the Tapestry – it is too near the beginning.

The second corner is not as obvious as the first, but the third side probably opens with ships appearing awkwardly from behind a tree (**Plate 15**). This third side is occupied entirely with the invasion: the launching and loading of ships, the crossing of the Channel and the preliminaries to the Battle of Hastings. The uncharacteristically stiff and spread-out style immediately before the Hastings feast suggests the foraging and cooking scenes and the scrap between two men with spades may represent an expansion, perhaps some of this non-heroic material being added at a secondary stage in the design to make the banquet appear at the right point. The additions may have been unauthorized: though they are captioned in Latin there is a subversive tone to the graphics. The figure of *Labor* from a Canterbury Prudentius manuscript (London, BL, Cotton Cleopatra C. viii, 27r) is copied and transformed into a man labouring: *Labor* is, in Prudentius's *Psychomachia*, a companion of *Avaritia*, 'Greed'.[52] The association would have revealed the Normans as greedy pillagers to anyone familiar with the illustration and its accompanying text. As the Normans prepare for their banquet they catch, kill and hump farm animals – a cow, a sheep and a pig. The scene occurs right opposite the lordly English hunters carrying their hawks and hounds into a ship, to the detriment of the Norman rabble. The Hastings banquet too, suggests an ironic eye. Odo may have intended to have himself depicted as presiding over a scene of holy austerity to counter Harold's lavish secular banquet opposite. Taken, as already noted, from a Last Supper illustration, the Hastings feast puts Bishop Odo in Christ's place, and despite the meat and poultry that have been prepared, the table bears simple loaves and fishes. Yet the replacing of Christ by Odo might be seen as presumptuous, and the artist replaces the orderly disciples with a sprawling, untidy group. The loaves and fishes may imply that the Normans, like Christ, were feeding the five thousand,[53] but as we have seen, they have fed their army by pillage. The respectful servant, with his bowl and napkin, who waits on the Norman feasters, is an image probably taken from the Old English *Hexateuch* (London, BL, Cotton Claudius B. iv, 57v).[54] There, the figure with the napkin is Joseph, who is serving Potiphar's wife; she will shortly make a false accusation

[51] The arrangement also slightly alters Bernstein's picture of the Tapestry as a drama in two acts, which sees the Norman family conference as beginning Act 2.

[52] *Psychomachia*, lines 629–30: *Metus et Labor et Vis/ et Scelus et placitae fidei Fraus infitiatrix*: H. J. Thomson, *Prudentius*, Loeb Classical Library, 2 vols (London and Cambridge, MA, 1949–53), I. 322. Thomson translates (p. 323) 'Fear and Suffering and Violence, Crime and Fraud that denies accepted faith'. 'Suffering' is an unusual translation for *Labor*. Perhaps what is meant is 'toil'.

[53] Owen-Crocker, 'Telling a tale', pp. 53, 58 n. 27.

[54] One of a number of similarities between the Tapestry and the manuscript demonstrated in the introduction to Dodwell and Clemoes, *Hexateuch*, pp. 72–3, Plate XIII (c), (d).

against Joseph and cause him to be imprisoned for a long time. The implication of the borrowing is that English who wait on the Normans can expect no favours or justice.

The third side ends when both leaders have been told the enemy is at hand (**Plate 20**, top).[55] From the third corner, as William exhorts his troops to behave *viriliter et sapienter* (**Plate 20**, bottom), all the figures move in the same direction as the Norman horses accelerate from walk to trot to gallop, full tilt into battle with the English infantry. After some spectacular carnage, Odo of Bayeux makes a dramatic appearance on the battlefield to rally the troops at the central point of the fourth side; shortly after, William moves his helmet to show his face and prove he is still alive. The battle continues through the deaths of Harold's brothers Leofwine and Gyrth, to Harold's own arrow in the eye and death by sword. The English are fleeing as the frieze breaks off.

Prefiguring, Brotherhood and Rivalry

If we arrange the Tapestry in a square, the placing of the images suggests their interrelationship. We find a mesh of brotherhoods and rivalries, echoes and ironies. On the second side, Odo, seated, responsibly advising his brother (**Plate 15**), comes like a mirror image at the opposite end to another discussion where Harold, vehement, and standing, addresses William (**Plate 8**). Opposite one another, on the second and fourth sides, Harold's acceptance of the throne on the deathbed of his brother-in-law Edward the Confessor, faces the deaths of Harold's blood brothers Leofwine and Gyrth whom he had led into the disaster that was the Battle of Hastings.

Odo's depiction as a man of action is an answer to Harold's heroism, particularly to the rescue of men at Mont-Saint-Michel. The Brittany campaign is a prefiguring of the Battle of Hastings, both of them ending in a defeat for Harold. Though ostensibly a hero in Brittany, Harold accepted subordination to William. At Hastings it is Odo who is depicted as the hero and Harold's campaign ends in death as he yields his kingdom to William. Harold had stretched out his arms in an oath to William but perjured himself. Odo now extends his horse and his *baculus* to save the day for his brother, to raise morale and hold the army together until the rumour of William's death is dispelled. It may not be coincidence if another brother-in-law of Edward's, Eustace of Bologne (tentatively identified by the text *E . . . TIVS*),[56] is present to identify William and share the moment when the tide turns in favour of the Normans. Eustace was an old enemy of the Godwine family.

Harold's own heroism is reduced to hubris as we look from one side of the Tapestry to the facing scene and find, opposite the Brittany campaign, his death. Odo, supposed patron of the Tapestry, has disposed of his rival. It is generally, though not

55 For a slightly different placing see Chris Henige, 'Putting the Bayeux Tapestry in its place', in this volume.

56 The identification appears to be accepted by Wilson, *BT*, p. 194, and is developed by Andrew Bridgeford, *1066: the Hidden History of the Bayeux Tapestry* (London and New York, 2004), though the gap as it is at present (see **Plate 22**) is longer than would be occupied by the four letters that would complete the name *EVSTATIVS*.

universally, agreed that Harold is shot in the eye and blinded, a presumed fate which has provoked considerable discussion.[57] There would be an ironic kind of justice in such an end for Harold: Edward the Confessor's younger brother, Alfred, had been blinded and tortured to death in 1036, evidently at the instigation of Earl Godwine, Harold's father. This is the reason the childless Edward had no brother to be his heir. Harold, his brother-in-law, son of the villain who ordered the blinding, is no substitute for a blood brother, and meets the same fate as Ætheling Alfred. The source of the blinding image, where Harold grasps at an arrow in his face, is probably a scene from the Harley Psalter (London, BL, Harley 603, 2r). If we had any doubts about the final judgement given by the Tapestry on Harold, the text from the psalm which the illustration accompanies should dispel it. It concerns God's punishment of the presumptuous: 'The kings of the earth stood up . . . against the Lord . . . The Lord shall deride them. Then he shall speak to them in his anger and trouble them in his rage.'[58]

Odo's fraternal superiority may not have been a theme of the Tapestry at the stage when the basic text was composed, but it certainly seems to have been part of the graphic design. I make no claim as to how or where it was hung. Chris Henige's paper in this volume will take up this point in relation to the display of the frieze in a Norman architectural setting. However, even if the Tapestry were originally hung in a building for Odo's gratification, this does not mean his 'heroism' would always have been openly displayed; that might have been tactless in front of King William. Even if the Tapestry were displayed in the square in which it was designed it only took only a small movement to change the centrality of an image; William, confirming that he is alive (**Plate 22**), could easily be moved a little to take central place at the Battle of Hastings; or the viewer could be directed (by, for example, moving the furniture in the room) to a different focus: William, on a high seat, watches Harold at his oath taking and is the most powerful person in the frame (**Plate 11**). We could see Harold's mortification as a manifestation of William's power if we chose to, rather than considering it in relation to the temporary frustration of Harold's ambition.

Later in the Middle Ages wall hangings became popular as portable furnishings for wealthy owners moving from one residence to another.[59] Although the length of the Bayeux Tapestry's first piece of linen, creating as it does a 'short' first side of a presumed square, suggests that it may have been measured out with one particular structure in mind, it might never have been intended to be confined only to that place. In the centuries between its manufacture and its documentation at Bayeux in the fifteenth century it may have been displayed in different buildings, in different countries, with different effect. The 'brotherhood' geometry would be lost when hung round walls of different dimensions; and there are many other internal patterns in the

57 Bernstein, *Mystery*, pp. 144–61, sees the blinding of Harold as imagery, a symbol of divine punishment.

58 Psalms II. 2–5; translation from *The Holy Bible translated from the Latin Vulgate* [Douai Version] (first published 1582, Dublin, 1847, reprinted 1888).

59 'Tapestries were easily portable and therefore well-suited to the peripatetic life-style of the northern courts [in the late-fourteenth and early-fifteenth centuries] providing a means for insulating and decorating the coldest and gloomiest castles': Thomas Campbell, 'Tapestry', in *5000 Years of Textiles*, ed. Jennifer Harris (London, 1995), pp. 188–99, at p. 188.

Tapestry[60] which other contexts might highlight. Since Odo's day the Tapestry has, we know, been hung in various ways. In the fifteenth century it was suspended in a rectangle around the nave of Bayeux Cathedral (not Odo's church, but a later one). In modern times the Tapestry was once kept on a roller so that the pictures, and the story, unwound. Subsequently it was displayed round the outside and inside of an angled enclosure and currently it is exhibited in a great left-handed curve. All of these modern techniques of display would appear natural to an audience raised on the concept that narrative moves sequentially. Perhaps a twenty-first-century audience brought up on hypertext editions and the internet novel with alternative plots and consequences, will show more sensitivity to the subtleties and flexibility of the medieval design.

60 See Owen-Crocker, 'Telling a tale', *passim*.

8

Putting the Bayeux Tapestry in its Place

CHRIS HENIGE

A Square Installation

IN her paper entitled 'Brothers, rivals, and the geometry of the Bayeux Tapestry', Gale Owen-Crocker has presented an intriguing theory on the original installation of the Tapestry.[1] Her focus is on four scenes: Harold swearing his oath (**Plate 11**) and Bishop Odo of Bayeux urging on the troops in battle (**Plate 22**), and their relationship; and the banquet at Bosham (**Plate 1**) and the banquet at Hastings (**Plate 16**), and their relationship. Building on her earlier recognition of a thematic and spatial relationship between the oath scene and the two banquet scenes, Owen-Crocker noticed that in both the oath scene and the Odo-in-battle scene, the figures are stretched laterally, in an exaggerated fashion, and that each image is almost exactly the same width. To Owen-Crocker, this indicated a potential relationship, both in meaning and in space.

To test her theory, Owen-Crocker laid out a printed reproduction of the Tapestry, and arranged it so that the two banquet scenes and the oath/Odo scenes were opposite one another. The first seam in the Tapestry suggested itself as the location of the first corner. The others were less obvious, and irregular shrinkage and stretching of the Tapestry may have confused the issue. However, placing the oath scene at the center of the second wall, Owen-Crocker suggested that the second corner occurred at the mooring of William's ships, at a point where the front ends of several ships emerge awkwardly from a tree (**Plate 15**). Given the presumed relationship between the oath scene and that of Odo with his *baculus*, the third corner must occur at the onset of the battle, and in this paper it is assumed that the corner came at the point where Harold is informed that William is approaching (**Plate 20** top).[2] In this configuration, the

1 In this volume.

2 Gale Owen-Crocker suggests that the corner occurred at the beginning of the next scene, where William spurs on his men and they begin to ride into battle (**Plate 20** bottom). Assuming Odo was centred opposite the Oath, and measuring back from the centre of the figure of Odo on his horse, the corner should occur somewhere within the scene of Harold and his scout, neither exactly at the beginning of it nor exactly at the end. The tree separating this scene from the next does not lend itself to a position in the corner nearly so well as the relatively dead space to the left of the scout. The figure of the scout is also repeated at this point – first looking through the woods, then turning to Harold to report. Furthermore, in decoration the upper border at this point is quite unlike that on either side, again seeming empty by comparison. As such, I am inclined to place the location of the third corner before the scout/Harold scene rather than after.

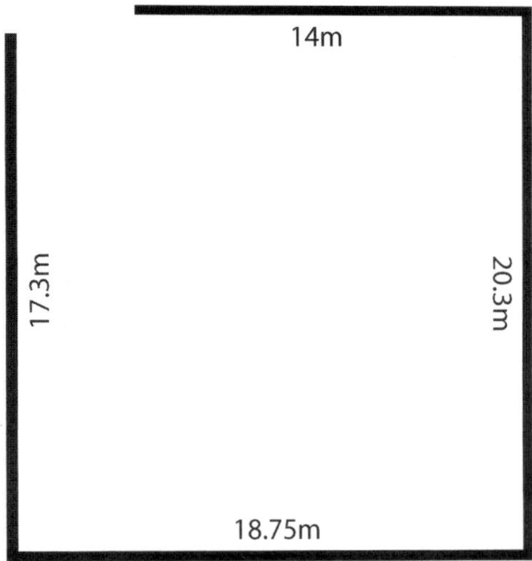

Fig. 9 Configuration of square installation with dimensions

Tapestry would have been divided over four walls: the first containing the narrative from the beginning to the point where Harold is 'rescued' by William; the second running through to the decision to invade; the third running to the onset of the battle; and the fourth running to the end of the Tapestry. Not only did this arrangement seem viable in terms of the locations of the corners, it seemed also to reflect the quadripartite division of the narrative: the Voyage of Harold; the Oath, Before and After; the Invasion; and the Battle of Hastings.

Owen-Crocker postulated only design. She did not try to explain why the Tapestry apparently began part way along a wall or to relate the square design to any building. Nonetheless, her hypothesis suggests to the historian of architecture that a square installation for the Tapestry was a distinct possibility. However, several potential problems needed to be resolved, including identifying a compatible setting for the installation. The lengths of tapestry occupying each of the sides of the configuration established by Owen-Crocker measure about 14m (45ft 11in) 20.30m (66ft 7in), 18.75m (61ft 6in), and 17.30m (56ft 9in) respectively, necessitating a very large room.[3] Architecturally speaking, in order to house the proposed installation a building would have had to measure about 20.40m (66ft 11in) per side on the *interior*, a considerable size for any structure in the eleventh century (**Fig. 9**). Her proposed installation requires that the Tapestry begin almost 4.75m (15ft 7in) from the corner of the room, suggesting the presence of some obstacle that interfered with the possibility of beginning the frieze at a corner, and forced the beginning of the Tapestry about a quarter of the way down the first wall. Finally, the embroidery at its current length would have ended nearly 3m (9ft 10in) short of the last corner, a greater distance than most have been willing to attribute to the missing fragment.

3 All measurements were taken from the 1:7 reproduction, and then recalculated using a total length of 230ft 11in per Stenton, *BT*.

In addition to the physical requirements, the building in question must have had some connection with Odo, as it seems apparent that it was he who commissioned the Tapestry. Was there a structure in post-Conquest England that fitted these requirements? Or, more accurately, might such a building have existed at the time of the creation of the Tapestry?

The Norman Timber Keep

As Wolfgang Grape notes, most modern commentators have favoured a secular building as the original location for the Tapestry:

> . . . recent scholarship has been unanimous that the Tapestry was designed to adorn the great hall of a palace, a hypothesis that takes no account of the historical fact of the consecration of a new cathedral.[4]

Since the Tapestry was housed in the Treasury of the cathedral of Bayeux at least as early as 1476, earlier scholars had argued that it was designed to be displayed in that cathedral from the start and Grape returned to this point of view:

> If the Bayeux Tapestry was designed to adorn a palace, then why was this elaborate narrative so painstakingly embroidered in the first place? Why did the patron not commission mural paintings (*al fresco*) instead? . . . It is unlikely that the Tapestry ever formed part of the permanent decorative programme of a hall.[5]

Most scholars, however, have envisioned the Tapestry installed in a palatial hall of secular character, and as known examples of this building type were rectangular, ranging from 1:2 to 1:4 in proportion, a square solution did not seem to fit the profile architecturally.[6] Dodwell's words sum up conventional thinking:

> I would suggest that the Bayeux Tapestry was a memorial to . . . ostentation and that it formerly decorated one of Odo's great palaces. Even if we allow for its present incompleteness, a hall of about 85 feet by 35 feet would have provided an appropriate setting.[7]

Both arguments hinge on issues of content, usually centred on the question of whether the seemingly erotic scenes found in the borders would have been

4 Wolfgang Grape, *The Bayeux Tapestry* (New York, 1994), p. 78.

5 *Ibid.*

6 Bernstein mentions Westminster Hall, measuring 240ft by 67.5ft, and the refectory of the monastery of Saint Martin at Dover, measuring 100ft by 27ft. See Bernstein, *Mystery*, pp. 105–6. Wilson also mentions Westminster Hall, as well as the Hall of the Exchequer at the Royal Castle at Caen, which measured 30.7m by 11m. See Wilson, *BT*, p. 203. Wilson also cites Margaret Wood, who includes two eleventh-century examples, Cheddar Palace at 110ft by 60ft, and Westminster Hall. See Margaret Wood, *The English Mediaeval House* (New York, 1965), p. 45. Finally, Swanton used the ducal hall at Caen for the purposes of his discussion, a building which measures 30m by 11m. See Michael Swanton, 'The Bayeux Tapestry: Epic Narrative, not Stichic but Stitched', in *The Formation of Culture in Medieval Britain*, ed. Françoise H. M. Le Saux (Lewiston, 1995), p. 164.

7 Dodwell, 'BT and the French secular epic', p. 48.

appropriate for an ecclesiastical setting. Few have considered the implications of the space on the reading of the Tapestry, the majority assuming that it was meant to be read from left to right, beginning to end, and that the actual shape of the installation was simply a product of known architectural types. In either case, the nave of the cathedral or the walls of a palatial hall, the result would have been a rectangular installation.

One building type which has eluded scholarly attention concerning the installation of the Tapestry, and the one which would lend itself best to the proposed square installation, is the Anglo-Norman keep or donjon. Primarily a defensive structure, the keep became a common feature of the post-Conquest landscape. Although there were a few keeps constructed entirely of stone – the White Tower in London, for example – the vast majority of early Anglo-Norman keeps were small timber towers raised on earthen mottes. Physical evidence for these timber castles is scant, although some recently excavated examples such as the keep at Hen Domen have added considerably to our understanding of the type.[8] Hen Domen is much smaller than would have been necessary to house the proposed installation of the Tapestry, and to date there are no known timber keeps having the necessary dimensions.

How wonderful it would be if we could point to the remains of an early Anglo-Norman keep which had all of the features necessary for the proposed installation of the Tapestry, but alas we shall not be so fortunate. No structure related to Odo and dating to the period of the creation of the Tapestry, *c.* 1067–1082, survives.[9]

The timber keep was normally a small-scale solution to the problem of local defence. Its size was often limited by the size of the motte which could be raised. However, the absence of direct evidence for large timber keeps does not automatically rule out the possibility that such structures may have existed at certain key sites, and were simply destroyed by subsequent fortifications. In areas which required more sophisticated defences, larger timber structures must have existed. There were many sites which had no mottes but still had documented fortified structures of some sort. These structures, like the smaller keeps on mottes, would have occupied the most defensible positions, and as such were often directly replaced by later stone defences. This is particularly true of those sites which would have been important enough strategically to require more substantial defences than the simple motte and wooden keep. The construction of these later fortifications would have eradicated all evidence of earlier timber keeps on the same site.[10] It is only where sites were abandoned altogether that we have evidence of the original timber fortifications, such as at Hen Domen, which was rendered obsolete by the regional defences offered by the newly built Montgomery Castle nearby.

Although direct evidence of a suitable timber keep is lacking, a review of the existing castles in south-eastern England reveals two twelfth-century stone keeps which have a configuration consistent with the requirements of the proposed installa-

[8] See Robert Higham and P. A. Barker, *Hen Domen, Montgomery: a Timber Castle on the English Border. A Final Report* (Exeter, 2000).

[9] These dates assume that the Tapestry was begun after the consolidation of power following the invasion and before Odo's imprisonment.

[10] For a discussion of the scant survivals of mixed stone and timber castles, see Robert Higham and Philip Barker, *Timber Castles* (London, 1992), pp. 171–93.

tion: Rochester and Dover. Both have nearly square interior spaces, and both have a stair tower in one corner. Both also had connections to Odo.

At Rochester, both the city and castle were placed in the hands of Odo until his imprisonment in 1082. An early keep, constructed just after the Conquest, is mentioned in the *Domesday Book* (1086) but almost nothing is known about it.[11] Scholars had assumed that the first keep was located to the south of the existing keep on a site known as Boley Hill, but there has been no archaeological proof of this, and recent scholarship holds that the original keep was probably on the site of the current one.[12] Odo's castle must have been a fairly substantial construction, as at least sixty fees were assigned to it, each owing the service of one knight to the garrison. It was replaced by a more permanent structure in stone by Gundulf, bishop of Rochester, begun between 1087 and 1089, to which was added the present keep, begun in 1127. In 1088, Rochester was besieged by William Rufus, after Odo had reneged on his promise to turn over the fortified place to the new king. In the end Odo was stripped of his properties in England and sent back to Normandy. While the later keep at Rochester is consistent with that required by the proposed installation, Rochester was not Odo's primary headquarters in England. That distinction belongs to Dover.

The keep which now stands at Dover was not begun until 1154, and so cannot have been the original site of the installation of the Tapestry. However, it is clear that Dover had a much earlier fortification, one that was contemporary with the Conquest.[13] According to the *Domesday Book*:

> Dover before 1066 paid £18, of which pence King Edward had two parts and Earl Godwin the third . . .
> . . . All these customs were there when King William came to England . . .
> . . . At his first arrival in England the town was burnt. Its valuation could not therefore be reckoned, what its value was when the Bishop of Bayeux acquired it. Now it is assessed at £40; however, the reeve pays £54, that is £24 of pence, which are 20 to the *ora*, to the King and £30 at face value to the Earl.[14]

John of Worcester mentions a castle as early as 1051:

> Meanwhile, Godwin and his sons, with their respective armies, entered Gloucestershire after the feast of the nativity of St. Mary, and encamping at a place called Langtreo, sent envoys to the king at Gloucester, demanding the surrender of count Eustace and his followers, as well as of the Normans and men of Boulogne, who were in possession of the castle [*castellum*] on the cliff at Dover, on pain of hostilities.[15]

11 *Domesday Book*, ed. Philip Morgan, I, *Kent* (Chichester, 1983), fol. 1, paragraph 2.

12 See Plantagenet Somerset Fry, *Castles of Britain and Ireland* (New York, 1996), pp. 174–5.

13 Dover has not been completely overlooked by scholars. Bernstein explored an installation in the refectory of the priory of Saint Martin in Dover – again a rectangular space: see Bernstein, *Mystery*, p. 106.

14 *Domesday Book*, *Kent*, folio D, paragraphs 1, 6 and 7.

15 This is based on *ASC* 1052 (1051) D which mentions the *castelle* at an unmentioned location, which John of Worcester clarifies. Quoted from the version in Thomas Forester, *The Chronicle of Florence of Worcester* (London, 1854), p. 151. Darlington and McGurk (R. R. Darlington and P. McGurk, *The Chronicles of John of Worcester*, 3 vols (Oxford, 1995–), II (1995). 560–1) inexplicably identify Canterbury as the site of the castle on the cliff, though clearly the passage refers to Dover. The Latin reads: *qui castellum in Doruuernie cliuo tenuerunt.*

Eadmer notes the importance of Dover in Harold's oath to William in 1064, and thereby establishes a possible date for its reconstruction:

> William: 'If you on your side undertake to support me in this project and further promise that you will make a stronghold [*castellum*] at Dover with a well of water for my use . . .'[16]
>
> Harold: 'As for the stronghold [*castellum*] at Dover and the well with water in it, I have completed that according to our agreement although for whose use I cannot say.'[17]

William of Poitiers also states that as part of Harold's oath,

> . . . the castle of Dover [*castrum Doveram*] should be fortified by his care and at his expense for William's knights . . .[18]

Immediately after the battle, according to William of Poitiers, Duke William

> . . . went to Dover, where he heard that a great multitude had gathered because the place seemed impregnable . . . When, however, the garrison were preparing to make humble surrender, the squires in our army, greedy for booty, set the place on fire. The duke, not wishing to injure those who had begun to parley with him for surrender, paid for the repair of the buildings and gave compensation for other losses . . . After the surrender of the castle [*castro*], he spent eight days fortifying it where it was weakest.[19]

Wace's account varies somewhat:

> Proceeding thence, he rested no where till he reached Dover, at the strong fort he had ordered to be made at the foot of the hill. The castle on the hill was well garrisoned, and there all the goods of the country round were stored, and all the people had collected. The place being well fortified, and being out of the reach of any engines, they had made ready to defend themselves, and determined to contest the matter with the duke; and it was so well fenced in, and so high, and had so many towers and walls, that it was no easy matter to take it, as long as provisions should last.
>
> The duke held them besieged there eight days; and during that time there were many fierce and bold assaults of the men and esquires.[20]

William of Poitiers also informs us of Odo's connection to the castle: 'As for the castle of Dover, he entrusted it to his brother Odo, together with the adjacent south coast, which goes by the old name of Kent.'[21] Almost immediately, internal strife led to the 'inhabitants of Kent' persuading Eustace of Boulogne to attack Dover castle '. . . with their help. If indeed he had been able to gain possession of that strong site

16 Geoffrey Bosanquet, *Eadmer's History of Recent Events in England* (London, 1964), p. 7.

17 *Ibid*., p. 8.

18 William of Poitiers, I. xlii: *The Gesta Guillelmi of William of Poitiers*, ed. and trans. R. H. C. Davis and Marjorie Chibnall (Oxford, 1998), pp. 70–1.

19 William of Poitiers, II. xxvii: Davis and Chibnall, *Gesta Guillelmi*, pp. 142–5.

20 Edgar Taylor, *Master Wace: His Chronicle of the Norman Conquest from the Roman de Rou* (London, 1837), pp. 262–3.

21 William of Poitiers, II. xxxvii: Davis and Chibnall, *Gesta Guillelmi*, pp. 164–5.

with its seaport his power would have been extended more widely and that of the Normans correspondingly diminished.'[22]

Odo eventually lost the favour of his brother William and was imprisoned in 1082. This appears to have ended Odo's connections with Dover, as upon his release, when he set out to re-establish his holdings in England, he centred his activities at Rochester, which was better suited to defend Kent from within rather than from without. After William's death in 1087, conflict over the succession led to the siege of Rochester, and Odo's subsequent capture after retiring to Pevensey. Odo's connections with England ceased at that point – he returned to Normandy and eventually died on the First Crusade. It is clear, however, that Odo was closely linked to Dover in the years between the Conquest and his imprisonment in 1082. Might the Tapestry have been designed for the earlier castle on the site?

Dover was a site of considerable importance, and its fortifications must have been more elaborate than a simple timber keep on a raised motte. The problems of terminology associated with the various manifestations of the fortifications at Dover have been explored in some detail by R. Allen Brown.[23] Brown concluded that the *castellum* or *castrum* of 1051 and 1064 mentioned by these chroniclers actually refers to an Anglo-Saxon *burh*, or fortified town, and that only that constructed by William in 1066 should be considered a 'castle', presumably built within the enclosure of the *burh*. Contrary to the belief of early scholars that the Saxon and Anglo-Norman fortifications mentioned by William of Poitiers and others were located on the site of the current church of Saint Mary in Castro, recent excavations in the area of the church have led scholars to the conclusion that the original fortification was located in the same position as the current castle:

> There is now no question of [the Saint Mary in Castro] earthworks having formed the motte or defensive core of the castle erected by Harold in 1064–1066, though the area may have been included within defences of this date. The site of Henry II's keep can thus be seen probably to represent the original, as well as the subsequent and logical center of the castle.[24]

It is interesting to note that the exterior dimensions of the current keep, at over 26m (85ft 3in) square, exceed those required by the 20-metre-square installation by a considerable margin, and that the configuration of the keep matches that which would be required by the proposed installation of the Tapestry (**Fig. 10**). Might the earlier keep have been on the same foundations, but constructed of wood rather than stone? Thinner timber-frame walls on the same foundations would have allowed the greater interior dimensions required (**Fig. 11**). Grape's questions concerning tapestry versus fresco are resolved in a timber-framed structure. The timber frame with impermanent wattle and daub infill would have been unsuitable for fresco, but would have been ideal for hanging a tapestry.

22 William of Poitiers, II. xlvii: Davis and Chibnall, *Gesta Guillelmi*, pp. 182–3.

23 See R. Allen Brown, 'The Norman Conquest and the genesis of English castles', in R. Allen Brown, *Castles, Conquest and Charters* (Woodbridge, 1989), pp. 85–6.

24 David M. Wilson and D. Gillian Hurst, 'Medieval Britain in 1962 and 1963', *Medieval Archaeology* 8 (1964), 254.

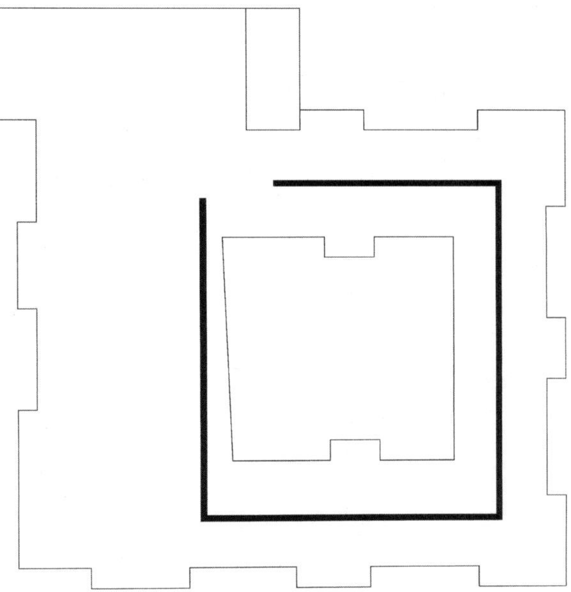

Fig. 10 Square installation superimposed over the current plan of Dover Castle (to scale)

A row of central supports would have been necessary to obviate the problem of spanning such a great distance with timbers, and to cut the spans to a more manageable 10 metres. The location of these earlier supports may well be reflected in the north-south wall which currently divides the interior space of the keep. At the troublesome corner, from which the Tapestry was apparently excluded, one might easily envision a stair tower of stone, serving as an anchor for the structure, and a safe escape if the timber portion of the keep caught fire. The stone construction of this tower would have been much thicker than the remaining timber portion of the keep, and would have intruded into the interior spaces at all levels. It would have been seen as an obstacle both practically and iconographically, as its short, solid walls would not have been friendly either to the installation or to establishing important spatial relationships.

Taking into account the gross configuration of the building, the location of the stair tower and the intermediate bearing wall, the current keep at Dover may well reflect almost exactly its predecessor – a literal translation of a successful wooden structure into one of stone. Such a theory can, of course, never be proven, and even if it is demonstrated at some point that the core of the foundations of the current keep date back to the Conquest, we can never be sure what the upper portions might have looked like. It is sufficient at this point to demonstrate that the type of building that the proposed installation of the Tapestry required *could* have existed, and the similarity of the current keep at Dover with that suggested by the proposed installation of the Tapestry seems more than happy coincidence. When combined with the connections Odo had with the site, Dover Castle becomes a leading candidate in the search for the original home of the Bayeux Tapestry.

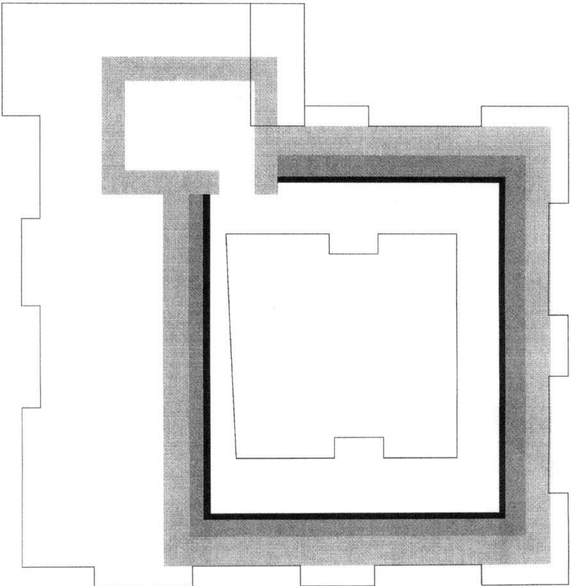

Fig. 11 Supposed timber walls superimposed over the existing foundations of Dover Castle, providing the requisite support for the square installation of the Tapestry

A final tantalizing link may be found in the Tapestry itself. In the scene, where Harold returns to England – *HAROLD DVX REVERSVS EST AD ANGLICAM TERRAM* – a scout views the ship from the balcony of a tower (**Plate 12**).[25] The lowest level of the structure is of stone, while the upper portions appear to be of timber. A garrison of soldiers can be seen in the windows. The most likely target for Harold's landing in England must have been Dover, a major port and one which must have been well garrisoned. Might we be treated here to a glimpse of the keep as it existed at the time of the creation of the Tapestry?

Iconographic implications

While the four scenes initially cited by Owen-Crocker and her further suggestions of interrelationships offer tantalizing hints toward a square installation, the argument for a square installation would be greatly strengthened if it could be demonstrated that there were relationships between nearly every scene in the Tapestry with their counterparts across the room. In fact, there are numerous significant relationships that exist across the room, and it would be worth summarizing them under the proposed installation scheme (the scenes in brackets indicate likely content for the missing fragment at the end of the Tapestry):

25 Scene 24. For a colour reproduction see Wilson, *BT*, Plate 27.

Subject	*Scenes*	*Subject Counterpart*
Edward meets with Harold	1 vs. 52	A House is Burned
Prayer at Bosham	3 vs. 50	William, Odo, Robert
Banquet at Bosham	4 vs. 49	Banquet at Hastings
Harold's Captivity	8/16 vs. 39/45	William's Invasion
Riding to William's Palace	17 vs. X	[Interruption by stone stair turret]
Harold and William Negotiate	18 vs. [76]	[William Enthroned]
A Cleric and Ælfgyva	19 vs. [75]	[William is Given the Crown]
William Rides to Brittany	20/21 vs. [74]	[William Rides to London]
Conan's Escape at Dol	23 vs. 71/72	Death of Harold
Rennes	24 vs. 71	A Cleric is Slain
Harold Swearing his Oath	29 vs. 68	Odo Inspiring the Troops
Harold Reporting to Edward	31 vs. 64	Deaths of Leofwine and Gyrð
Harold's Usurpation	34 vs. 62/63	The Two Forces Collide

There are also more general relationships from wall to wall. Most scholars have seen the Tapestry as a two-part story, one of betrayal and retribution – Bernstein calls it 'a play in two acts', with the first act ending with the vision of the ghostly ships.[26] Owen-Crocker's square installation offers the possibility of a four-part interpretation, with each part relating to one wall of the proposed installation.

The earliest scenes of the Tapestry, on the first wall, which I will call the Captivity Wall, relate the story of Harold's journey to France and his subsequent captivity by Guy de Ponthieu. This story line ends with the transfer of Harold into the hands of Duke William. The scenes on this wall establish two key elements of the story: first, that Harold came to France at the request of Edward, setting up Harold's subsequent betrayal; and second that he was captured and held hostage by one of William's less amiable vassals, Guy de Ponthieu, creating the opportunity for William to position himself as saviour of Harold – and his overlord.

The second wall, or Oath Wall, deals with the bonding between Harold and William, which climaxes at the central scene – Harold's oath. The story then continues with the 'betrayal' – Harold's usurpation of the throne of England – and ends with William's subsequent decision to invade England. This is the focal wall, and I would suggest that if the Tapestry hung in a banquet or reception hall within the timber keep, Odo sat directly under Harold's oath. There has been little disagreement that this is the key scene in the narrative, and in the proposed installation it forms the visual focal point of the Tapestry.

The third wall, or Invasion Wall, depicts the invasion of England, from the mooring of the newly constructed fleet to the sighting of the enemy at the battlefield.

In this segment, there are numerous scenes that have the appearance of being filler material, and may serve both to position certain important scenes across others on the facing wall, and to push the start of the battle to the fourth wall.[27]

The fourth wall, or Battle Wall, begins with William's army riding into battle,

26 Bernstein, *Mystery*, p. 16.

27 See Owen-Crocker 'Brothers, rivals' in this volume.

continues with all of the carnage of the battle, and ended (probably) with William enthroned. It now ends with the Normans chasing the English off the battlefield.

It should be noted that the Captivity Wall presents Harold's journey to France, while opposite, the Invasion Wall depicts William's journey to England. A similar opposition occurs in the themes of the Oath Wall and the Battle Wall: action versus consequence – betrayal versus retribution. The Tapestry might therefore be read in terms of four acts rather than two, with each act corresponding to one of the walls of the installation.

Scholars also have been unanimous in their reading of the narrative quality of the Tapestry, that it was meant to be understood, even 'read', remorselessly from left to right. This is demonstrated by the discussions that have occupied a number of scholars on the so-called 'retrograde' scenes, where the actions seem to occur in reverse chronological order, presumably because they seem to fly in the face of the conventional left-to-right narrative format.[28] Owen-Crocker's proposed square installation is not inconsistent with a strictly narrative understanding of the content, and in light of the numerous relationships that exist across space, it allows also for the possibility of foreshadowing and flashback, devices in the Tapestry that have not been addressed with any conviction to date. Some of these relationships are quite general, but others seem very specific and intentional. An analysis of two of these relationships may shed considerable light on scenes that have vexed scholars since the study of the Tapestry began: Who is Ælfgyva and why is she presented here? What was the content of the missing scenes at the end of the Tapestry?

The scene containing a cleric and a woman identified as Ælfgyva – *VBI VNVS CLERICVS ET ÆLFGYVA* (**Plate 8**) – has been the subject of so much debate that it would be impractical to revisit all of the arguments here.[29] Instead, the solution offered by J. Bard McNulty will be supported, that the scene depicts Ælfgyva of Northampton and the cleric from whom she was rumoured to have procured the child Swein and passed him off as the legitimate son of King Cnut.[30] Inspiration for this interpretation comes from John of Worcester:

> Before his death, Cnut, king of the English, made Swein king over the Norwegians. He was said to be his son by Ælfgifu of Northampton, that is the daughter of Ælfhelm the ealdorman, and the noble lady Wulfrun. However, several asserted that he was not the son of the king and that same Ælfgifu, but that Ælfgifu wanted to have a son by the king, and could not, and therefore ordered the new-born child of some priest's concubine to be brought to her, and made the king fully believe that she had just borne him a son. Also, he set up as king over the Danes Hardacnut, his son by Queen Ælfgifu. . . . Harold claimed to be the son of King Cnut by Ælfgifu of Northampton, but that is quite untrue, for some say that he was the son of a certain cobbler, but that Ælfgifu had acted in the same way with him as she is said to have done with Swein. But, because the matter concerned is open

28 See Michel Parisse, *The Bayeux Tapestry* (Vitry-sur-Seine, 1983), pp. 74–7; Stenton, *BT*, pp. 177, 180; Wilson, *BT*, pp. 176–7, 198; Bernstein, *Mystery*, pp. 19–21, 120–4.

29 See Catherine E. Karkov, 'Gendering the battle? Male and female in the Bayeux Tapestry', in this volume, p. 142 n. 13.

30 J. Bard McNulty, 'The Lady Aelfgyva in the Bayeux Tapestry', *Speculum* 55 (1980), 659–68.

> to doubt, we have been unable to make a firm statement about the parentage of either.[31]

McNulty argued that this scene served to undermine the Norwegian claims to the English throne by going right to the source of the argument: that all of these claims went back to Swein, and that he was not the legitimate son of Cnut to begin with. This argument was dismissed almost immediately by M. W. Campbell,[32] who argued that the identity of the woman in question must conform to the following criteria: that she was English, as Ælfgyva is clearly an English name; and that all of the scenes in the Tapestry are contemporary, and so this woman must have been present at William's court when Harold was there. The first argument is reasonable, but the second deserves further scrutiny.

The columns which flank Ælfgyva , with their spiral treatment on columns, peculiar capitals and large animal heads, are without precedent in the Tapestry and as such are perhaps meant to indicate an unfamiliar architecture, one that was neither Norman nor Saxon. I would tentatively suggest it was meant to represent a Norwegian structure.[33] This would make sense only if the Ælfgyva in question was Ælfgyva of Northampton, and the scene was intended to undermine the Norwegian claims to the English throne.

If we take this thesis further, and envision which scene would have been opposite the Ælfgyva scene in a square installation, we have a problem, for the Ælfgyva scene would have been opposite the missing last scenes of the Tapestry. If we take the first four scenes of the Oath Wall – Duke William with Harold riding to his palace, Harold negotiating for the hostages, the cleric and Ælfgyva, and William riding off to Brittany – we might imagine an arrangement of four scenes on the opposite wall. Although no one can agree on the number of missing scenes, scholars generally agree that one of the last scenes would have depicted William enthroned. If this story follows the precedent set when Harold took the throne, then we might expect to see at least two scenes, one of William receiving the crown, and the next of William enthroned. Preceded by William riding to London (opposite William riding to Brittany), the crowning would have occurred opposite Ælfgyva, and the enthronement opposite the hostage negotiations.[34] Here we have a seemingly perfect juxtaposition of themes – the legitimate opposite the illegitimate.[35] If we accept that the designer of

31 John of Worcester, 1035: Darlington and McGurk, *John of Worcester*, II. 520–1.

32 M. W. Campbell, 'Aelfgyva: the mystery lady of the Bayeux Tapestry', *Annales de Normandie* 34 (1984), 127–45.

33 Examples of Norwegian woodwork may be found in M. Blindheim, *Norwegian Romanesque Decorative Sculpture 1090–1210* (New York, 1966).

34 The first scene of the Oath Wall, William and Harold riding to Rouen, would not have had a counterpart; instead the stone stair tower might have interfered here as well.

35 The notion of the Tapestry as a vehicle for undermining the illegitimate claims of the 'usurpers' and for advancing the legitimate claims of William finds its earliest narrative manifestation in the first scene, assuming it depicts Edward instructing Harold to go to Normandy and inform William that he had been chosen to succeed Edward as king of England. If Harold indeed had designs on the throne at this time (see N. J. Higham, 'Harold Godwinesson: the construction of kingship', in this volume), this must have been a distasteful duty. On the opposite wall, directly opposite this scene, is the enigmatic house-burning scene (**Plate 17**). It has been consistently described as depicting refugees and 'the perils of war'. It is difficult to accept an argument that the house was 'in the way of the battle' and if the

the Bayeux Tapestry wished to undermine the legitimacy of both Harold Godwinesson's *and* Norwegian claims to the throne, the device that could achieve the latter in the simplest and most effective terms was the story of Ælfgyva of Northampton, a 'flashback' story that may well have come up in the hostage discussions depicted in the previous scene.[36]

Conclusion

The iconographic evidence for a square installation presented by Gale Owen-Crocker and augmented herein is compelling, and the sheer number of relationships that would have existed across the room in such an installation is impressive. And although we cannot point to an existing or excavated structure and state with certainty that the Tapestry could have been installed within it, it is clear that the Anglo-Norman keep would have been the likely home for such an installation, and that as such the castle at Dover is the strongest candidate for the original home of the Bayeux Tapestry.

burning represents Norman reprisals on the Saxons it is strange that it appears before, and not after, the battle. However, in the preceding scene, William is informed of Harold's activities (*HIC NVNTIATVM EST WILLELM̊ DE HAROLD*, 'here William is informed about Harold'), the messenger apparently gesturing towards the next scene with the hand that holds his lance. Harold had been absent from the south of England because he was engaged in defeating Harold of Norway at the Battle of Stamfordbridge. Might the house-burning scene, like the Ælfgyva scene, be a metaphorical 'flashback' to Stamfordbridge where Harold destroyed the claims of the Norwegian royal house to the English throne? (*HIC DOMVS INCENDITVR*, 'here a [royal] house is burned') *Domus*, as well as its literal meaning of a residence, could be applied to kindred (see for example Isidore of Seville, *Est . . . domus genus, familia sive coniunctio viri et uxoris*, '*Domus* is kindred, family or the union of man and wife': *Isidori Hispalensis Episcopi Etymologiarum sive Originaum*, ed. W. M. Lindsay, 2 vols (Oxford, 1911), IX. iv. 3). Since the Norwegian claim to the throne might be traced back to the sons of Cnut, might the mother and child in the burning house represent Ælfgyva and her (allegedly illegitimate) son, Swein? (For the Scandinavian role in the succession crisis see Ian Howard, 'Harold II: a throne-worthy king', in this volume.)

36 See Owen-Crocker, 'Brothers, rivals', in this volume, p. 119.

9

Gendering the Battle? Male and Female in the Bayeux Tapestry

CATHERINE E. KARKOV

MUCH has been written about the women in the Bayeux Tapestry, who they are and what they might mean. While in this article I will offer some suggestions as to their meanings, my primary interest is in the way in which they function formally within the Tapestry's larger composition and visual narrative.[1] At what points in the story do they appear, and are there significant similarities or differences in their poses, gestures or situations? We may not agree on the identification or meaning of most of the women depicted in the Tapestry, but we can at least agree that there are not very many of them: only three in the main narrative panel, and three more (not counting the centaurs) in the borders. Only one of these women, Ælfgyva, is identified by name (**Plate 8**), ironically making her the most problematic of all. I have no intention here of adding to the speculation surrounding which historical Ælfgyva she might or might not represent, and will note here only that the name form identifies her as English.[2]

Given the carefully constructed nature of the Tapestry as a *visual* narrative, and the designers' use of repeated figures, scenes and motifs as a means of advancing that narrative,[3] we might ask what, if anything, links these somewhat intrusive women together. Let us begin with the women in the main panel. Firstly, context or inscription identifies them all as English: Edith, wife of Edward the Confessor (**Plate 13**), the mysterious Ælfgyva, and the anonymous English woman fleeing her burning home (**Plate 17**). Secondly, they are all in vulnerable positions: the queen's husband has just died, and the succession will be difficult to say the least, Ælfgyva is having her face fondled by a cleric, and the anonymous woman has just lost her home (and possibly her husband). Thirdly, all three are placed at key turning points in the pictorial and historical narrative. The *Vita Ædwardi* does record that Edith was present at Edward's

1 It is impossible for a work of visual art ever to be understood exclusively in terms of the textual, hence the Tapestry cannot be interpreted simply as a 'narrative' for 'reading'. On the tension between the visual and the textual see Nicholas Mirzoeff, *An Introduction to Visual Culture* (London and New York, 1999).

2 Emma of Normandy, for example, was given, or took, the name Ælfgyfa (Ælfgifu) as her official English name at the time of her marriage to Æthelred II.

3 On the formal aspects of the Tapestry's narrative see Brilliant, 'Stripped narrative'.

death and that she sat on the floor warming his feet,[4] so the artists, if they knew the *Vita*, may well have included her in the death scene as a note of historical reality. That does not, however, mean that we should see this as the only reason for her inclusion, or the *Vita* as the only source for her pose. Edith's presence may also serve as a means of highlighting Edward's lack of an heir, or perhaps his saintliness (her pose echoing that of Mary at the Crucifixion, or the Marys at the tomb of Christ), and she does also appear at a significant turning point in the narrative – it is only with Edward's death that the confrontation between William and Harold becomes inevitable. Edith's gesture of sorrow may also serve to alert us to the grim events to come, particularly as it echoes and is echoed by a series of similar gestures, perhaps most notably those of the first of the marginal nude women, and of Harold at Hastings.[5] Ælfgyva appears at the point at which Harold enters William's court, and the anonymous fleeing woman appears between the scenes of William receiving news of Harold, and of William and his troops setting forth for battle. As far as repetition is concerned, one might also note that Ælfgyva is similarly framed in a doorway between scenes of William receiving Harold, and of William and Harold setting off on the campaign in Brittany, scenes very similar to those which frame the woman fleeing her home.[6] In this case the visual similarity of the two episodes is echoed in the inscriptions: the ambiguous *VBI VNVS CLERICVS ET ÆLFGYVA* ('Where Ælfgyva and a cleric'), followed by *HIC VVILLEM DVX ET EXERCITVS EIVS* (*VENERVNT AD MONTE[M] MICHAELIS*) ('Here Duke William and his army [came to Mont-Saint-Michel]'), and the ambiguous *HIC DOMVS INCENDITVR* ('Here a house is burned') (whose house? and by whom?),[7] followed by *HIC MILITES EXIERVNT DE HESTENGA* ('Here soldiers set out from Hastings'). Whatever the historical reasons, if any, for their inclusion in the Tapestry, the intrusion of these women into its predominantly male world provides a visual clue that something significant is about to happen. While they do not participate directly in the political and military action, they are visual examples of the 'betweenness' that Carol Clover has shown to be characteristic of women out of place in an early medieval warrior world.[8]

The women in the borders are all halves of couples. To be sure, all of the women in

4 Barlow, *Vita Ædwardi*, pp. 116–24.

5 On the use of repeated gestures in the Tapestry see Brilliant, 'Stripped Narrative'.

6 The figures of William and Harold, and William and the messenger bringing news of Harold placed before the scenes depicting the threatened two women are very close in composition, while both scenes are followed by figures of horsemen departing on military campaigns.

7 J. Bard McNulty (*The Narrative Art of the Bayeux Tapestry* (New York, 1989), p. 48) suggests that the scene is a reference to Harold's implementation of a scorched earth policy, though given the documentation of William's destruction of the land around Hastings by William of Poitiers and the poet of the *Carmen de Hastingae Proelio*, this seems unlikely to be the case. See William of Poitiers, II. xv: *The Gesta Guillelmi of William of Poitiers*, ed. and trans. R. H. C. Davis and Marjorie Chibnall (Oxford, 1998), pp. 124–5; Guy of Amiens, lines 145–55: *The Carmen de Hastingae Proelio of Guy Bishop of Amiens*, ed. Catherine Morton and Hope Muntz (Oxford, 1972), pp. 10–12. See also Richard Gameson, 'The origin, art, and message of the Bayeux Tapestry', in Gameson, *Study*, pp. 158–9.

8 Carol J. Clover, 'Maiden warriors and other sons', in *Matrons and Marginal Women in Medieval Society*, ed. Robert R. Edwards and Vickie Ziegler (Woodbridge, 1995), pp. 75–87. Clover uses the term in a slightly different context from that in which I am using it here, but we both use it to describe women in a warrior world to which they do not normally belong.

the Bayeux Tapestry are parts of couples (queen and king, Ælfgyva and the cleric, mother and son), but the women in the marginal scenes are members of confrontational couples, and each of these couples appears at a point of confrontation. The first couple is placed directly beneath Harold as he comes face to face with William for the first time (**Plate 7**), and the second two are directly over the point at which the two armies prepare to confront each other at Hastings (**Plate 19**). The marginal women are doubly intrusive because of their nudity, and therefore they must also be considered in relation to the other nudes portrayed in the Tapestry, all of them confined to the borders. Most famously, a nude man chops wood beneath the depiction of Harold's audience with William, while in the very next scene a squatting figure beneath Ælfgyva and the cleric mirrors the cleric's dramatic pose and gesture (**Plate 8**). The only other nudes, again all male, appear at the end of the Tapestry, amongst the bodies of the dead who have been dismembered and stripped, or are being stripped, of their arms, and directly beneath the fall of the dragon-standard of Wessex and the death of Harold (**Plate 23**). Nudity, like the appearance of the women, serves to highlight conflict, confrontation and defeat, but it also serves to expand the relationship between the episodes it glosses. The figure of the man chopping wood is echoed by that of the nude man carrying an axe at the beginning of the battle (and possibly indirectly by the dead nudes being stripped of their weapons at its end).[9] The repetition of the two male nudes also serves as a visual bridge to the awkward transition from the scene of Harold before William to that of Ælfgyva and the cleric. Harold's pointing gesture does the same. While it has generally been accepted that Harold is pointing to Ælfgyva and the cleric, and that this is the subject of his conversation with William,[10] such a reading implies that (a) there must be a text (a story or a history) that explains the episode, and (b) that it is little more than an Anglo-Saxon form of thought-bubble. The composition of the scene within William's palace suggests that this may not in fact be the case. A group of William's men stands behind Harold, and the hand of the first soldier in the group touches Harold's own, while the group as a whole looks intently towards Harold and William. The positioning of the group stops the flow of the narrative, and keeps the action confined within the walls of William's palace; at the very least the composition problematizes the relationship between the two scenes.

The nudity and the pose of the man beneath Ælfgyva draw our attention not only to the likely impropriety of the encounter between her and the cleric, but also to the cleric's gesture. His arm thrusts dramatically forward to touch the side of Ælfgyva's face, and the framing device of the doorway keeps our eyes focussed on that touch of hand to face. In his analysis of formal patterns and repetition in the Bayeux Tapestry, Richard Brilliant commented on the fact that 'strong movements of the hand to the eye' seemed particularly significant and programmatic.[11] There are a number of such movements – mostly those of people raising their hands to their own faces or eyes – but only three points in the narrative where one person's face or eye is touched by the

9 While the pose of the figures is similar, the tools or weapons they carry are not.

10 E.g. Gale R. Owen-Crocker, 'Telling a tale: narrative techniques in the Bayeux Tapestry and the Old English epic *Beowulf*', in *Medieval Art: Recent Perspectives*, ed. Gale R. Owen-Crocker and Timothy Graham (Manchester, 1998), pp. 40–59, at p. 45.

11 Brilliant, 'Stripped narrative', p. 118.

hand, or an object from the hand, of another: Ælfgyva and the cleric, the scene in which William gives Harold arms (**Plate 10**), and the death of Harold. The cleric touching Ælfgyva's face precedes the start of the campaign in Brittany. That same campaign ends with the scene in which William gives Harold arms, touching his face in a manner similar to that in which the nameless cleric touches Ælfgyva's. William's grant of arms is followed by the scene of Harold swearing his oath before William at Bayeux (**Plate 11**), just as the image of Ælfgyva and the cleric is preceded by Harold's audience with William in his palace. The episodes frame the series of events through which Harold becomes William's vassal, his man, just as Ælfgyva is apparently about to become the cleric's woman. As noted by Gale Owen-Crocker,[12] these are the only two points in the whole of the Tapestry in which two figures touch each other in such intimate fashion, and the visual similarities suggest that we are meant to understand the relationships between the two figures as equivalent. In both cases we are dealing with hierarchical relationships of power in which the more aggressive figure is the one in control. If one wishes to identify the Tapestry's Ælfgyva with a particular historical Ælfgyva,[13] it is more than likely – given the candidates suggested to date – that she too would have been involved in a similar relationship of unequal power at some point.

In Brilliant's analysis the dramatic hand to eye (or face) gestures were designed to lead the eye of the viewer up to the dramatic high point of the historical narrative, the point at which Harold is shot in the eye with an arrow.[14] They also serve to highlight the role of looking, both within and at a work in which narrative is primarily pictorial, and in which composition cannot be reduced to narrative alone.[15] Lookouts routinely

12 Owen-Crocker, 'Telling a tale', pp. 48–9.

13 The main candidates suggested to date and major sources for discussion of each are as follows: Ælfgyva of Northampton (see Dodwell, 'BT and the French secular Epic'; J. Bard McNulty, 'The lady Aelfgyva in the Bayeux Tapestry', *Speculum* 55 (1980), 659–68); Queen Ælfgyva/Emma (see Eric F. Freeman, 'The identity of Ælfgyva in the Bayeux Tapestry', *Annales de Normandie* 41 (1991), 117–34; Martin K. Foys, *The Bayeux Tapestry Digital Edition* (Leicester, 2003), commentary to panel 39 scene 11); a conflation of Ælfgyva of Northampton and Queen Ælfgyva/Emma (Suzanne Lewis, *The Rhetoric of Power in the Bayeux Tapestry* (Cambridge, 1999), pp. 88–9); Ælfgyva, abbess of Wilton (John Gosling, 'The identity of the lady Ælfgyva in the Bayeux Tapestry and some speculation regarding the hagiographer Goscelin', *Analecta Bollandiana* 108 (1990), 71–9); Alfgyva, abbess of Barking (Henri Prentout, 'Essai d'identification des personnages inconnus de la Tapisserie de Bayeux', *Revue Historique* 176 (1935) 14–23); Eadgifu, abbess of Leominster (Miles W. Campbell, 'Ælfgyva: the mysterious lady of the Bayeux Tapestry', *Annales de Normandie* 34 (1984), 127–45); Harold's wife or potential bride (John Collingwood Bruce, *The Bayeux Tapestry Elucidated* (London, 1856), pp. 53–6; Owen-Crocker, 'Telling a tale', p. 45); one of Harold's sisters (Jean Verrier, *The Bayeux Embroidery Known as Queen Matilda's Tapestry*, trans. R. Schoedelin (Paris, 1946), p. 10; Richard D. Wissolik, 'Code in the Bayeux Tapestry', *Annuale Mediaevale*, ed. Frank Zbozny, 19 (Atlantic Highlands, NJ, 1979), pp. 69–97, at 83; Ian W. Walker, *Harold, the Last Anglo-Saxon King* (Stroud, 1997), pp. 93–5); William's daughter Adeliza (Simone Bertrand, *La Tapisserie de Bayeux et la Manière de Vivre au Onzième Siècle* (Saint-Leger–Vauban, Yonne, 1966), p. 87; Wolfgang Grape, *The Bayeux Tapestry: Monument to a Norman Triumph*, trans. David Britt (Munich, 1994), p. 40; Mogens Rud, *The Bayeux Tapestry and the Battle of Hastings 1066*, trans. C. Bojesen (Copenhagen, 1996), p. 49). For extensive bibliography on the scene see Foys, *Digital Edition*, commentary to panel 39 scene 11.

14 Brilliant, 'Stripped narrative', pp. 118–19.

15 The Bayeux Tapestry is also a non-narrative visual experience. The way in which the borders relate to the central panel, the shock with which the Ælfgiva and the cleric scene causes us to interrupt our

make this type of gesture, but it is also made by the nude woman in the first of the marginal couples, by Edith at Edward's death, by William when he proves to his troops that he is still alive, and by Harold when he is shot in the eye. The gesture of the cleric, and William when he grants Harold arms do, however, function slightly differently, as in both cases the person doing the touching is expressing power over the person being touched.

The formal patterns are easy to pick out, but what they might mean is not so easily discerned. The marginal nudes have been identified as references to specific Aesopic fables,[16] to the English soldiers' rush to battle and/or their last embrace with their wives,[17] to William's promise to his men that women would welcome them back from battle,[18] to the epithets that the Normans may have hurled at the English,[19] and as a subversive commentary on the male-dominated 'master narrative' by the female embroideresses.[20] Bard McNulty suggested simply that the marginal nudes served to gender the battle, with William and the Normans identified as the masculine victors, and Harold and the English identified as the feminized losers. In support of this basic argument, Madeline Caviness has written that 'the exclusion of women [from the Tapestry] allows a reconfiguration of gender, so that long-haired Anglo-Saxons, especially Harold, are constructed as feminised "other" or the enemy'.[21] She cites such details as William's 'carefully positioned' sword hilt and 'well-hung' stallion as signs of his triumphant masculinity and inevitable victory.[22] The suggestion that the marginal figures serve to gender the battle is theoretically attractive, especially given the generally later medieval practice of feminizing the 'other',[23] and given the fact that the Anglo-Saxons would have been familiar with the concept of gendered battle from such texts as Prudentius's *Psychomachia*. It was the Anglo-Saxons who began the practice of depicting the defeated Vices of the *Psychomachia* as women (as opposed to monsters),[24] and similarities between individual figures in the Tapestry

linear 'reading' of the flow of events, the expressive gestures of the lookouts, and the turmoil of the battle scenes, are all amongst the elements in the Tapestry that cannot be conveyed textually.

16 Léon Hermmann (*Les Fables Antiques de la Broderie de Bayeux* (Brussels, 1964)) links the first of the marginal couples to the fable of 'The Maiden and her Suitors' (p. 8), the second to 'The Widow and the Soldier' (p. 11), and the third to 'The Young Man and the Courtesan' (p. 11).

17 Frank Rede Fowke, *The Bayeux Tapestry: a History and Description* (London, 2nd ed., 1898), p. 116; Rud, *Bayeux Tapestry and the Battle of Hastings*, p. 76.

18 Michelle Bolduc, 'The disruptive discourse: women in the margins of the Bayeux Tapestry and the Hours of Catherine of Clèves', *Romance Languages Annual* 6 (1994), pp. 18–22.

19 Madeline H. Caviness, 'Obscenity and alterity: images that shock and offend us/them, now/then?' in *Obscenity: Social Control and Artistic Creation in the European Middle Ages* , ed. Jan M. Ziolkowski (Leiden, 1998), pp. 155–75, at 172.

20 Karen Rose Mathews, 'Nudity on the margins: The Bayeux Tapestry and its relationship to marginal architectural sculpture', in *Naked Before God: Cultural Constructions of the Unclothed Body in Anglo-Saxon England*, ed. Benjamin Withers and Jonathan Wilcox (Morgantown, 2003), pp. 138–61.

21 Caviness, 'Obscenity and alterity', p. 172.

22 Caviness, 'Obscenity and alterity', p. 169.

23 See e.g. Louise Mirrer, 'Representing "other" men: Muslims, Jews, and masculine ideals in medieval Castilian epic and ballad', in *Medieval Masculinities: Regarding Men in the Middle Ages*, Medieval Cultures 7, ed. Clare A. Lees (Minneapolis, 1994), pp. 169–86; Carol Clover, 'Regardless of sex: men, women and power in early northern Europe', in *Studying Medieval Women: Sex, Gender, Feminism*, ed. Nancy F. Partner (Cambridge, MA, 1993), pp. 61–85.

24 Catherine E. Karkov, 'Broken bodies and singing tongues: gender and voice in the Cambridge, Corpus

and those in one of the Anglo-Saxon illustrated *Psychomachia* manuscripts (London, BL, Cotton Cleopatra C. viii) have been noted.[25] Unfortunately, it is far from clear that Harold is consistently associated with the feminine, or William with the masculine. Some of the English are depicted with equally suggestive sword hilts, and it is not the women but the two men in the margins above the suggestively dressed William at the start of the battle who are identified as English by their hair and their moustaches. Moreover, Sarah Keefer has shown that the gender of the horses can shift from scene to scene.[26] William does always ride a stallion, but Harold also rides a stallion at Bosham and on his return to England from Normandy. As Keefer demonstrates, the gender of the horses is significant, but it is used to convey shifting power relationships rather than to equate Harold consistently with the feminine – although it remains true that power is equated with the masculine and lack of it with the feminine. Both women and Harold are ultimately disempowered within the discourse of the Tapestry, but that does not make them metaphorical equals. It seems most likely that the marginal nudes and the women in the main panel function as indexical signs rather than symbols, that is they point our way towards a meaning rather than literally embodying one (the other marginal images would of course function in the same way).[27] The women in the main panel of the Tapestry appear at key points in the shifting balance of power, but they do not enjoy power themselves, and their fate in the visual narrative is ultimately ambiguous. The situations in which they appear, however, are moments of disruption in the social or political order represented and maintained by king (be it Edward, Harold or William) and country (be it England or Normandy). The marginal nudes are equally, if not more disruptive as, while confined to the borders, they catch our eye, distracting it from the high historical narrative of the main panel. Much recent work has been done on the power of the obscene or the abject to disrupt the category of art. The marginal nudes may not be obscene, but they are bawdy, suggestive, perhaps even scandalous. They transgress, or lead us to transgress, the boundary between margin and centre, anecdote (or whispered aside) and master narrative. Like the hybrids and fabulous creatures with whom they share the

Christi College 23 *Psychomachia*', *ASE* 30 (2002), 115–36. It was also the Anglo-Saxons who first consistently depicted the Virtues as women instead of as armoured warriors; however the bodies of the Virtues remain clothed in spiritual armour, hence impenetrable and 'masculinized', while those of the Vices are open, penetrable and feminine (*ibid.*).

25 Wormald, 'Style and design', p. 32; Sarah Larratt Keefer, 'Body language: a graphic commentary by the horses of the Bayeux Tapestry', in this volume. See also David Hill, 'The Bayeux Tapestry and its commentators: the case of scene 15', *Medieval Life* 11 (Summer 1999), 24–6; Gale R. Owen-Crocker, 'Embroidered wood: animal-headed posts in the Bayeux "Tapestry"', in *Aedificia Nova: Studies in Honor of Rosemary Cramp*, ed. Catherine E. Karkov and Helen Damico (Kalamazoo, MI, forthcoming 2006).

26 Keefer, 'Body language'.

27 In this respect I would see them as functioning very differently from 'marginal' images such as the Irish sheela-na-gigs which confront the viewer rather than each other, and which do literally embody the shifting power relationships of a postcolonial Ireland. See Catherine E. Karkov, 'Sheela-na-gigs and other unruly women: images of land and gender in medieval Ireland', in *From Ireland Coming: Irish Art from the Early Christian to the Late Gothic Period and its European Context*, ed. Colum Hourihane (Princeton, 2001), pp. 313–31.

borders, they demonstrate that not 'all the particulars of the world [or the story] can be subsumed under the bounded categories we use to order it'.[28]

Finally, women are equated with fertility, sex and the maternal across Anglo-Saxon culture,[29] and the women of the Bayeux Tapestry are equated with the same. The marginal nudes and Ælfgyva are clearly engaged in sexual encounters of some sort, while both the woman fleeing her house and Edith are depicted as mothers – a metaphorical virgin mother in Edith's case as she is clearly modelled on the image of the grieving Mary. As such, they can also be read as signifiers of family and lineage, although I am not sure that I would agree with Gerald Bond's suggestion that 'only as a marker of status and a vessel of lineage would a woman, even a noblewoman, fit into such a story'.[30] Edith's lack of the child she should have produced is central to the history behind the Tapestry, and her portrayal as a sorrowing virgin is therefore all the more poignant.[31] Within the discourse of power represented in the Tapestry, it must also be understood in terms of Edward's budding saintliness; the fact that her pose is modelled on that of the mourning Virgin only adds to her husband's Christomimesis.[32] She and Edward represent the end of the royal line, but she is also Harold's sister, and a visual reminder of the powerful political family and royal marriage on which his claim to the throne was in part based. (We might also note here that it is through marriage and maternity that Edward, Harold and William are related to each other.) While women may not be part of the traditional Anglo-Saxon imagery of battle, family lineage is. In *The Battle of Maldon*, for example, Ælfwine is identified as the son of Ælfric and the grandson of Ealhelm,[33] Wulfstan son of Ceola is

28 The quotation is from Martin Jay, 'Must justice be blind? The challenge of images to the law', in *Law and the Image: the Authority of Art and the Aesthetics of Law*, ed. Costas Douzinas and Lynda Nead (Chicago and London, 1999), pp. 19–35, at p. 25. On the disruptive power of obscenity and the abject see Hal Foster, 'Obscene, abject, traumatic', in Douzinas and Nead, *Law and the image*, pp. 240–56.

29 See Clare A. Lees and Gillian R. Overing, *Double Agents: Women and Clerical Culture in Anglo-Saxon England* (Philadelphia, 2001).

30 Gerald A. Bond, *The Loving Subject: Desire, Eloquence and Power in Romanesque France* (Philadelphia, 1995), p. 26.

31 Mourning women appear in similar poses in the illustrations of the death of the descendants of Adam in the Old English *Hexateuch* (London, BL, Cotton Claudius B. iv, 10v–11v), and in the drawing of the death of Malaleel in the Junius 11 manuscript (Oxford, Bodleian Library, Junius 11, p. 59). In these images, however, children are included as signs that the dynasty will continue. See Catherine E. Karkov, 'The Anglo-Saxon Genesis: text, illustration and audience', in *The Old English Hexateuch: Aspects and Approaches*, ed. Benjamin C. Withers and Rebecca Barnhouse (Kalamazoo, MI, 2000), pp. 187–223; Catherine E. Karkov, *Text and Picture in Anglo-Saxon England: Narrative Strategies in the Junius 11 Manuscript*, Cambridge Studies in Anglo-Saxon England 31 (Cambridge, 2001), pp. 81–8; cf. Cyril Hart, 'The Canterbury contribution to the Bayeux Tapestry', in *Art and Symbolism in Medieval Europe – Papers of the 'Medieval Europe Brugge 1997' Conference*, V, ed. Guy de Boe and Franz Verhaeghe (Zellik, Belgium, 1997), 7–15, at 12.

32 The famous reversal of direction in the scene of Edward's funeral may also have been intended as a sign of his saintliness. His body, enshrined in its cross-covered bier, moves against the flow of the narrative to be received by the hand of God. Resisting the linear progress from life to death followed by Harold and the rest of the casualties of the Battle of Hastings, Edward remains hovering between life and death in the manner of any medieval saint or relic. See further Catherine E. Karkov, *The Ruler Portraits of Anglo-Saxon England* (Woodbridge, 2004).

33 'bearn Ælfrices . . ., Ælfwine, þa cwæð . . . "wæs min ealda fæder Ealhelm haten" ' (lines 209–18). All citations are from *The Anglo-Saxon Minor Poems*, ed. Elliott van Kirk Dobbie, Anglo-Saxon Poetic Records VI (New York and London, 1942). For a related discussion of death and dynasty in *The Battle*

valiant because of his family,[34] and Wulfmær is the nephew of Byrhtnoth, the son of Byrthnoth's sister.[35] Within the context of the poem, their deaths mark the end of their bloodlines; within the context of the Tapestry, the childless Edith and the death of Harold mark the end of theirs,[36] and their related gestures help to make this point. Edith raises her hand to her face to wipe the tears from her eyes, while Harold raises his hand to his face to grasp the arrow in his eye.

The blinding of Harold has an additional significance as a crippling form of punishment which made a king unfit to rule, a punishment (and a form of death) which might also have had a particularly ironic appeal in Harold's case as his father had been implicated in the blinding of the Ætheling Alfred in 1036. Both the arrow in the eye and the cutting of Harold's legs in the following scene are symbolic forms of castration, as Bernstein has pointed out, fitting ways to show that 'with the death of Harold a royal line came to an end'.[37] It is possible that the disarmed and dismembered bodies shown without genitals in the border beneath the scene of the death of Harold were meant to symbolize the same thing (**Plate 23**). It is surely significant that they first appear directly under the fall of the Wessex banner and Harold's death, and their lack of genitalia is in marked contrast to all the other nude men in the border; however, this section of the Tapestry is so heavily restored that it would be dangerous to read too much into the small details. Suffice it to say that Harold and the English have most clearly lost not only the battle but also all vestiges of power. If the restoration is accurate, these men, like the Tapestry's women, display their 'betweenness'; they are not fully masculine, but neither are they feminine.

Because of its length the whole of the Bayeux Tapestry could never have been taken in all at once. Its artists did, however, repeat scenes, figures and motifs as memory cues, and as a way of relating specific events or figures together. Within the overall composition of the Tapestry, the women tend to catch our eye because of their rarity, and their intrusiveness, the fact that we really do not expect to find them there. The women of the Bayeux Tapestry help to advance the visual narrative; they alert us to key turning points in the relationship of power that it documents; as repeated images they act as visual signposts, or echoes, which help to index the relationships between episodes; as English women, they reflect the political and military vulnerability of the English; and as vulnerable women, they become signifiers of land and

of Brunanburh see John M. Hill, *The Anglo-Saxon Warrior Epic: Reconstructing Lordship in Early English Literature* (Gainesville, FL, 2000), pp. 93–109. See also Gale R. Owen-Crocker, *The Four Funerals in Beowulf* (Manchester, 2000), pp. 220–7 where it is argued that *Beowulf* engages with the feminine side of heroic life.

34 'Wulfstan, cafne mid his cynne, þæt wæs Ceolan sunu' (lines 75–6).

35 'Wulfmær . . . Byrhtnoðes mæg . . . his swuster sunu . . .' (lines 113–15).

36 See further Shirley Ann Brown, 'The Bayeux Tapestry and the *Song of Roland*', *Olifant* 6 (1979), 339–50, esp. 343. Guy of Amiens, lines 472–80, 545–50: Morton and Munz, *Carmen de Hastingae Proelio*, pp. 30–1, 34–7.

37 Bernstein, *Mystery*, p.160. See also *Carmen de Hastingae Proelio*, as cited in n. 36 above; Robert Stein, 'The Trouble with Harold: the Ideological Context of the *Vita Haroldi*', *New Medieval Literatures* 2 (1998), 181–204; Lewis, *Rhetoric of Power*, p. 128. On castration and emasculation in general see Mathew Kuefler, *The Manly Eunuch: Masculinity, Gender Ambiguity, and Christian Ideology in Late Antiquity* (Chicago, 2001), esp. pp. 31–3, 49–69.

lineage, and the loss of the same. Each one of them might or might not carry further specific meaning(s), either historical or metaphorical, but as a group they have an important though subtle structural role to play within the narrative and our visual experience of that narrative, one that cannot be reduced to a simple gendering of the battle.

10

Cognate Imagery: the Bear, Harold and the Bayeux Tapestry

SHIRLEY ANN BROWN

IN developing his ideas on communications and culture, Marshall McLuhan argued that it is the way information is structured and relayed that determines perceptions of reality.[1] Erwin Panofsky, the art historian, insisted that visual art is perceptible only if it presents images that are already recognizable and that their deeper meaning is reliant upon already familiar ideas and texts.[2] Taken together, these basic principles form the underpinning for the process by which the viewer interprets visual art. But art not only reflects its societal context – it has been employed as a powerful and eloquent agent in the creation of historical memory and popular culture – those whom we now call 'spin doctors' have always recognized the value of intertextuality. One very good, recent example is the Overlord Embroidery which was created to commemorate and monumentalize the successful Allied landing in Normandy in June 1944. Exhibited in a purpose-built D-Day Museum in Portsmouth, this appliqué work keeps alive the memory of a great battle, placing it in the greater context of the Second World War. Financed by a private patron, Lord Dulverton, and created in 1968–73, it was deliberately meant to evoke the more famous Bayeux Tapestry. Longer and wider than its model – 80.46m x 1.01m (264ft x 40in) as opposed to 68.38m x 0.5m (224ft 4½in x 20in) – which it parallels in both general purpose and layout, as well as in particular details, it was meant to represent a sort of 'reverse Conquest', the successful English invasion of Normandy.[3]

Nine centuries earlier, the Bayeux Tapestry was itself a work of both art and propaganda. Depicting the Battle of Hastings and the events leading up to it, it was instrumental in creating contemporary history. Intertextuality and discourse with other cultural products of its time advanced its purpose.[4] Since 1732, when it was first published in its entirety,[5] the Bayeux Tapestry has often been regarded as an

1 Marshall McLuhan, *Understanding Media* (New York, 1964); *The Medium is the Message* (New York, 1967).

2 Erwin Panofsky, *Studies in Iconology* (New York, 1972), pp. 3–17.

3 Brian Jewell, *Conquest and Overlord: The Story of the Bayeux Tapestry and the Overlord Embroidery* (London, 1981).

4 Shirley Ann Brown, 'The Bayeux Tapestry: history or propaganda?', in *The Anglo-Saxons, Synthesis and Achievement*, ed. J. D. Woods and David A. E. Pelteret (Waterloo, ON, 1985), pp. 11–25.

5 Antoine Lancelot, 'Suite de l'explication d'un monument de Guillaume le Conquérant', *Mémoires de*

'historical document' because of the vividness of its visual reconstruction of a series of events which were still resonant in the minds of its intended audience. Probably commissioned by Odo, Bishop of Bayeux, for a long time it was thought that the Tapestry was created for the cathedral consecrated in Bayeux in 1077. More current opinion supports the notion that it was meant for a secular setting.[6] It would be fairly simple to accommodate the approximately 73.15m (240ft) length of the hanging in a large audience hall such as had been traditional in northern Europe.[7] According to fragmentary evidence, these halls were rectangular in shape, the length to width ratio varying from about 2:1 to almost 4:1. At 2:1 the hall would be approximately 24.38m x 12.19m (80ft x 40ft); at 3:1 it would be 27.45m x 9.15m (90ft x 30ft); and at 3.25:1 it would measure 28.96m x 7.32m (95ft x 24ft). A hall in any of these proportions could accommodate the Bayeux Tapestry. Two examples would be the Great Tower at Chepstow Castle (30.48m x 12.19m; 100ft x 40ft) built *c.* 1070 by William fitzOsbern,[8] and the timber palace at Cheddar, dated to before the end of the eleventh century.[9] Westminster Hall and the archiepiscopal palaces at Canterbury[10] and Croydon[11] also had great halls large enough to accommodate a hanging the size of the Bayeux Tapestry.[12]

Although it is possible, it is not essential to see the Embroidery as a site-specific work. It would have been fairly easy to transport it from place to place as its owner's entourage moved throughout his domaine.[13] Easily portable, this embroidery was well-suited to be a travelling show, ready to be exhibited wherever there was a large enough interior space, as in a great hall or church, in England or in Normandy.

Its long and narrow format indicates that the Bayeux Tapestry was not meant to function as a practical wall hanging to eliminate draughts in a lord's great hall or to decorate the alcove of a lady's bedroom.[14] It had a greater purpose: in the aftermath

littérature tirés des registres de l'Académie royale des Inscriptions et Belles-Lettres depuis l'année MDCCXXVI jusques et compris l'année MDCCXXX 7 (1732), 602–68.

6 This idea had actually been suggested by Albert Marignan, in *La Tapisserie de Bayeux. Étude archéologique et critique* (Paris, 1902), pp. 183–9.

7 Brilliant, 'Stripped narrative', p. 113 and n. 5; for an overview see Margaret Wood, *The English Mediaeval House* (London, 1965), pp. 35–48.

8 J. C. Perks, *Chepstow Castle* (London, 2nd ed., 1967); Suzanne Lewis, *The Rhetoric of Power in the Bayeux Tapestry* (Cambridge, 1999), p. 9 and n. 33; Joseph and Frances Gies, *Life in a Medieval Castle* (London, 1974), pp. 1–7.

9 Wood, *The English Mediaeval House*, pp. 35, 45.

10 T. Tatton-Brown, 'The Great Hall of the Archbishop's Palace', *The British Archaeological Association, Conference Transactions for 1979, V. Medieval Art and Architecture at Canterbury before 1220* (1982), 112–19. There are literary indications that the original Great Hall was built in the 1070s and 1080s by Lanfranc.

11 P. A. Faulkner, 'Some medieval archiepiscopal palaces', *ArchJ* 127 (1970), 130–46 at 133–8. Once again, it is thought that the original Great Hall dates from the time of Lanfranc.

12 William Rufus's Westminster Hall (*c.* 1097) and the great dining hall of Dover Priory (*c.* 1150) are often cited as possible examples even though they postdate the Bayeux Tapestry's creation. See Bernstein, *Mystery*, pp. 104–7 and Fig. 65.

13 The Tapestry has been moved many times in its known history and has spent much of its existence folded or rolled up in a wooden chest. The surprisingly small chest now in the Treasury in the Bayeux Cathedral is supposed to have accommodated it, but with the current lining, the embroidery will not fit into the chest.

14 Baudri de Bourgueil, 'Adelae Comitissae', lines 207–578, trans. by Michael W. Herren in Shirley Ann

of the Battle of Hastings and in the context of the continuing consolidation of 'foreign rule' in England, the Embroidery emerges as a deliberate and planned attempt to create a version of contemporary history which was to serve the purposes of the victors – in other words, it was Norman propaganda. The intended audience was the newly emerging Anglo-Norman aristocratic society, comprising people of Anglo-Saxon, Anglo-Danish and Norman blood, as well as the new generation of blended heritage springing from the marriages of England's recent heiresses to the immigrant Norman lords. The Tapestry's primary purpose was to promote morale and loyalty among the broad spectrum of the society upon whom the new rulers of England depended. This was to be accomplished by creating a version of events which both legitimatized Norman rule in England, particularly Odo of Bayeux's earldom in Kent, while at the same time *apparently* retaining the dignity and honour of an English king, however discredited, slain in battle.[15]

The Latin inscriptions give the Bayeux Tapestry the visual authority of an official document allied to the Norman bureaucracy, for under this new regime, Latin became the only language of document whereas previously vernacular English had co-existed with Latin.[16] In spite of the increasing use of the written word, late-eleventh-century Anglo-Norman society was still predominantly oral, for the skills of developed reading and writing, although cultivated by clerics and bureaucrats, could not have been universal among the dominant warrior class. The Latin inscriptions on the Tapestry are terse and often ambiguous, registering placenames and settings, identifying certain key players, but not really filling in any detailed explanation of what is being depicted and how it is to be understood. This creates the possibility of varying interpretations depending upon the experience and political positioning of the observer.

Many Tapestry scholars now accept that the embroidery was really a piece of 'performance art'. It is highly plausible that when it was exhibited, a narrator would have led the viewers through the story, perhaps reading the text aloud and using it as a guide for his expansion of the depicted sequence of events.[17] Since everybody was already intensely aware of the outcome of the struggle depicted, the drama relies not so much on the story itself but on the manner of its telling. The task of the Tapestry's designer was to create the opportunity for the colouring of history along desired lines. The images provide many moments when the audience is required to fill in the silences, such as the numerous discussions indicated in the narrative for which no details of content are given. The story begins with one such instance, the meeting between Edward and Harold. The interlocutor, in retelling the story and expanding on the silences in the visual imaging, creates contemporary history by resetting past

Brown, *The Bayeux Tapestry: A History and Bibliography* (Woodbridge, 1988), pp. 167–77. An English translation of the entire poem is now available: Monika Otter, 'Baudri of Bourgueil, "To Countess Adela" ', *The Journal of Medieval Latin* 11 (2001), 60–141 at 66–99.

15 Lewis, *The Rhetoric of Power*, p. 131.

16 Lewis, *The Rhetoric of Power*, pp. 10–11; M. T. Clanchy, *From Memory to Written Record: England 1066–1307* (Oxford, 2nd ed., 1993), p. 27.

17 Brilliant, 'Stripped narrative', 128–34. Most of us do just this when we introduce undergraduate classes to the Bayeux Tapestry, as does the modern visitor who takes advantage of the audio guide in the Bayeux exhibition site.

events in the context of the vocal present. The strategy of combining actual image clues with the written and spoken word to serve in the construction of imagined images and reconstructed story are analogous to devices present in more purely literary genres connected to history-telling, genres such as the Norman *gestae*, the epic *chansons de geste* and panegyric.[18]

The Bayeux Tapestry presents its material in two visually distinct but related schemas. In the larger central register, the main narrative displays a sequence of chosen events which appears to establish the main storyline. The upper and lower borders contain animal figures, anecdotes and fabliaux which have been interpreted as examples of treachery and betrayal, meant to comment upon and augment the moral interpretation of the Tapestry's narrative.[19] When the fables are viewed as a whole, it becomes apparent that they were chosen because the animals break their promises and through trickery and brute force rob others of what is rightly theirs.[20] They are all brutal, covetous and betrayers – obvious parallels to Harold's motivations, at least in the eyes of the Normans. This internal intertextuality is particularly operative in the first half of the embroidery. Once the battle at Hastings begins, the effects of the carnage spill over into the lower border and the representation of the fables ceases, for they have served their purpose.

Looking at the expanse of images presented in the Bayeux Tapestry, the narrator and the audience are invited to draw upon their familiarity with other culturally embedded genres in order to recreate the full implications of the 'history' being unfolded before their eyes. Oral material would have had a much larger and more immediate audience than written histories and the rhetorical devices seen in the Bayeux Tapestry align it very closely with the realm of poetry and epic. The narrative structure of the Bayeux Tapestry has been compared to that found in *Beowulf*,[21] *The Battle of Maldon*[22] and even the *Völsunga Saga*.[23] It has been suggested that the text as it appears on the Tapestry was a distillation of a longer, prepared text which no longer exists – a sort of *Gesta Guillelmi* composed for Odo of Bayeux.[24] Although it is an intriguing idea, there is no real evidence for the existence of this work.

The relationship between the embroidery's narrative strategies and the French

18 Lewis, *The Rhetoric of Power*, pp. 10–29.

19 Opposition, with which I do not agree, to this viewpoint certainly exists; most recently see Michael Lapidge and Jill Mann, 'Reconstructing the Anglo-Latin Aesop: the literary tradition of the hexametrical Romulus', in *Latin Culture in the Eleventh Century: Proceedings of the Third International Conference on Medieval Latin Studies, Cambridge, September 9–12, 1998*, 2 vols, Publications of the Journal of Medieval Latin 5, ed. Michael W. Herren, C. J. Mcdonough, and Ross G. Arthur (Turnhout, 2002), II. 1–33 at n. 47.

20 J. Bard McNulty, *The Narrative Art of the Bayeux Tapestry Master* (New York, 1988); Emily Albu, *The Normans in their Histories* (Woodbridge, 2001), pp. 88–105.

21 Gale R. Owen-Crocker, 'Telling a tale: narrative techniques in the Bayeux Tapestry and the Old English epic *Beowulf*', in *Medieval Art: Recent Perspectives. A Memorial Volume for C. R. Dodwell*, ed. Gale R. Owen-Crocker and Timothy Graham (Manchester, 1998), pp. 40–59.

22 Dolores Warwick Frese, '*Worda ond Worca*: The Battle of Maldon and the lost text of Aelfflaed's Tapestry', *Mediaevalia* 17 (1994), 27–51 at 41–51.

23 George Henderson, *Early Medieval* (Harmondsworth, 1972), pp. 171–3.

24 Bernard Bachrach, 'Some observations on the Bayeux Tapestry', *Cithara: Essays in the Judeo-Christian Tradition* 1 (1988), 5–28; also, René Louis, 'Y a-t-il eu une "geste de Guillaume" le Conquérant?', *Annales de Normandie* 3 (1953), 15–21.

chansons de geste, in particular the *Song of Roland*, has been an issue since the beginning of the twentieth century.[25] The discussion was sparked by the mention in William of Malmesbury and Wace that the *Song of Roland* was sung or recited to the Norman troops at Hastings, just before the onset of battle. In *c.* 1120–30, William of Malmesbury wrote:

> Tunc, cantilena Rollandi inchoata, ut martium viri exemplum pugnaturos accenderet, inclamatoque Dei auxilio, praelium consertum, bellatumque acriter, neutris in multam diei horam cedentibus.[26]
>
> (Then, the song of Roland was begun, so that the warlike example of that man might stimulate the soldiers, and calling on God for assistance, the battle commenced, and there was a bitter fight with neither side retreating for many hours of the day.)[27]

Wace subsequently wrote his version of the pre-battle event sometime between 1160 and 1174:

> Taillefer, qui mult bien chantout,
> sor un cheval qui tost alout,
> devant le duc alout chantant
> de Karlemaigne e de Rollant,
> e d'Oliver e des vassals
> qui morurent en Rencevals.[28]
>
> (Taillefer, singing very well, on a horse which moved ahead rapidly, came before the duke singing of the exploits of Charlemagne and Roland and Oliver and his vassals who died at Roncevaux.)

The twelfth-century belief that the struggle between William of Normandy and Harold of England could be valorized in the same framework as that employed in the *Roland* to characterize the struggle between Charlemagne and his vassals can be convincingly transposed back to the time when the Bayeux Tapestry and the *Chanson de Roland* were being formed and absorbed into cultural consciousness. The embroidery must have been created sometime between 1067 and Odo of Bayeux's death in 1097, most likely in the 1070s or 1080s. It is generally agreed that the Oxford text of the *Song of Roland*,[29] composed by a man named Turoldus, dates from the early twelfth century and that it was a reworking of an earlier form created towards the middle of the eleventh century in Norman French. There is much argument and no real scholarly consensus on the form that this earlier version took and whether or not

25 Marignan, *La Tapisserie de Bayeux*, pp. 133–82; more recently, Dodwell, 'BT and the French secular epic'; and Shirley Ann Brown, 'The Bayeux Tapestry and the *Song of Roland*', *Olifant* 6:3/4 (1979), 339–50.

26 William of Malmesbury, *De Gestis Regum Anglorum*, ed. and trans. R. A. B. Mynors, R. M. Thomson and M. Winterbottom, 2 vols (Oxford, 1998), I. 454. Note that these editors realign the contents of the books in the *Gesta*. The quotation appears at III. ccxlii in this edition.

27 Translation by M. W. Herren.

28 Wace, *Roman de Rou*, III, lines 8013–18: *Le Roman de Rou de Wace*, ed. A. J. Holden, 3 vols (Paris, 1970–3), II. 183.

29 Oxford, Bodleian Library, Digby 23.

it was sung or recited before an audience.[30] Whether part of the *jongleur*'s repertoire or a clerical work, it would have been part of the feudal culture of the Norman military aristocracy by the time of the invasion of England and the creation of the Bayeux Tapestry. The *Roland* epic would have provided a suitable reference in any scheme to place the recently transpired events in an 'historical' context.

The interrelationship of the Bayeux Tapestry and the *Song of Roland* is apparent from the many similarities in narrative and rhetorical strategy which are embedded in the two works. In addition to the similar broad outline of an epic struggle within the feudal order, the parallels can be perceived through the shared devices of the *récit* (or main storyline) and *chant* (or commentary),[31] and the characterization of the hero-villain.

As to the first point, in the Tapestry the central band acts like the *récit* in the epic, unravelling a series of episodes and characters, which combine to present the story as real, historical event. The borders with their animals, fables and anecdotes function as the *chant* or commentary, to reflect upon the moral significance of the actions and occasionally to foretell the future consequences.[32] Since the essential elements of the *récit* are already known to the audience, it is the *chant* that presents and augments the narrative elements in unexpected ways in order to produce surprise and pleasure in the viewers as they hear and see known facts take on new and unforeseen inflections.[33] As to the second point, the notion that it was Harold Godwinesson's perfidious character which led to his downfall was well-established as an important aspect of the Norman justification for the invasion of a sovereign country.

Allusions to the Roland legend would link Harold with another of the great hero-villains in contemporary parlance: Count Ganelon. The similarities in these constructed portrayals are remarkable. Harold and Ganelon were both brothers-in-law to their sovereigns, respectively Edward and Charlemagne; they were both powerful nobles who had spent many years in royal service and who were entrusted with dangerous missions into hostile territory; they were both depicted as the epitome of manhood and their bravery was carefully asserted. But, in the end, Harold and Ganelon suffered from the same fatal personality flaw. They both betrayed their trust as ambassadors and vassals for reasons of personal gain and had to face death because of their acts, destroying their families in the process.

These parallel character constructions can easily be invoked from the main story-line of the Bayeux Tapestry (the *récit*), as well as being augmented in the border scenes (the *chant*). There is one curious vignette in the lower border which has so far not been convincingly interpreted, which, it can be suggested, provided a key opportunity for an interlocutor to create the Harold-Ganelon link for his audience.

This vignette is connected to the first episode of Harold's journey to Normandy in

30 Gerard J. Brault, *The Song of Roland*, 2 vols (University Park and London, 1978) 1. 3–6; more recently, Andrew Taylor, 'Was there a Song of Roland?', *Speculum* 76.1 (January 2001), 28–65.

31 Stephen G. Nichols, Jr, 'The generative function of chant and récit in Old French epic', *Olifant*, 6/3 and 4 (Spring and Summer 1979), 307, 313.

32 Shirley Ann Brown, 'Prolepsis in the Bayeux Tapestry', in *Le futur dans le moyen age anglais*, ed. Anne Mathieu and Wendy Harding, 2 vols (Paris, 1999), I. 21–53.

33 Nichols, 'The generative function', p. 306.

1064, when, for whatever reason, the English ship landed in Ponthieu. In the Tapestry, when he was informed that the English delegation was being held for ransom, William of Normandy sent messengers, including the man named Turold, who succeeded in securing their release. This is one remarkable instance in the Tapestry of the ambiguity which can foster different readings on the part of the audience. It is suggested that the sequence runs chronologically from right to left, in reverse reading fashion. But since we read naturally from left to right, the scene can easily be interpreted in two ways. If viewed from right to left, it would appear that the same set of messengers is shown twice, first setting off to Ponthieu at high speed, and then shown standing in parley with someone in the camp of Guy de Ponthieu. But if read, as is more natural, from left to right, the viewer sees something dramatically different: there is one set of messengers, including the man named Turold, in negotiation with Count Guy or his representative (**Plate 4**), and then a second, different set of messengers who are riding with great urgency and flying hair to their destination in Ponthieu (**Plate 5**). The implication is that the first entreaty failed and that the subsequent mission was sent with more urgency. This second reading adds greatly to the presentation of the 'fact' that William of Normandy took extraordinary pains to rescue Harold and his companions from the clutches of their avaricious captor, thereby increasing the debt which Harold owed the Norman duke. William of Poitiers, writing about 1070, mentioned only that Harold was handed over to William after threats had come into play.[34] He did not indicate the number or the identity of the Norman envoys who carried out this mission. In the presentation of the sequence, the Bayeux Tapestry artist allowed different interpretations, perhaps even different versions of the events to be alluded to, without actually making a definitive 'historical statement'. The audience would read the scene as it wished.

Below the representation of the 'second pair' of messengers who are rushing to Ponthieu with hair flying, the designer inserted the vignette showing a muzzled bear chained to a tree while a man with a shield raises his sword as if to strike the captive animal (**Plate 6**). Scholars have generally disagreed in their interpretations of the bear scene. In 1914, Wilhelm Tavernier suggested that it was part of a series which was meant to depict the kind of rural life enjoyed by the Norman barons. Bear-baiting, deer hunting, farming, bird snaring were reflections of the manner of life in which the Normans, including Turold, took pleasure. He even suggested that the landowner and hunter of the bear was none other than the father of a younger Turold, who was both the Tapestry's designer and the *Roland* poet.[35]

34 William of Poitiers, I. 41: *The 'Gesta Guillelmi' of William of Poitiers*, ed and trans. R. H. C. Davis and Marjorie Chibnall (Oxford, 1998), pp. 68–71.

35 W. Tavernier, 'The author of the Bayeux Embroidery', *ArchJ* 21 (1914), 184–6. He further suggested that this Turold the younger was portrayed as the boy lookout in the tree above the bear scene and that he later became chaplain to King William Rufus in England. This clerical Turold, he postulated, was the designer of the Bayeux Tapestry, and the same Turoldus who signed the Oxford *Song of Roland*. This Turold/Turoldus theory has no support today but reflects the close correspondence between the Tapestry and the *Roland* seen by other scholars. Rita Lejeune, in 'Le caractère de l'archévêque Turpin et les événements contemporains de la *Chanson de Roland* (Version d'Oxford)', *Société Rencesvals – IVe Congrès International, Heidelberg, 28 août – 2 septembre 1967, Actes et Mémoires* (Heidelberg, 1969), 9–21 suggests that the Turold who was a close relative of Odo of Bayeux and abbot of Peterborough, a man known for his military exploits and warrior personality, was the author of the

In 1957, Francis Wormald reasserted that the bear-baiting scene was a genre element, but that along with the fabliaux, it was purely decorative and had no relationship to the main narrative.[36] Richard Wissolik took a somewhat different stance. He identified bear-baiting as a popular English, rather than Norman, sport. Furthermore, he suggested that under the guise of a genre scene, the English artist sneaked in a coded Anglo-Saxon message. He believed that the chained bear being antagonized by the armed Norman knight stands for Harold under duress – for the bear would certainly feel himself in immediate danger under the circumstances – and reflects the Anglo-Saxon view that Harold took the oath at Bayeux under great duress, a condition which would invalidate it.[37] The motif would then become a proleptic device referring to the oath scene shown later in the Tapestry and does not relate specifically to the scene it accompanies.

I am suggesting instead that the bear-baiting scene *is* related directly to the Ponthieu incident which it accompanies, and that it can best be explained as a rhetorical device alluding to a motif in the *Song of Roland*, helping to establish Harold's infamy and undermining the image of an apparently noble and heroic Harold presented in the main register.

In the epic poem, the bear is given special significance in Charlemagne's dreams. In the second dream sequence, the emperor saw that:

> . . . il ert en France, ad Ais, a un perrun,
> En dous chaeines s'i teneit un brohun.
> Devers Ardene veeit venir .XXX. urs,
> Cascun parolet altresi cume hum.
> Diseient li: 'Sire, rendez le nus!
> Il nen est dreiz que il seit mais od vos,
> Nostre parent devum estre a succurs.'
>
> (. . . he was at Aix, in France, before a pillar,
> A bear was being restrained there by two chains.
> He saw thirty bears coming from the Ardennes,
> Each speaks like a man:
> They said to him: 'Sire, give him back to us!
> It isn't right that he stay with you,
> We must come to the aid of our kinsman.') (laisse 186)[38]

This is a clear, proleptic allusion to Ganelon's later humiliation and trial, and to the thirty relatives who stand as *pleges*.

In the Bayeux Tapestry, the chained bear is a reference to Harold and the dangerous situation in which he found himself in Ponthieu. The rapacious nature of the inhabitants of this part of the French coast and the merciless treatment of captives was high-

Norman version of the *Song of Roland* and was probably the Turold referred to in the Bayeux Tapestry, which he may very well have designed at an earlier date. As neat as package as it is, there are no real adherents of this Turold theory today.

36 Wormald, 'Style and design', pp. 27–8.

37 Richard D. Wissolik, 'The Saxon statement: code in the Bayeux Tapestry', *Annuale Medievale* 19 (1979), 69–97.

38 Brault, *The Song of Roland*, II. 156–7, lines 2556–62.

lighted by William of Poitiers.[39] The knight menacing Harold would be an allusion to the decidedly hostile Guy of Ponthieu. The duke of Normandy sent his envoys to come to the aid of Harold, and one can almost hear the quotation from the *Roland* emanating from the silent image of the negotiations in progress: 'Sire, give him back to us! It isn't right that he stay with you. We must come to the aid of our kinsman.'

There are several more instances of the bear image in the *Song of Roland*, images in which the bear is a metaphor for evil, treachery, violence and betrayal. In one instance there is a direct reference to Ganelon, Charlemagne's perfidious brother-in-law. In laisse 137, the rough treatment meted out to Ganelon even before his trial is described thus:

> Ben le me guarde, si cume tel felon!
> De ma maisnee ad faite traïsun.
> . . .
> Icil li peilent la barbe e les gernuns,
> Cascun le fiert .IIII. colps de sun puign;
> Ben le batirent a fuz e a bastuns,
> E si li metent el col un caeignun,
> Si l'encaeinent altresi cum un urs.

> ('Guard him well, as befits the felon that he is!
> He has betrayed my household.'
> . . .
> They pluck out his beard and his moustache,
> Each strike him four blows with his fist;
> They thrash him soundly with rods and sticks,
> They put an iron collar around his neck,
> And they chain him like a bear.)[40]

In an earlier dream, Charlemagne saw himself attacked by a bear which bit him on the right arm:

> Aprés iceste altre avisiun sunjat
> Qu'il ert en France, a sa capele, ad Ais,
> El destre braz li morst uns uers si mals.

> (After this vision he dreamed anew,
> This time that he was in France, in his chapel, at Aix,
> A fierce bear bit him on the right arm.) (laisse 57)[41]

– another foretelling of Ganelon's treachery and the destruction of Roland, the emperor's right arm.[42] Charlemagne's dreams are fulfilled when Ganelon is arrested, and the bear imagery is fully explained.

[39] William of Poitiers, I. 41: Davis and Chibnall, *Gesta Guillelmi*, pp. 68–71. The fact that, according to William of Poitiers, the payment of money and lands occurred after Harold's release rather than before simply indicates that Duke William was a very prudent man. There must have been earlier negotiations about the size of the 'reward' since the duke was not in the habit of giving away land and money easily.

[40] Brault, *The Song of Roland*, II. 112–13, lines 1819–20, 1823–7.

[41] Brault, *The Song of Roland*, II. 46–7, lines 725–36.

In one other dream sequence, bears are included in an ominously demonic frame, as hell-beasts attacking the Franks:

> En grant dulor i veit ses chevalers,
> Urs e leuparz les voelent puis manger,
> Serpenz e guivres, dragun e averser;
> Grifuns i ad, plus de trente millers,
> N'en i ad cel a franceis ne s'agiet.
>
> (He sees his knights in great agony.
> Then bears and leopards try to devour them,
> Serpents, vipers, dragons, and devils;
> There are more than thirty thousand griffins,
> All throw themselves upon the French.) (laisse 185)[43]

Gerard Brault, in his commentary on the *Song of Roland*, postulated that the bear is probably also a symbol for the violent side of Ganelon's nature, one of the results of his greed. Brault refers to the *Hortus Deliciarum* in which a bear is one of the animals surrounding *Avaritia*'s chariot; it bears a scroll proclaiming, *Violentia est ursus* ('Violence is a bear') and *Terret clamore minisque avaritia* ('Avarice threatens with shouts and threats').[44] The late date of the sketch, 1159–1205, would weaken the connection with the Bayeux Tapestry bear, but it is possible that the association of the bear with violence was long-established.

It would have been apparent to a skilled narrator commenting on the Tapestry's narrative that both Harold and Ganelon were symbolized by a bear. The fact that the bear in the Tapestry is chained would make the Harold-Ganelon link more obvious. The only difference is that in the Embroidery the poem's cudgels have been replaced by the knight's sword, a weapon more in line with a count's status. It would be fitting that the two felons – Harold and Ganelon – who committed similar treasonous crimes against the feudal loyalty required between lord and vassal, be referred to in the same manner. A late-eleventh-century audience would surely pick up the coincidence, or be guided to do so.

As everybody knew, Harold did not meet his end in Ponthieu, nor was he torn asunder by horses as was Ganelon. According to the *Carmen de Hastingae Proelio*, a poem written in 1067 by Guy of Amiens, Harold was hacked into pieces, another unpleasant form of dismemberment.[45] Since the audience was already aware of what lay ahead, the chained bear scene, with its constructed intertextual reference to the *Song of Roland* and Ganelon, would both foretell Harold's treason and his fate at Hastings and indicate his motivation. Just as the poetical bear symbolized Count Ganelon's greed and violence, so the Tapestry's little bear would, by association, comment upon Harold's avaricious nature which, according to the Norman viewpoint, led him to seize the English crown, thereby precipitating the carnage at Hastings.

42 Brault, *The Song of Roland*, I. 93.

43 Brault, *The Song of Roland*, II. 154–5, lines 2541–6.

44 Brault, *The Song of Roland*, I. 102 and Fig. 29.

45 Guy of Amiens, lines 545–50: *Carmen de Hastingae Proelio of Bishop Guy of Amiens*, ed. Catherine Morton and Hope Muntz (Oxford, 1972), pp. 34–7.

The placement of the bear scene in the sequence of fables allies it with *their* narrative strategy: they all manage to say something without assuming the obvious responsibility for having said it. They lead the audience and give the viewer of the Bayeux Tapestry the opportunity to bring an additional dimension to the sparseness of the written text and the gaps in the visual sequencing. Like the *chant* elements in epic poetry, the fables and vignettes accompany the sequential development of the Bayeux Tapestry's story to pose questions concerning the significance of the actions witnessed in the main scenes. These elements 'are reflexive rather than transitive signs, soliciting us to focus on the whole context of the passage in which they appear, and beyond that, to the larger structure of the story'.[46] Their role is to provide insight into the larger significance of a long narrative, an intuitive understanding of what has transpired and of the consequences for the future. This is important since the main narrative shows much of Harold's noble and aristocratic character, and indicates that he was an anointed king of England. Indeed, he was shown in every external way to be a foe fitting to do battle with the Duke of Normandy. His ignoble double-cross of the visually silent oath of loyalty at Bayeux is shown as inexorably leading to the slaughter at Hastings. The fabliaux and indeed the bear-baiting scene allow an additional dimension to be added to the discourse.

It is all too easy to forget that the Middle Ages must have had a thriving and lively market for secular art, poetry and music, and that entertainment value would have been a consideration in their formulation. The tradition of oral entertainment and story-telling is clearly indicated in existing sources and the *jongleur* played an important role in court circles. The Bayeux Tapestry was meant for close viewing and certain elements of the borders were devices by which the patron, the designer and the interlocutor could comment and expand upon the history which was being recreated for the audience. Using the Latin text stitched onto the Tapestry as a guide and as a set of clues, a narrator could render the story into whichever vernacular was best suited to the immediate audience. The Bayeux Tapestry would have made a striking setting out of a space in which the *chanson de geste*, or more particularly, the legend of Roland was recited. Both were meant for the same aristocratic warrior audience, people who enjoyed being entertained in their castles after the evening meal, in their gardens, or while on prolonged journeys. Feudal lords undoubtedly enjoyed visualizing themselves accomplishing great deeds, striking mighty blows and achieving the fame of the epic heroes. In the Bayeux Tapestry, Odo of Bayeux is depicted not only as a valued and powerful advisor to his brother William, but also as an active participant in the fighting at Telham Hill. This latter representation flies in the face of the known facts. The aristocratic audiences were certainly sophisticated enough to appreciate aesthetic effects and to recognize literary allusions, particularly the clerks among them.

It has been suggested that the Oxford *Roland* is a literary text, basically a 4002-line poetical text meant for reading aloud, and not necessarily a transcription of a *jongleur*'s song which was written down as it was performed. The Roland legend probably existed as a series of shorter versions or snatches which could be recited (or

[46] Nichols, 'The generative function', p. 313.

sung) in sessions of short duration, short songs of which the broader context existed in the minds of the people.[47] Given that scenario, it is entirely possible that the imagery and allusions which found concrete form in the written version were fully present in the earlier forms, probably oral, which existed as part of the *jongleur*'s repertoire in the late eleventh century, when the Bayeux Tapestry was being created and exhibited. The suggestions of manuscript sources for individual figures and motifs on the Embroidery, such as the bear-baiting scene,[48] in no way indicate the meaning and interpretation that would have been attached to the image. The apparently analogous usage of the bear image as a metaphor for violence and betrayal in the Bayeux Tapestry and in the *Song of Roland*, would indicate that we can talk of cognate imagery in contemporary epic contexts.

Unlike the *Song of Roland*, the Bayeux Tapestry narrative was dealing explicitly with current events, but the relationship between the two allowed the audience to perceive their situation in the light of historical precedent, retold in contemporary terms. Today, contemporary history is recreated by works of art such as the Overlord Embroidery with its references to the Bayeux Tapestry, and the public media – newscasts, television mini-series, newspapers, and website and e-mail interchanges. In the eleventh century, contemporary history was created by *its* public media – visual art and oral poetry, as well as written discourse. Intertextual, cognate imagery served to induce medieval viewers to become actively complicit in the Bayeux Tapestry's narrative project, and thus to recreate recent past events in the context of the totality of their current cultural experience.

47 Taylor, 'Was there a Song of Roland?', pp. 64–5.

48 Wormald suggested that it is related to an initial in a Canterbury manuscript (London, BL, Arundel 91, 47v, from St Augustine's, Canterbury) which includes a man with a club fighting with a bear which has broken its chain. The date of *c.* 1100 for the manuscript makes this problematic. See also Cyril Hart, 'The Bayeux Tapestry and schools of illumination at Canterbury', *ANS* 22 (1999), 117–67, and 'The *Cicero-Aratea* and the Bayeux Tapestry' in this volume pp. 165–6, **Fig. 15(d)**.

11

The *Cicero-Aratea* and the Bayeux Tapestry

CYRIL HART

IN recent years it has been suggested that the Bayeux Tapestry was designed and manufactured at Canterbury about a decade after the Norman Conquest.[1] In a paper published in 1997 these opinions were confirmed beyond reasonable doubt.[2] In a later paper I showed how the motifs used to depict a large proportion of the events shown in the Tapestry, and also many of the decorative figures in its borders, were taken from illustrated manuscripts stored in the libraries of the two great monasteries of the town, at Christ Church Cathedral and at St Augustine's Abbey a couple of hundred yards to the east, just outside the city walls.[3]

For a century before the Conquest, the scriptoria at these two centres had been producing large, ambitious codices containing illuminated pictures of the highest quality, unrivalled not only in England but also on the Continent as a whole.[4] Many of these have of course since been lost, but a surprisingly large number remain. It is evident that Canterbury specialized in the production of texts requiring great cycles of illustrations, such as psalters, the Old English *Hexateuch* (the first six books of the Bible), and calendars picturing the agricultural activities associated with each month. All of these were made use of as sources for scenes in the Bayeux Tapestry, and it should be mentioned that the same sets of motifs were almost certainly used in other kinds of art-work being produced at Canterbury at this time, including sculpture in stone, carving in wood and ivory, metal-work, stained glass, ornamental enamels, wall paintings, and of course embroidery of wall hangings, altar cloths and

1 Brooks and Walker, 'Authority and interpretation', p. 77.

2 C. R. Hart, 'The Canterbury contribution to the Bayeux Tapestry', in *Art and Symbolism in Medieval Europe – Papers of the 'Medieval Europe Brugge 1997' Conference* V, ed. Guy de Boe and Frans Verhaeghe (Zellik, Belgium, 1997), 7–15.

3 C. R. Hart, 'The Bayeux Tapestry and schools of illumination at Canterbury', *ANS* 22 (2000), 117–67.

4 T. A. M. Bishop, 'Notes on Cambridge manuscripts, Part VII: The Early Minuscule of Christ Church, Canterbury', *Transactions of the Cambridge Bibliographical Society* 3.5 (1963), 413–23; N. P. Brooks, *The Early History of the Church of Canterbury* (Leicester, 1984), pp. 273–8; Richard Gameson, 'Manuscript art at Christ Church, Canterbury, in the generation after St Dunstan', in *St Dunstan, his Life, Times and Cult*, ed. Nigel Ramsay, Margaret Sparkes and Tim Tatton-Brown (Woodbridge, 1992), pp. 187–220; Nigel Ramsay, 'The Cathedral Archives and Library', in *A History of Canterbury Cathedral*, ed. Patrick Collinson, Nigel Ramsay and Margaret Sparks (Oxford, 1995), esp. pp. 342–6; Sandy Heslop and John Mitchell, 'The arts and learning', in *St Augustine's Abbey, Canterbury*, ed. Richard Gem (London, 1997), esp. pp. 87–92.

ecclesiastical vestments. Unfortunately, apart from ivories, very few examples of these other art media survive to the present day.[5]

This article concerns only a very small part of this huge output, namely a series of illustrated compilations known as the *Cicero-Aratea*. The *Aratea* is a work by the Greek poet Aratus, which was written to accompany twenty-seven drawings illustrating a star map and catalogue of antique origin. It was translated into Latin verse by Cicero, and a number of commentaries were made, which travelled with the poem during its transmission. Of these, the most important companions to the English versions were the *scholia* of Hyginus, which also survive as independent manuscripts. Each of these *scholia* consists of a fable, followed by a list of stars for the particular constellation. The fables are peculiar to Hyginus, and do not appear in any other classical source known to me.

The hyparchetype and ultimate exemplar of all the English versions is London, BL, Harley 647, a ninth-century carolingian manuscript which reached Canterbury from the great abbey of Fleury-sur-Loire in the last quarter of the tenth century.[6] In this manuscript, the star catalogue itself (36r–44v) is accompanied by a number of other texts, mostly computistical. Four of the English copies include this material in varying detail.[7] At least two of these (London, BL, Harley 2506 and Cotton Tiberius B. v, Part I) were kept at Canterbury.[8] Details of English copies of the *Cicero-Aratea* appear in Appendix 1 below.

In order to locate the various constellations in the night sky, small copies of each of them were drawn on a circular map of the heavens (now usually termed a planisphere) which appears to have accompanied most copies of the *Cicero-Aratea* collection since classical times. These planispheres are absent from all the English versions, either having been omitted as unnecessary by the copyists, or, though originally included, having been lost. The only surviving Canterbury manuscript which still includes a planisphere is the carolingian prototype itself, Harley 647. As we shall see, it was this planisphere, rather than the separate drawings of the constellations, which was used as the exemplar for the majority of the motifs from the *Aratea* used in the Tapestry. The remaining motifs rely on illustrations of individual constellations in Harley 2506 for their exemplars.

The Harley 647 planisphere (**Fig. 12**)

Some of the constellations drawn in the planisphere are familiar today from modern depictions of the night sky. The Pole Star is at the centre, and just beneath it appears

5 C. R. Hart, 'Carolingian motifs from the school of ivory carving at Canterbury', in *Centre, Region, Periphery. Papers of the Third International Conference of Medieval and Later Archaeology. Medieval Europe Basel 2002*, ed. Guido Helmig, Barbara Scholkmann and Matthias Untermann, 3 vols (Basel, 2002), I. 302–6, revised and reprinted in C. R. Hart, *Learning and Culture in Late Anglo-Saxon England and the Influence of Ramsey Abbey on the Major Monastic Schools*, 2 vols (Lewiston, NY, 2003), I. 563–76.

6 Elżbieta Temple, *Anglo-Saxon Manuscripts 900–1066*, vol. 2 of *A Survey of Manuscripts Illuminated in the British Isles*, ed. J. J. G. Alexander (London, 1976), 22, 104.

7 *An Eleventh-Century Anglo-Saxon Illustrated Miscellany*, ed. P. McGurk, D. N. Dumville, M. R. Godden and Ann Knock, Early English Manuscripts in Facsimile 21 (Copenhagen, 1983), esp. 67.

8 Temple, *Anglo-Saxon Manuscripts*, Cat. 42, 87.

Fig. 12 The Harley Planisphere, London, BL, MS Harley 647, fol. 21v, after Otley (cited in note 16 below), Plate XXII

Ursa Major, the Great Bear. As we shall see, a version of this figure appears in the Tapestry, as does that of *Centaurus* holding a hare; but the well-known representation of *Orion*, which can be found in the planisphere at five o'clock, was not utilized in the Tapestry. Other figures, such as *Serpentarius*, *Duo Pisces*, *Taurus*, *Leo*, *Hydra*, *Sirius*, *Lepus*, *Ara* and *Eridanus* were all utilized as motifs. In the large majority of cases they appear in the Tapestry borders.

Duo Pisces (**Fig. 13**)

The distinctive features of this constellation provide the most convincing evidence that the *Cicero-Aratea* was used as a source for the Tapestry. Paired representations of fishes appear twice in the Tapestry borders (**Plate 9**, Wilson *BT*, Plate 33) and the first and larger version has a line joining the two mouths. The line derives from a fable by Hyginus about the fishes, which is written in the body of the drawing in

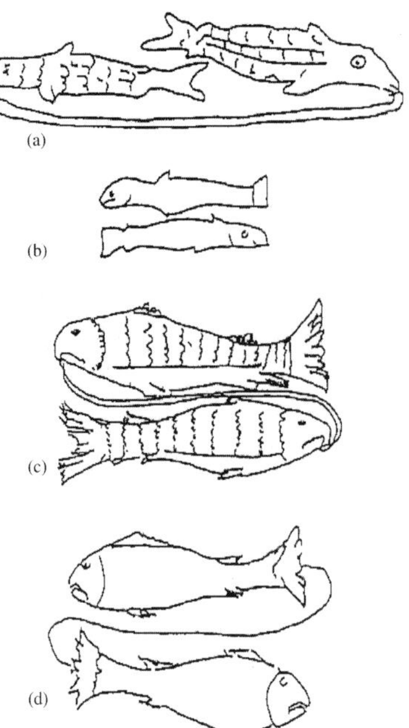

Fig. 13 (a) the Bayeux Tapestry, lower border (**Plate 9**); **(b)** the Bayeux Tapestry, lower border (Wilson *BT*, Plate 33); **(c)** *Duo Pisces*, detail from the *Cicero-Aratea*: London, BL, MS Harley 2506, fol. 36v; **(d)** *Duo Pisces*, detail from the *Cicero-Aratea*: London, BL, MS Harley 647, fol. 3r

Fig. 14 (a) the Bayeux Tapestry, lower border (Wilson, *BT*, Plate 20); **(b)** *Centaurus*, detail from London, BL, MS Harley 647, fol. 21v, planisphere

Harley 647, and to either side of the drawing in one of its copies, Harley 2506. We need not spend time here on the details of this story, but it is significant that the line linking the fishes, which joins the two tails in Harley 647, follows the same course in all of its copies except Harley 2506, in which it runs from mouth to mouth. It is this unique variant that is reproduced in the Tapestry, and it is difficult to account for its presence there without assuming that Harley 2506 was the direct source. The second pair of fishes in the Tapestry has no line joining them, and one postulates that this particular version depended for its exemplar on the representation of the constellation in the Harley 647 planisphere, in which the line from fish to fish is also missing.

Fig. 15 (a) the Bayeux Tapestry, lower border (**Plate 6**); **(b)** *Boötes*, from London, BL, MS Harley 647, fol. 21v, planisphere, after Otley (cited in note 16 below) Plate XXII; **(c)** *Arcturus*, from London, BL, MS Harley 647, fol. 21v, planisphere; **(d)** lower half of initial B in London, BL, MS Arundel 91, fol. 47v

Centaurus (**Fig. 14**)
The story of *Centaurus* and the hare is another of the fables of Hyginus. Here the Tapestry version resembles that of the Harley planisphere rather than that of the original constellation. The large size and odd shape of the hare in the Tapestry figure are not readily explained, but one needs to appreciate that all the figures in the border had to be modified to fit them into its cramped space.

Ursa Major (**Fig. 15**)
One of the better-known figures in the Tapestry borders is that of a soldier with shield and sword, menacing a bear which is chained to a tree. Bear-baiting was a popular pastime in the medieval period. Because of the restricted space, the soldier in the Tapestry had to be depicted as kneeling. The Tapestry figure of the baited bear is similar to that of *Ursa Major* in the Harley 647 planisphere, and the concept of the soldier menacing him derives, I suggest, from the separate constellation of *Boötes* (the herdsman) wielding a stick, placed just to the west of *Ursa*. A closer version of this scene as shown in the planisphere appears in the illustrated initial ‘B’ on folio 47v of the Arundel Passional (London, BL, Arundel 91), another Canterbury manuscript,

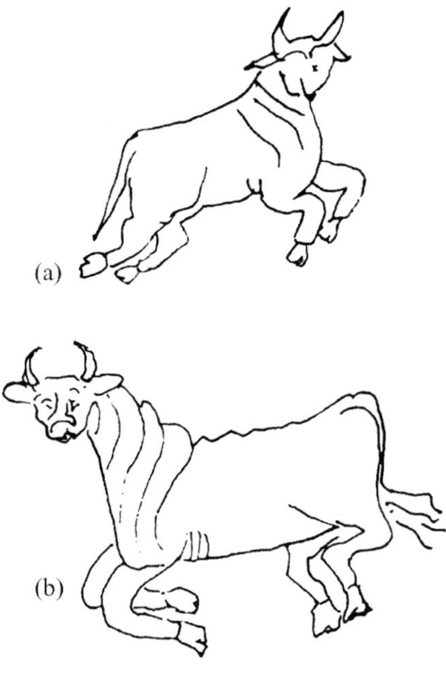

Fig. 16 (a) the Bayeux Tapestry, lower border (**Plate 2**); **(b)** the Bayeux Tapestry, main register (Wilson, *BT*, Plate 45); **(c)** *Taurus*, detail from London, BL, MS Harley 647, fol. 21v, planisphere

written fifty years after the Tapestry was made. Here the bear is being threatened by a man holding a cudgel in the fashion of *Boötes* as in the planisphere, but instead of being chained to a tree the bear is restrained by a rein held by his tormentor. It seems that this was the version of the motif favoured at Canterbury, but the man was changed to a soldier wielding a sword to suit the requirements of the Tapestry. It is probably significant that the figure of the chained bear in the border appears at the point where the main story of the Tapestry tells of Harold's seizure by Guy, count of Ponthieu, who escorts him to Duke William.[9]

Taurus (**Fig. 16**)

The origin of the two peculiar figures of bulls with bended knees which appear in the Tapestry (**Plate 2**, Wilson, *BT*, Plate 45) has been the subject of much speculation. I suggest that they derive from the Harley planisphere, which shows only the front half of *Taurus*. The back halves of the bulls are due to the Tapestry artist, the end-result being most odd-looking beasts which do not fit in well with their surroundings. Gale

9 For a thematic interpretation of the Tapestry's bear-baiting scene see Shirley Ann Brown, 'Cognate imagery: the bear, Harold and the Bayeux Tapestry', in this volume.

Fig. 17 (a) The Bayeux Tapestry, main register (**Plate 11**); **(b)** *Ara*, detail from London, BL, MS Harley 2506, fol. 43v

Owen-Crocker has suggested that the animal in the main register (Wilson, *BT*, Plate 45) is supposed to be dead, having been pillaged for food by the Norman soldiers.[10]

Ara (**Fig. 17**)

One of the most famous scenes in the Tapestry is that of Harold taking an oath, with his right hand on a portable reliquary and his left on an altar (**Plate 11**). The custom of placing a hand on an altar when swearing an oath goes back to Roman times, and possibly to still earlier in the classical era. Our interest here lies with the altar itself, which has a design very close to that depicted for the constellation *Ara* (= altar) in Harley 2506. This has four dots representing stars, two on top and two at its base. The Tapestry version has three dots. The centre one is usually interpreted as the Host, displayed on a monstrance.[11] The significance of the other two dots has long been debated; they may now be identified as copies of stars shown in the exemplar.

10 Personal communication.

11 Brooks and Walker, 'Authority and interpretation', p. 66.

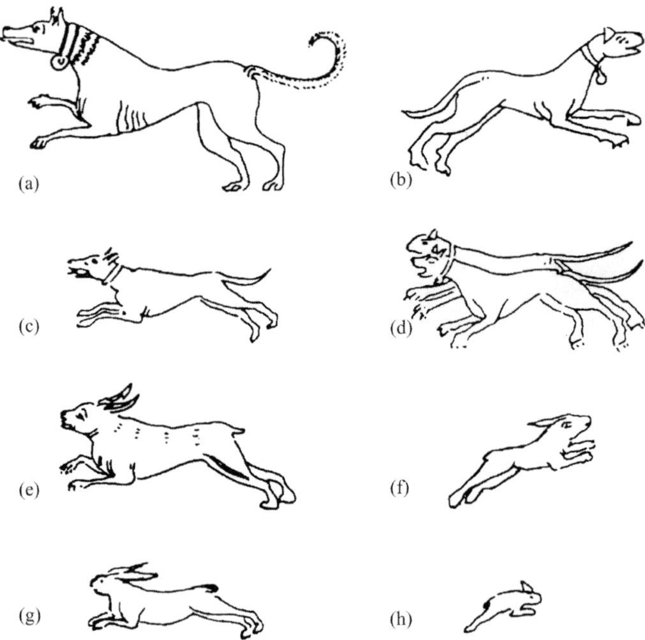

Fig. 18 (a) *Sirius*, from London, BL, MS Cotton Tiberius B. v, fol. 42r; **(b)** the Bayeux Tapestry, main register (**Plate 1**); **(c)** *Sirius*, from London, BL MS Harley 2506, fol. 41r; **(d)** the Bayeux Tapestry, lower border (Wilson, *BT*, Plate 13); **(e)** *Lepus*, from London, BL, MS Cotton Tiberius B. v, fol. 42r; **(f)** the Bayeux Tapestry, lower border (Wilson, *BT*, Plate 54); **(g)** *Lepus*, from London, BL, MS Harley 2506, fol. 41v; **(h)** the Bayeux Tapestry, lower border (Wilson, *BT*, Plate 6)

Lepus, Leo, Sirius, Hydra (**Figs 18, 19**)

With these suggested identifications in mind, it seems reasonable to hypothesize further that four other constellations depicted in the *Aratea* provided exemplars for figures which appear in the Tapestry, namely a lion in the upper border, hares and hunting dogs in the lower border, and eels swimming in the River Couesnon. Note that in the Tapestry as in the *Aratea*, the hunting dogs have collars with rings to take the leash, and that the eels appear in the Tapestry next to the motif of *Duo Pisces* taken from the *Aratea*.

Serpentarius (**Fig. 20**)

The end of the Tapestry is in a very tattered state. Some of the figures are heavily restored and their iconography has received little attention. The theme is that of the Normans pursuing the defeated English forces, and two of the Tapestry figures appear to show Englishmen hiding themselves in trees and shrubs. The first man seems to be wrapping lengths of foliage around himself as camouflage. Presumably the exemplar for this curious figure was the drawing of the constellation *Serpentarius* as shown in the Harley planisphere.

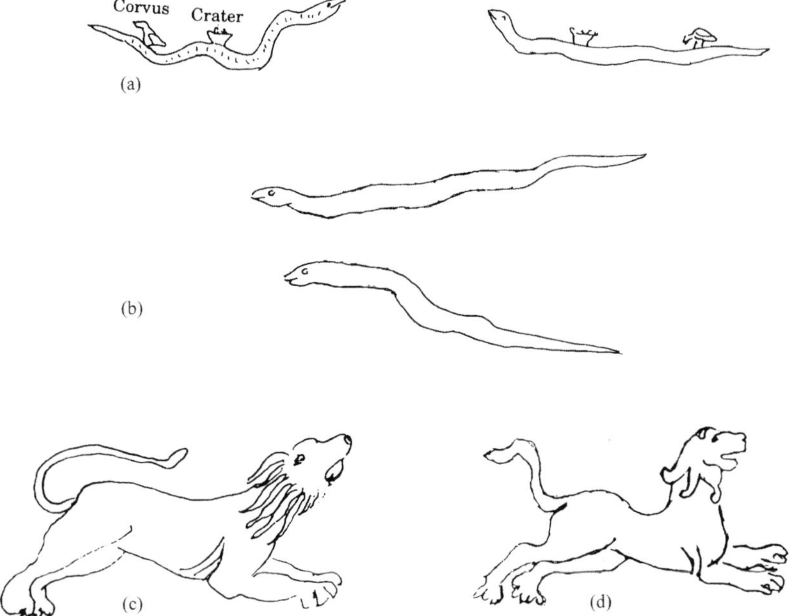

Fig. 19 (a) *Hydra*, from London, BL, MS Harley 647, fol. 21v, planisphere, and fol. 12v; **(b)** the Bayeux Tapestry, lower border (**Plate 9**); **(c)** *Leo*, from London, BL, MS Harley 647, fol. 21v, planisphere; **(d)** the Bayeux Tapestry, upper border (Wilson, *BT*, Plate 46)

Fig. 20 (a) Man in bush, from the Bayeux Tapestry, main register, incomplete (Wilson, *BT*, Plate 73); **(b)** *Serpentarius*, from London, BL, MS Harley 647, fol. 21v, planisphere;

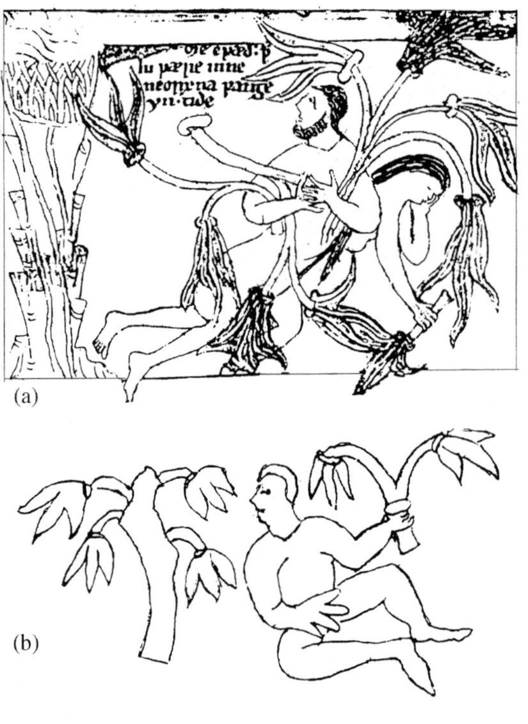

Fig. 21 (a) Genesis III. 8: 'Adam and his wife hid themselves from the presence of the Lord God among the trees of the garden.' London, BL, MS Cotton Claudius B. iv, fol. 7v; **(b)** the Bayeux Tapestry, lower border (Wilson, *BT*, Plate 73); **(c)** *Eridanus*, from London, BL, MS Harley 2506, fol. 42v

Eridanus (**Fig. 21**)

The second of these representations of defeated Englishmen hiding from the Normans is even more bizarre. The last surviving figure in the bottom border of the Tapestry consists of a man sitting on the ground and attempting to cover his nakedness with a hand placed over his genitalia. I have suggested elsewhere that the main exemplar for this figure was the picture of Adam in the Garden of Eden as shown in the Canterbury *Hexateuch* (London, BL, Cotton Claudius B. iv, 7v).[12] However, this does not account for the branch of a tree held in his left hand, and I think that this particular element derives from the picture of the river-god *Eridanus* shown in Harley 2506. Some may consider that the derivation is far-fetched, but in fact this figure of *Eridanus* also appears on a notable ivory book-cover sculpted at Canterbury in the

12 Hart, 'The Bayeux Tapestry and schools of illumination', p. 160.

Fig. 22 Ivory book-cover from Canterbury, front: Paris, Bibliothèque Nationale, Cod. lat. 323

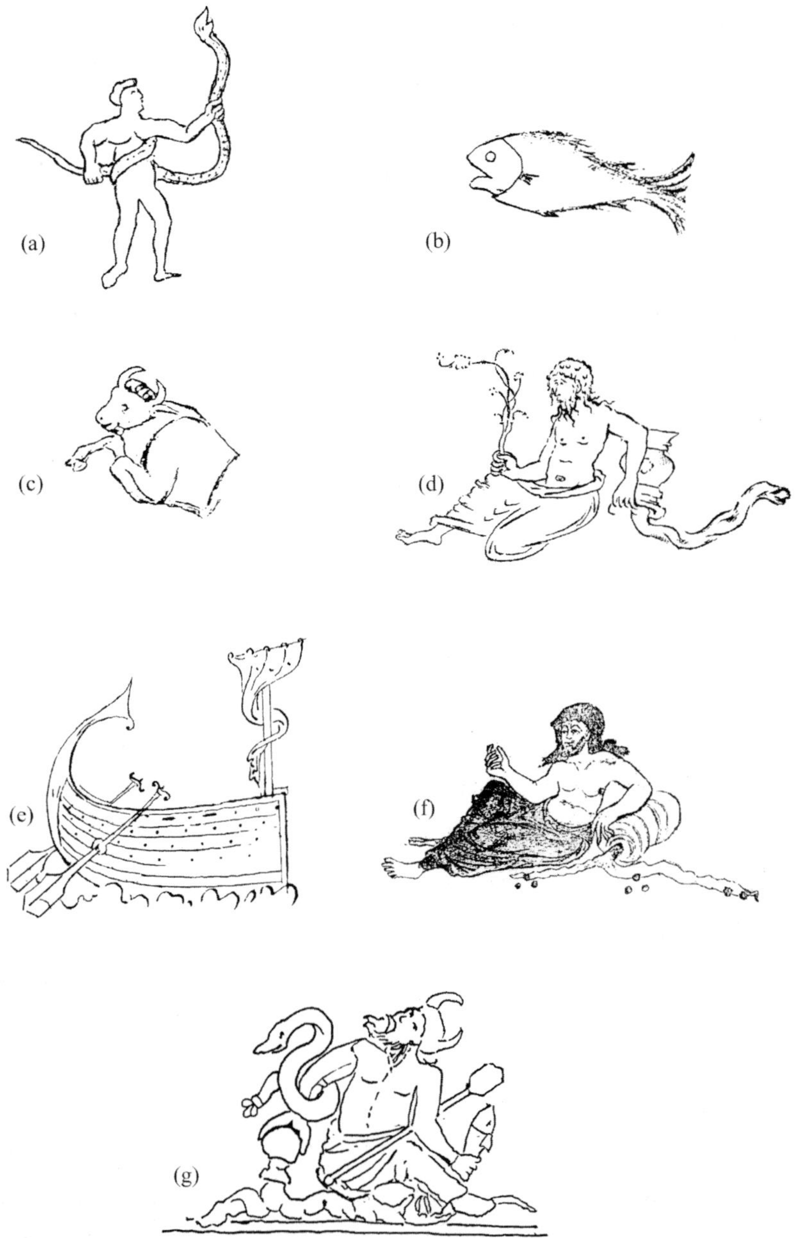

Fig. 23 (a) *Serpentarius*, from London, BL, MS Harley 647, fol. 21v, planisphere; **(b)** *Piscis*, from London, BL, MS Harley 647, fol. 21v, planisphere; **(c)** *Taurus*, from London, BL, MS Harley 647, fol. 21v, planisphere; **(d)** *Eridanus*, from London, BL, MS Harley 2506, fol. 42v; **(e)** *Argo*, from London, BL, MS Harley 2506, fol. 26v; **(f)** *Eridanus*, from London, BL, MS Cotton Tiberius B. v, fol. 44v; **(g)** Composite figure made up from constellations to represent the heavens, detail from an ivory book-cover from Canterbury (**Fig. 22**): Paris, Bibliothèque Nationale, Cod. lat. 323

late-tenth century (**Fig. 22**, Paris, Bibliothèque Nationale, Cod. lat. 323), and here it can be shown even more convincingly that the drawing of *Eridanus* in the Harley 2506 version of the *Aratea* was the exemplar (see Appendix 2 below).

The Cicero-Aratea *as an exemplar for the Tapestry*
The derivation of Tapestry images from Canterbury astrological manuscripts is consistent with what is known of the Tapestry designer's practice: at least six other illuminated manuscripts from Canterbury have been shown to have provided exemplars for the Tapestry.[13] The use of *Aratea* images at Canterbury is confirmed by the appearance of *Aratea* figures in a tenth-century Canterbury ivory (see **Fig. 23**). The unique Tapestry figure of the two fishes joined by a line to their mouths can only derive, mediately or immediately, from Harley 2506, a Canterbury copy of the *Cicero-Aratea*. The cumulative evidence that the designer of the Tapestry copied figures from the *Cicero-Aratea* is overwhelming.

Appendix 1

English Copies of the Cicero-Aratea

The English copies of the *Cicero-Aratea* have been described many times, notably by Elżbieta Temple in 1976[14] and by Patrick McGurk in 1983,[15] to whose accounts (both of which include extensive bibliographies) I am much indebted. Since they wrote, work on the series has continued, and an interim revision of their accounts of the transmission of the text in England is now desirable.

London, BL, Harley 647
The prototype of the English copies is a ninth-century Lotharingian manuscript notable for the late antique character of its twenty-three drawings personifying the constellations.[16] The drawings are thought to be copies of an exemplar from the fourth

13 CCCC 286 (*St Augustine Gospels*); Utrecht, Bibliotheek der Rijksuniversiteit, 32, Eccl. 484 (*Utrecht Psalter*); Oxford, Bodleian Library, Junius 11 (513) (*Cædmon Manuscript*); London, BL, Harley 603 (*Harley Psalter*); London, BL, Cotton Claudius B. iv (Old English illustrated *Hexateuch*); London, BL, Cotton Tiberius B. v. Part I, 3r–8v (the calendar series in the Canterbury illustrated Old English miscellany). These exemplars are all described in Hart, 'The Bayeux Tapestry and schools of illumination', pp. 119–25.

14 Temple, *Anglo-Saxon Manuscripts*, Cat. 65–6.

15 McGurk *et al.*, *Miscellany*, pp. 68–78.

16 For accounts of Harley 647 and its English copies, in addition to the bibliographies by Temple and McGurk already referred to, the lavishly illustrated, 1836 paper by Otley should be consulted (W. Young Otley, 'On a manuscript . . . Containing the translation of Aratus' astronomical poem by Cicero, accompanied by drawings of the Constellations', *Archaeologia* 26 (1836), 145–214). It is verbose, but still remarkably useful. The engravings of figures in Harley 647 are highly accurate, and beautifully executed. Comparative folios from Cotton Tiberius B. v. are included. See also A. Van de Vyver, 'Les

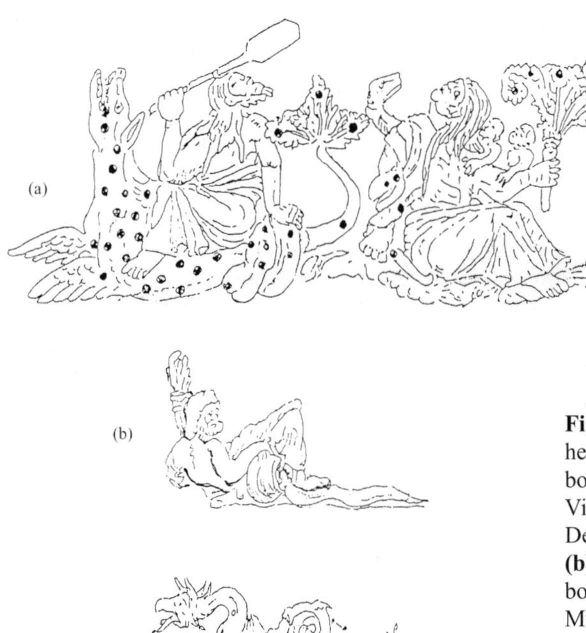

Fig. 24 (a) Water, earth and the heavens from the base of an ivory book-cover from Metz: London, Victoria and Albert Museum, Dept. of Sculpture, 250–1867; **(b)** *Eridanus*, from an ivory book-cover from Rheims: Munich, Staatsbibliothek, MS Cod. lat. 4452; **(c)** *Coetus*, from London, BL, MS Harley 2506, fol. 42v

century. Each constellation is given a page; the *scholia* are written within the drawings and the Ciceronian verses beneath. The *scholia* are excerpts from Hyginus, and each consists of a fable, followed by a list of stars for the particular constellation. Harley 647 was annotated, possibly by Abbo of Fleury, and eventually reached St Augustine's Canterbury, where additions were made in the late-tenth century, mostly supply copies replacing the early folios.

London, BL, Harley 2506

This manuscript was written at Fleury-sur-Loire in about 975, by a number of English and continental scribes. It contains astronomical texts, some by Abbo of Fleury. Its account of the *Cicero-Aratea* is based on that of Harley 647, but its star list and *scholia* depend on different exemplars. Personifications of the constellations were drawn by the Master of the Ramsey Psalter, an English monk and renowned illustrator, then working at Fleury.[17] A few of these (notably *Cœtus*, **Fig. 24(c)**) use Harley 647 as an exemplar, but most of them are original, with no known exemplar, and represent some of the finest line drawings ever to have come from the pen of an English artist. It is noteworthy that the positions of the stars shown in these illustrations vary widely from those in Harley 647. The Ramsey Master was concerned not

Œuvres inédites d'Abbon de Fleury', *Revue Bénédictine* 47 (1935), 123–69; 'Les plus anciennes traductions latines médiévales (Xe–XIe siècles) de traités d'astronomie et d'astrologie', *Osiris* 1 (1936), 658–91.

17 Hart, *Learning in Anglo-Saxon England*, II. 542–3.

with scientific accuracy, but with producing a work of art; he made his drawings first, and added the stars later, almost haphazardly. Harley 2506 reached Canterbury from Fleury together with Harley 647, before the end of the tenth century. They may have been taken there by Abbo himself when he visited Canterbury and Ramsey in 985–7, but it is perhaps more likely that they formed part of the exchanges of manuscripts between the three houses which followed Abbo's visit.

London, BL, Cotton Tiberius B. v, Part I

The *Aratea* forms a comparatively small section of this manuscript, which has been described comprehensively by McGurk.[18] Much of its very complicated content derives from other carolingian manuscripts, now lost, which were available to copyists at Canterbury when the recension in Cotton Tiberius B. v was written there in the second quarter of the eleventh century. However, the compilation of the archetype may have occurred several decades before this. Presumably, many of the sources came from Fleury. Most of the text is from the pen of a single scribe, working probably at Christ Church, Canterbury. Bishop thought that, as with other Canterbury copies of the *Aratea*, the exemplar was Harley 647;[19] but this is not satisfactory, as Tiberius B. v shares some illustrations with London, BL, Cotton Tiberius C. i which are omitted from Harley 647. The illustrations of Tiberius B. v show clear indications of the Canterbury style.

One concludes that Cotton Tiberius B. v was a copy by a Canterbury scribe of a lost text of the *Cicero-Aratea*, at least one step away from Harley 647. Conceivably, it shared its exemplar with Cotton Tiberius C. i, below.

London, BL, Cotton Tiberius C. i

This is the Peterborough Abbey copy of the Ramsey Scientific Compendium.[20] The *Cicero-Aratea* appears on folios 19r–42r of the manuscript. Although the text of the Peterborough copy is close to that of Cotton Tiberius B. v, it seems that the artists responsible for drawings of the constellations tried to follow slavishly those of Harley 647. In reaching this conclusion, account has been taken of the fact that the Peterborough copyist was a very poor draughtsman. On the other hand, *Aquarius* and *Capricornus*, missing in Harley 647, are both present in Tiberius B. v and Tiberius C. i, as are the drawings of *Sol* and *Luna*. Several other items common to these two texts do not appear in Harley 647.

In my opinion Tiberius C. i copied a version of the *Cicero-Aratea* which was still kept at Ramsey Abbey at the end of the eleventh century, but has since been lost. This lost version was very close to that of Harley 647, but it contained illustrations which were missing from Harley 647 at an early stage after its arrival at Canterbury.

18 McGurk *et al.*, *Miscellany*, pp. 107–9; Temple, *Anglo-Saxon Manuscripts*, Cat. 104, with full bibliography.

19 T. A. M. Bishop, 'Notes on Cambridge manuscripts, Part IV: MSS connected with St Augustine's, Canterbury', *Transactions of the Cambridge Bibliographical Society* 2.4 (1957), 332–6. In a recent paper ('The Bayeux Tapestry and schools of ilumination', pp.121–3), I suggested that Harley 2506 was the main exemplar for the Cotton Tiberius B. v. *Aratea*, but I am increasingly doubtful about this. There may have been other texts then available at Canterbury, since lost. Further work is needed.

20 Described in Chapter 26 of Hart, *Learning in Anglo-Saxon England*, II. 357–70.

Presumably it was a copy of Harley 647 made while that manuscript was still at Fleury. One cannot be sure when this copy reached Ramsey, but probably it had arrived by the time of Abbo's visit in 985.

Cambridge, Trinity College R. 15. 32 (945)

A Table of Contents of this manuscript was published recently.[21] According to N. R. Ker, the two quires occupying folios 8r–15v and 16r–19v were written by the scribe Ælfsige of Newminster (*fl.* 1020 onwards).[22] The calendar occupying most of the first of these quires has indications of a Winchester location. However, this may have been added to the bulk of the manuscript, written in a similar but not identical hand, which appears to be a copy of computistica kept at Ramsey. The *Aratea* section has no illustrations. Without these, the text could have had very little meaning in astronomical terms, for the distribution of the stars (and therefore the ability to recognize each constellation in the sky) would remain unknown. The exemplar of the *Aratea*, incompletely copied, may have been the same lost Ramsey text, close to that of Harley 647, as that which served for Cotton Tiberius C. i, above.

Appendix 2

Ivory Carvings from Northern Europe and Canterbury which used the Cicero-Aratea *as an Exemplar*

In 1952 when Beckwith published his pioneer corpus of 166 early medieval English ivories, he identified a small group as being associated with the tenth-century continental Benedictine Reform. He noted: 'Unlike some Continental schools, the different styles and layers of stylistic influence cannot be associated with any particular locality. It is improbable that it will ever be possible to make a distinction of this kind.'[23]

Recently I noticed the dependence of a particular motif in one of the finest ivories of this group on illustrations appearing in English copies of the *Cicero-Aratea*. This ivory appears to have been sculpted at Canterbury, where the manuscripts were first located, and it provides an important example of the use of the *Cicero-Aratea* as an exemplar by Canterbury artists. It is described briefly below.

21 Hart, *Learning in Anglo-Saxon England*, II. 557–62.

22 N. R. Ker, *Catalogue of Manuscripts Containing Anglo-Saxon* (Oxford, 1957), p. 135.

23 John Beckwith, *Ivory Carvings in Medieval England* (London, 1972), p. 50.

Paris, Bibliothèque Nationale, Cod. lat. 323[24]

These paired, late-tenth-century, English ivory plaques are used as book-covers for a carolingian Evangelistary dating from the mid-ninth century.[25] The front cover is a representation of Christ within a mandorla, enthroned and supported by two angels, presenting a book to St Paul and keys to St Peter (see **Fig. 22**). The abbey church of St Augustine's, Canterbury, was originally dedicated to these two saints,[26] and from this it may be inferred that if these ivories are of Canterbury origin, they were in fact sculpted at St Augustine's. Perhaps they were designed specifically as covers for the carolingian service book. Beneath the central mandorla of the front cover appears a composite figure representing *Eridanus*, a classical river god, adorned with a horned helmet and accoutred with a paddle, a serpent, and a fish. These items all derive from motifs taken from illustrations of star constellations in Canterbury copies of the *Cicero-Aratea*, as shown in **Fig. 23**. The whole panel is executed with great artistry, and its components follow the Harley 647 tradition so closely that one is tempted to suggest that the ivory was sculpted by the Ramsey master himself, while on a visit there.

The companion-piece (Beckwith, Cat. 24), used as the back cover, is clearly from the same workshop. Here the stylistic item pointing most definitely to a Canterbury origin is the Virgin's veil, wound round the head like a turban, with the free end hanging over one shoulder. Beckwith compared this with the headdress of *Luxuria* illustrating one of the Canterbury copies of the *Psychomachia* of Prudentius.[27] It is still closer to the veil of *Luna* on folio 47r of Cotton Tiberius B. v, a Canterbury copy of the *Cicero-Aratea*. The veiled Winchester figures of this period are in a different tradition.

Finally, it is to be noted that *Eridanus*, occasionally adorned with representations of figures of other constellations in the *Cicero-Aratea*, appears in the same position on several surviving ninth-century Carolingian book-covers. The two examples illustrated in **Fig. 24** come from Rheims (Munich, Staatsbibliothek, Cod. lat. 4452)[28] and Metz (London, Victoria and Albert Museum, Dept. of Sculpture, 250–1867).[29] The Rheims figure shows *Eridanus* emptying a water pot and holding a branch. It forms part of the decoration of a cover, carved in the third quarter of the ninth century, which was used for a Book of Pericopes executed for the Emperor Henry II before 1014. The base of the Metz cover, sculpted at approximately the same date, is occupied by the joint figures of *Eridanus* and *Mater Terra* (Mother Earth or *Rhea* in Greek mythology, carrying the twins *Romulus* and *Remus* on her left arm).[30]

Both figures from the Metz book-cover carry symbols derived from the cycle of illustrations in the *Cicero-Aratea*. *Eridanus* rides *Coetus* and brandishes a paddle from *Argo*. *Mater Terra* holds a branch from *Eridanus* in her left hand and has

24 Dimensions: 15.8cm x 11.3cm (7.2in x 4.5in): Beckwith, *Ivory Carvings*, Cat. 23, 24.

25 Hart, *Learning in Anglo-Saxon England*, II. 563.

26 Gem, *St Augustine's Abbey*, p. 20.

27 Beckwith, *Ivory Carvings*, p. 28.

28 Facsimile in John Beckwith, *Early Medieval Art* (London, 2nd reprint, 1974), p. 109.

29 I am grateful to Ted Williams for drawing my attention to this ivory.

30 Robert Graves, *The Greek Myths*, 2 vols (Harmondsworth, 1955 reprint), I. 223.

Serpentarius entwining her right arm (in one of the Greek myths, *Rhea* herself was transformed into a serpent).[31] The whole of this cover has numerous small cavities which were occupied originally by gold studs, now lost. There can be no doubt that the figures of *Eridanus* and *Mater Terra* symbolize Water and Earth, and the gold studs represent the stars of mythological constellations inhabiting the Heavens. Taken together, these motifs may be thought to personify the Universe as portrayed in classical times, populated by pagan gods, which formed the back-drop upon which the religious figures depicted on the rest of the cover were sculpted. The Canterbury cover, described already, is in the same tradition. Thus the allegorical theme underlying this group of book-covers may be the replacement of ancient classical mythology by a new Christian art, depicting ecclesiastical events of the early medieval period.

It is evident therefore that the use of illustrations from the *Cicero-Aratea* as motifs for drawings and ivory sculptures was of carolingian origin, and that the tradition passed to Canterbury as part of the exchanges of the late-tenth-century Benedictine Reform.[32] The utilization of these motifs in the Bayeux Tapestry represents the final phase of a long process of development, reaching right back to the earliest classical times.

31 *Orphic Fragment* 58; Graves, *Greek Myths*, I. 53.
32 Hart, *Learning in Anglo-Saxon England*, II. 528.

12

The Bayeux Tapestry and Eleventh-century Material Culture

MICHAEL LEWIS

SCHOLARS have generally, and rightly, had a high opinion of the designer of the Bayeux Tapestry. The fact that the Tapestry provides a detailed account of a contemporary event has encouraged the view that he 'had a catholic interest in the contemporary scene', and that the Tapestry itself 'is a record of first hand observation'.[1] The shortage of alternative visual sources for eleventh-century life, especially in areas where archaeological survival is poor, adds to its appeal. Arms and armour are a prime example, for – paradoxically – less military culture remains from the tenth and eleventh centuries than from earlier periods.[2] Similarly, the only clothing to survive from the early medieval period is (shoes excepted) highly fragmentary, and of limited use for reconstructing the nature of eleventh-century garments.[3] There are also few surviving Anglo-Saxon domestic structures: most buildings, apart from churches, were constructed of wood, and hence little remains but post-holes and, very occasionally, foundations or wall fabric.[4] The archaeological survival of ships,

1 Wolfgang Grape, *The Bayeux Tapestry* (Munich, 1994), pp. 28–9. This view is embodied in Simone Bertrand, *La Tapisserie de Bayeux et la manière de vivre au onzième siècle* (La Pierre-qui-Vire, 1966).

2 There is more evidence from the fifth to seventh centuries, when grave-goods were interred with the dead (Sam Lucy, *The Anglo-Saxon Way of Death* (Stroud, 2000), pp. 48–51). There are occasional finds of weapons deposited in rivers and streams, as votive or ritual offerings. James Graham-Campbell, *Viking Artefacts* (London, 1980), Cat. 265, p. 74, shows axeheads like those in the Bayeux Tapestry, dating from the second half of the tenth century to the early twelfth.

3 For surviving textiles, mostly fragments, see Penelope Walton, *Textiles, Cordage and Raw Fibre from 16–22 Coppergate*, The Archaeology of York 17/5 (York, 1989); A. MacGregor, *Anglo-Scandinavian Finds from Lloyds Bank, Pavement and Other Sites*, The Archaeology of York 17/3 (York, 1982), 102–38 and (from London) Elisabeth Crowfoot, Frances Pritchard and Kay Staniland, *Textiles and Clothing c.1150–c.1450* (London, 1992), p. 1. Pre-Conquest shoes are discussed by A. MacGregor, *Anglo-Scandinavian Finds*, pp. 138–42 and Patricia Reid, 'Knowing people through their feet: the shoes of Lundenburg', *London Archaeologist* 9.10 (2001), 267–74. See also Francis Grew and Margrethe de Neergaard, *Shoes and Pattens* (London, 1988), pp. 9–13, for a discussion of early- to mid-twelfth-century footwear.

4 Survivals of Anglo-Saxon stone churches are numerous (see H. M. Taylor and J. Taylor, *Anglo-Saxon Architecture*, 2 vols (Cambridge, 1965–8)). Timber rarely survives into modern times (Greenstead, Essex, is an exception). For the debate on Anglo-Saxon use of stone for secular structures see (*contra*) Margaret Wood, *Norman Domestic Architecture* (Leeds, 1974), p. 67; also Julian D. Richards, *Viking Age England* (London, 1994), pp. 58, 68; and (*pro*, citing Porchester and Sulgrave) Andrew Reynolds, *Later Anglo-Saxon England: Life and Landscape* (Stroud, 1999), pp. 124–9; also (citing the 'Anglian Tower', York) Mary and Nigel Kerr, *Anglo-Saxon Architecture* (Aylesbury, 1983), pp. 6–7.

another once common type of object, is equally poor, especially in England and Normandy.[5] However, the fact that the designer was a skilful narrator who well understood how to evoke the world around him does not mean that he was concerned to create an accurate record of contemporary life. The point is well made by a *Punch* cartoon of 1966, where we see the artist actually on the field of battle, frantically working away in an epic effort to capture every detail as it happens.[6] This is obviously ridiculous; yet the view that this was essentially what the designer did, albeit working at a more leisurely rate, is implicit in much of the literature.

Some anomalies in the Tapestry's depiction of objects have of course been identified, the most famous example being the trousered hauberks.[7] However, even these discussions proceed from the assumption that the Tapestry is basically a reliable source for the nature of contemporary artefacts, and that such unusual errors are to be explained by the circumstances of the commission. Thus, trousered hauberks, it was concluded, were drawn in error by an English designer unaccustomed to some aspects of Norman armour. Yet, paradoxically, the basic assumption that is made in relation to other early medieval depictions is precisely the reverse: that is to say, they are held to derive, to a greater or lesser extent, from inherited visual sources.[8] The Bayeux Tapestry obviously differs from most surviving early medieval artworks in that it portrays contemporary events. However, is this likely to have led the designer to a complete departure from traditional working methods: to have made him a 'proto-realist'? The answer is surely not. A glance at any scene should be sufficient to remind us that his principal objective was to tell a story, evoking the contemporary world, and not to provide an accurate record of it.

Hitherto there has been little systematic study of the relationship between the material culture depicted in the Bayeux Tapestry, that found in contemporary art, and that known through archaeological survival. Yet this is imperative if we are to understand the art and artistry of the Tapestry, and its authority for archaeological detail. In order to evaluate the extent to which the Tapestry reflects the contemporary scene we must compare its artefacts with, on the one hand, the relevant archaeological remains and, on the other, the way such items are shown in contemporary manuscript illumination. In the present context our investigation will be limited to three test cases, but in the conclusion, we will attempt to outline some of the broader implications of this research.

5 Valerie Fenwick noted that fewer tangible remains have been 'found in the British Isles than in almost any other North European country' (*The Graveney Boat*, ed. V. Fenwick (Greenwich, 1978), p. 195). The boat remains from Graveney, Kent, date from *c.* 1000. The Sutton Hoo mound 1 ship burial dates to *c.* 620–5 (R. L. S. Bruce-Mitford, *The Sutton Hoo Ship Burial*, 3 vols (London, 1975–83), I (1975). 584–8). In Normandy there is nothing of comparable antiquity.

6 Reproduced in Bernstein, *Mystery*, p. 37.

7 Brooks and Walker, 'Authority and interpretation', pp. 19–20.

8 Demonstrated by M. O. H. Carver, 'Contemporary artefacts illustrated in Late Saxon manuscripts', *Archaeologia* 108 (1986), 117–46, in his comparison of the *Harley Psalter* (London, BL, Harley 603) with the *Utrecht Psalter* (Utrecht, Bibliotheek der Rijksuniversiteit, 32, Eccl. 484).

Conical Helmets

Arms and armour are widespread in the Bayeux Tapestry, which is hardly surprising given that warfare is fundamental to the narrative. One distinctive element of the armour in the Tapestry is the conical helmet. Most such helmets appear to be segmented (each part usually a different colour) and many have a brow band, which supports the segmented plates of the helm and helps hold them together. The helmets are all fitted with nasal guards, some of which are ornately decorated. Other embellishments include circles on the crown and supporting bars around the chin.

Surviving helmets, though few in number, provide good evidence that the artist attempted to reflect elements of contemporary fashion in his design. An example in the Royal Armouries, Leeds, and another in the Metropolitan Museum of Art, New York, compare well with the segmented helmets depicted in the Bayeux Tapestry.[9] Whereas all the Tapestry helmets are shown with nasal guards, only the Wenceslas helm preserves this as an original feature.[10] This helmet also has a brow band, an element which is common in the Tapestry.[11]

Turning to pictorial representations in Anglo-Saxon art we find that, from about the tenth century, classical and crested helmets give way to those of a conical type, suggesting that artists were responding to changing fashions in arms and armour.[12] Conical helmets are found on Viking Age stone sculpture in Yorkshire,[13] and it is not impossible – albeit hardly likely – that the Tapestry designer may have seen these or others like them. A more plausible influence is contemporary manuscript illumination, where segmented conical helmets are common, such as that worn by Goliath in

9 The helmet in the Royal Armouries (on loan from Liverpool Museum) is Polish and probably tenth-century. That in the Metropolitan Museum of Art is from northern France, or possibly the River Thames, and probably tenth- or eleventh-century. Also comparable are the ninth- or tenth-century St Wenceslas helmet, Prague Cathedral, Czech Republic, and an eleventh- or twelfth-century helmet from Olmütz, Moravia, exhibit A 41, Kunsthistorisches Museum Hofjagdund Rüstkammer, Vienna, Austria. (See Christopher Gravett, *Norman Knight 950–1204 AD* (London, 1993), pp. 6–7.) The unpublished helmet found in 1788 in the River Witham at Washingborough, Lincolnshire (Lincoln Museum accession number 9734.06), may date to the time of the Norman Conquest.

10 It is an integral part of a highly decorated brow-band, but the brow-band itself may be a later addition (A. Merhautová, 'Der St. Wenzelshelm', *Bimonthly of the Institute of the History of Art of the Czechoslovak Academy of Sciences* 20.3 (1992), 170–8, at 172). The nasal guard on the New York helmet is a restoration.

11 The Polish, Olmütz and Witham helmets all have holes around the rim, possible evidence for brow bands.

12 Some conical helmets in Anglo-Saxon art curve towards the top, as in Oxford, Bodleian Library, Douce 296, 40v (?Crowland, s. xi$^{2/4}$) and British Library, Cotton Tiberius B. v, 85v (?Winchester, s. xi$^{2/4}$) (Elżbieta Temple, *Anglo-Saxon Manuscripts 900–1066* (London, 1976), Cat. 79, Ill. 260; Cat. 87, Ill. 275). This feature is absent from the archaeological record, but probably originates from the Phrygian cap.

13 Middleton 2a, 4a and 5a, all tenth-century (James Lang, *York and Eastern Yorkshire*, Corpus of Anglo-Saxon Stone Sculpture 3 (Oxford, 1991), Plates 676–7, 686, 688). Similar helmets appear on the runestone from Ledberg, Östergötland, and a carved antler fragment from Sigtuna, Sweden: Dominic Tweddle, *The Anglian Helmet from Coppergate*, The Archaeology of York 17/8 (York, 1992), 1129–31.

Fig. 25 (a) Goliath in segmented helmet, from London, BL MS Cotton Tiberius B. vi, fol. 9r; (b) Tapestry helmet

Plate 25 Helmet-type coin of Edward the Confessor issued by Eadwerd of Canterbury

the Tiberius Psalter (**Fig. 25**).[14] Nonetheless, it is a phenomenon of early medieval illumination that helmets are never shown with nasal guards. Indeed, since nasal guards are not found in manuscript art until the twelfth century,[15] their abundance in the Tapestry is of particular interest. Another significant visual parallel for the type of helmets depicted in the Bayeux Tapestry is eleventh-century coinage, on which nasal guards are sometimes shown (**Plate 25**). However, it is doubtful that the relevant coins would still have been in circulation by about 1070,[16] and therefore could not have been a model for the Tapestry artist.

In brief, in this case (conical helms with nasal guards) the close correspondence between the design in the Tapestry and the known form of the contemporary artefact, allied to the circumstances that the visual tradition in manuscript illumination was not as faithful to that form, strongly suggests that the designer was here responding to 'real life'.

Gap Amidships

There are thirty-seven ships in the Bayeux Tapestry, fulfilling various functions. Some are shown with horses aboard, and by implication seem to be cargo vessels. The designer does not otherwise, or obviously, make the distinction between cargo vessels and warships; both appear broadly similar in form.

Although archaeologists have compared the Tapestry ships with medium-sized warships, such as Skuldelev 5,[17] these would have had little room for storage or cargo. Whilst a reconstruction of the Ladby boat was put to sea with four horses,[18] such a vessel could not have accommodated the large numbers of animals shown aboard the Tapestry's ships.[19] Moreover, the Ladby exercise tested whether horses could embark on, and disembark from, a shallow-drafted vessel, rather than the sailing capabilities

14 London, BL, Cotton Tiberius C. vi, fol. 9r (uncertain, s. xi^{med}) (Temple, *Anglo-Saxon Manuscripts*, Cat. 98). T. A. Heslop convincingly argued that this manuscript was post-Conquest (T. A. Heslop, 'A dated Late Anglo-Saxon illuminated psalter', *AntJ* 72 (1992), 171–4, at 171). Segmented conical helmets also appear in Tiberius B. v, fol. 85v (?Winchester, s. xi$^{2/4}$) (Temple, *Anglo-Saxon Manuscripts*, Cat. 87, Ill. 275).

15 Examples include London, BL, Royal 6 C. vi, 79v (Rochester, s. xii$^{1/4}$) and NewYork, Pierpont Morgan Library, M 724r (?Canterbury, Christ Church, s. xii$^{2/4}$): C. M. Kauffmann, *Romanesque Manuscripts 1066–1190* (London, 1975), Cat. 15, Ill. 37; Cat. 66, Ill. 173.

16 Cnut's 'helmet type' coinage, *c.* 1024–30, depicts a segmented helmet with nasal guard, as do the 'helmet type' coins of Edward the Confessor, *c.* 1053–6 (J. J. North, *English Hammered Coinage, 1: Early Anglo-Saxon to Henry III c.650–1272* (London, 1994), Cat. 787–9; Cat. 825–6^{2}). Gareth Williams (British Museum, Department of Coins and Medals, personal communication 22 May 2001) agrees these are intended to represent conical helms with nasal guards (though not apparent on all coins of these types), but regards it unlikely that the Tapestry designer was influenced by coinage since neither type was in circulation at the supposed time of the Tapestry's production. Conical helmets next appear on English coins a hundred years later: see North, *Coinage*, Cat. 922, 929, 932.

17 Wilson, *BT*, p. 226; Grape, *The Bayeux Tapestry*, p. 38.

18 For the Ladby experiment see Knud Thorvildsen, *The Viking Ship of Ladby* (Copenhagen, 1975), p. 26. C. M. Gillmor convincingly argued that the Ladby ship was 'too narrow and too shallow draughted' to transport horses across the Channel: C. M. Gillmor, 'Naval logistics of the cross-Channel operation, 1066', *ANS* 7 (1984), 105–31, at 110.

19 Up to ten horses are shown on a single ship in the Bayeux Tapestry.

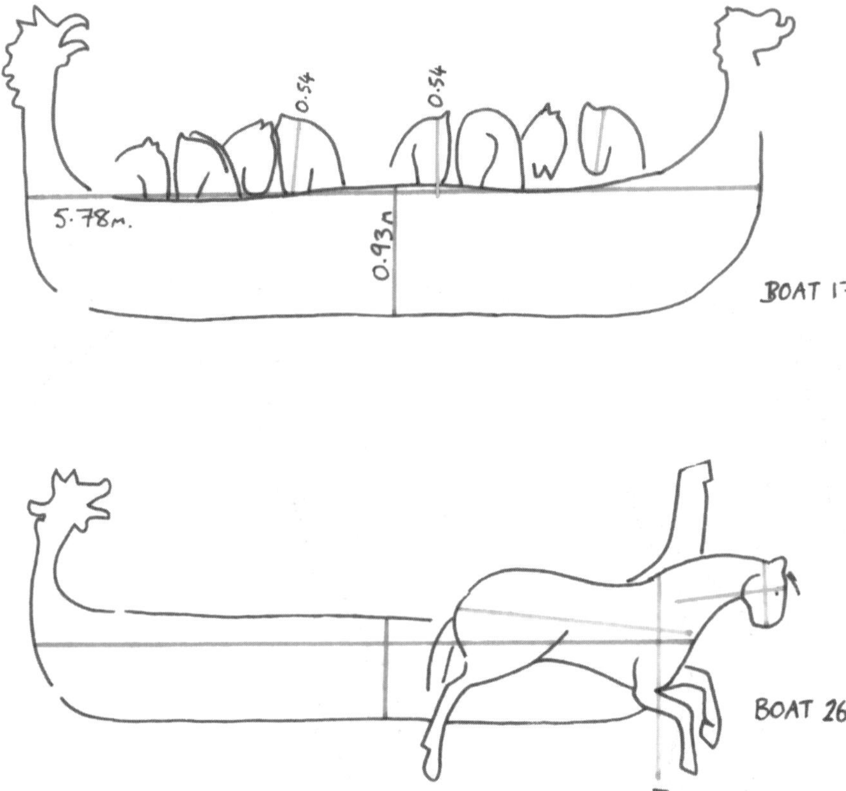

Fig. 26 (a) Horses on board ship: the Bayeux Tapestry

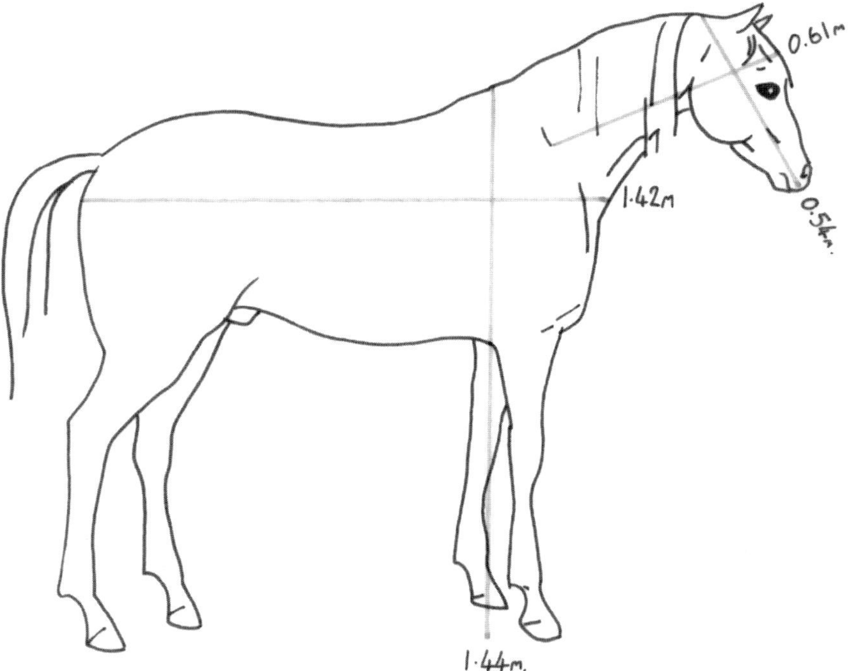

Fig. 26 (b) Eleventh-century horse

of a ship laden with up to ten horses and undertaking a Channel crossing. Incidentally, given that the average European warhorse was a medium-sized animal of between 14.2 and 15 hands, the distance between the base of the hull and the gunwale of a ship transporting them should be at least 1.5m (4ft 11in).[20] It is quite clear then (if there were any doubt) that the horses and ships in the Tapestry are not drawn to the same scale (**Fig. 26**).

Some ships in the Tapestry are depicted with a gap in the gunwale amidships, and it is possible that the designer thought this to be a diagnostic feature of contemporary cargo vessels.[21] Certainly some ships in the Tapestry do seem to share the basic characteristics of the Skuldelev traders, having the same hull form, central sail, gap amidships and, in three cases, oar ports both forward and aft.[22] However, it is perplexing that in the Tapestry horses are never shown on ships with a gap amidships, while those ships with the gap (which we would naturally assume to be traders) are never shown with cargo. It is apparent that horses have a limited role in the earlier part of the Tapestry, and this might explain why they are not illustrated aboard ships with a gap amidships. Nonetheless, this still does not explain why, if cargo vessels are shown with a gap amidships in the earlier part of the Tapestry, they do not have gaps in the Norman invasion fleet.

The point at which the gap amidships appears within the Tapestry seems to be important for understanding its significance. Since, in all but one instance, the gap amidships is associated with English vessels, it may be the case that the Tapestry designer deliberately used this feature to differentiate between English and Norman ships.[23] Interestingly, both the vessel from mound 1 at Sutton Hoo and the Graveney boat may have had a gap amidships.[24] Yet caution is still needed, since this feature is

[20] Given that the average European warhorse was between 144.27 and 152.40cm (56.8 and 60in) high from from hoof to withers (Ann Hyland, *The Medieval Warhorse from Byzantium to the Crusades* (Stroud, 1996), pp. 85–6), we can calculate that the largest ship in the Bayeux Tapestry (Ship 17) – immediately after the inscription *MARE* (Scene 38, Wilson, *BT*, Plate 40) – is only 0.93m deep: well below the 1.5m required to ensure that only the horses' heads are showing above the gunwale.

[21] Ships 1 to 6 (Scenes 4–6 and 23–4, Wilson, *BT*, Plates 4–6 and 26–7). This seems to be a common feature of traders from the ninth century onwards. For example, Skuldelev 1 had a small number of oars, fore and aft, which would have been used when the wind dropped (Olaf Olsen and Ole Crumlin-Pedersen, 'The Skuldelev ships', *Acta Archaeologia* 38 (1967), 74–153, at 106–7). Wilson, *BT*, p. 226, compared the Tapestry ships with Skuldelev 3, which has two oar ports forward starboard, three forward port, and a single oar-hole (which shows little sign of wear) on each side aft. Evidence from Roskilde, Denmark (excavated 1996) supports the view that oars no longer played much part in the propulsion of trading vessels from the eleventh century onwards: Angela Croome, 'Museum Report: the Viking Ship Museum at Roskilde: expansion uncovers nine more early ships; and advances experimental ocean-sailing plans', *The International Journal of Nautical Archaeology* 28.4 (1999), 382–93, at 384.

[22] For example, Ships 3, 5 and 6 (Scenes 4–6 and 23–4, Wilson, *BT*, Plates 4–6 and 26–7). Gillmor, 'Naval logistics', p. 114, compares the Tapestry ships with the Gokstad ship, and Skuldelev 1 and 3.

[23] Wilson, *BT*, pp. 181 and 226, suggested this distinction might have been based on verbal description or personal observation.

[24] The Graveney boat 'may have had a break amidships in the hold area' (Fenwick, *Graveney Boat*, p. 251). Rupert Bruce-Mitford noted an 'absence of gunwale spikes or tholes in the midship area' of Sutton Hoo 1 might suggest that the vessel had a central gap in the rowing positions from the outset: Bruce-Mitford, *The Sutton Hoo Ship Burial*, I. 352); see also Edwin and Joyce Gifford, 'The sailing performance of Anglo-Saxon ships as derived from the building and trials of half-scale models of the

not exclusive to Anglo-Saxon boat-building; as we have seen, it appears in the Skuldelev traders.[25]

The only English ship shown without a gap amidships appears in Scene 33 (Wilson, *BT*, Plate 33), after one of the 'joins' in the Tapestry (between Sections 2 and 3).[26] It is possible, then, that the distinction between the ships in the earlier part of the Tapestry and those depicted after Scene 24 is due to the tastes of different workshops, rather than representing a purposeful attempt to express characteristics of national identity.[27]

This said, since the gap amidships is unparalleled in early medieval art, this feature encourages the speculation that the Tapestry designer was here drawing upon first-hand observation.[28] Even so, these ships must be stylized: their lean appearance, and the fact that they do not carry cargo (in this case horses), is atypical for most medieval cargo vessels. Here, then, we seem to see some independent response to the real world, presented according to the needs of the narrative, and probably somewhat stylized.

Bosham Church and Mont-Saint-Michel

The Bayeux Tapestry is rich in architecture. There are thirty-three buildings, of which four are churches. Of these Bosham church (**Plate 1**) and the abbey church of Mont-Saint-Michel (**Plate 9**) are shown as rectangular buildings with trapezoid pitched roofs. This form is used elsewhere in the Tapestry for secular structures,[29] suggesting that the designer did not intend it to be diagnostic of church architecture. It is only the small crosses on the roofs of the buildings at Bosham and Mont-Saint-Michel that unequivocally indicate their ecclesiastical function.[30]

The early fabric that survives at both Bosham and Mont-Saint-Michel reveals that the Tapestry designer did not take the appearance of the contemporary structures for

Sutton Hoo and Graveney ship finds', *The Mariner's Mirror, The Journal of the Society for Nautical Research* 82/3 (1996), 131–53, at 133.

25 Both Skuldelev 1 and 3 had cargo space amidships, and oar ports forward and aft.

26 Boat 7 (Wilson, *BT*, Plates 33–4). If the gap amidships is considered an English attribute then the Tapestry designer might be forgiven for omitting it in this instance, as he had already described this vessel as *NAVIS ANGLICA*. This raises the question of whether this feature was diagnostic of English ships, or just adopted for the purposes of the narrative.

27 At the same point in the Tapestry the moustaches of 'Englishmen', which in previous scenes had been used to distinguish between Anglo-Saxons and Normans, disappear.

28 One possible exception is Oxford, Bodleian Library, MS Junius 11 (?Canterbury, Christ Church, s. x/xi, but for a *c.* 960–90 date see Leslie Lockett, 'An integrated re-examination of the dating of Oxford, Bodleian Library, Junius 11', *ASE* 31 (2002), 141–73), where, at p. 68, a vessel is shown with a doorway cut through the upper two strakes (Ohlgren, *Illustration*, p. 564). For a note on the gap amidships see A. C. Evans, *Sutton Hoo Ship Burial* (London, 1994), p. 29, and Fenwick, *Graveney Boat*, p. 251. For a discussion of horses aboard ship see Wilson, *BT*, p. 187 and Grape, *Bayeux Tapestry*, p. 38.

29 For example Buildings 25, 26, 27 (Scene 41; Wilson, *BT*, Plates 45–6) and 32 (Scene 47; Wilson, *BT*, Plate 50).

30 Crosses also appear on the reliquary box upon which Harold makes an oath in Scene 23 (**Plate 11**), and at the ends of the catafalque bearing the Confessor's body in Scene 26 (Wilson, *BT*, Plate 29).

Plate 26 The church of St Laurence, Bradford-on-Avon, Wiltshire

Fig. 27 The Tapestry's depiction of Bosham church (**Plate 1**)

the basis of his design.[31] Even though the aisles, porch, and most of the chancel which dominate Bosham church today are later additions which disguise much of the Anglo-Saxon fabric, it is apparent that the ground plan of the original Saxon church has little in common with the building illustrated in the Tapestry.[32] The suggestion that the central 'doorway' shown in the Tapestry might be the present Bosham's magnificent chancel arch ignores the fact that rounded arches are not unique to this building.[33] Indeed, any relationship between the surviving Anglo-Saxon parts of the church at Bosham and the representation in the Tapestry could well be coincidental. However, the rectangular structure of Bosham as shown in the Tapestry compares well with that of several Anglo-Saxon churches, and this may indicate that the designer took a standard Anglo-Saxon church form as the basis for his design.[34] Moreover, one can move beyond the plan to compare individual aspects of the church in the Tapestry with (for example) the surviving fabric of St Laurence, Bradford-upon-Avon, Wiltshire, which has similar features and decoration (**Plate 26**, **Fig. 27**).[35] Of course, this is not to say that the Tapestry designer knew of this particular building first-hand, rather that the upper arcading, arched windows and doorway are typical features of many late Anglo-Saxon churches from which he could have drawn inspiration.

The Tapestry shows Mont-Saint-Michel on a hill, but there resemblance to the eleventh-century building ends. The carolingian church, built in the tenth century, comprised a rectangular nave and square chancel built on the summit of the rock, with a lower sanctuary (the chapel of Notre-Dame-sous-Terre) on the terrace below. In about 1023 Abbot Hildebert II began work to replace (and incorporate) these buildings within an ambitious and complex Romanesque edifice. Although the structure in the Tapestry has some ancillary buildings, it is difficult to reconcile this depiction with the eleventh-century abbey complex.[36] The nave, which consisted of seven bays, was not yet finished by 1085, and it is possible that the tenth-century carolingian

31 R. Allen Brown, 'Architecture of the Bayeux Tapestry', in his *Castles, Conquest and Charters – Collected Papers* (Woodbridge, 1989), pp. 214–26, at pp. 216–17.

32 John Pollock, *Bosham: Ecclesia as Shown in the Bayeux Tapestry* (Selsey, 1995), in contrast, attempted to demonstrate that the surviving fabric of Bosham is comparable to the depiction in the Tapestry, arguing that the present bell tower was built using some of the fabric of an earlier watch tower which is depicted in the Tapestry. Pollock's evidence for this structure, which focused on the apparent remains of the earlier building, is dubious: cf. Taylor and Taylor, *Anglo-Saxon Architecture*, I. 81–2.

33 Implied by James Campbell in *The Anglo-Saxons*, ed. James Campbell (London, 1991), p. 232. It could also be suggested that the outer arch in the Tapestry depiction mimics the arch of the chancel itself. See H. M. Taylor, *Anglo-Saxon Architecture* III (Cambridge, 1978), 775–98, for a discussion of arches in Anglo-Saxon churches.

34 The ground plans of Heysham, Ledsham i, Thornage and Wharram Percy ii (Taylor and Taylor, *Anglo-Saxon Architecture*, I. 969–1005) show particular resemblance. It is, however, unlikely that a Canterbury-based designer would have first-hand experience of any of these specific cases.

35 Taylor and Taylor, *Anglo-Saxon Architecture*, I. 86–7 and 799–868, dated Bradford-on-Avon as follows: chancel, and nave with flanking porches period A2 (*c*. 650–700), altered in periods C1 to C3 (*c*. 950–1100). E. Fernie, *The Architecture of the Anglo-Saxons* (London, 1983), pp. 145–9, however, convincingly argued for an eleventh-century date.

36 Some differences between the Tapestry's depiction of Mont-Saint-Michel and the surviving eleventh-century fabric of this church are discussed in Maylis Baylé, Pierre Bouet *et al.*, *Le Mont-Saint-Michel: histoire et imaginaire* (Paris, 1998), p. 112.

church still survived when the Tapestry was produced: whatever the case, neither the new nave nor the earlier church is suggested in the Tapestry.[37]

Art, not the real world, informed much of the Tapestry's architecture. Rectangular-shaped buildings with trapezoid pitched roofs are commonly illustrated in contemporary illumination,[38] and it was these, as well as contemporary reliquary shrines,[39] which probably influenced the Tapestry's depiction of Bosham church and Mont-Saint-Michel. This is logical, given that such artistic creations will have been more immediately available to the designer – whatever his identity and circumstances – than the actual buildings themselves. Arched doorways and windows are widespread in contemporary illuminations, as well as in surviving architectural fabric. The Junius 11 manuscript of Old English poetry, for example, shows steps reminiscent of those leading up to the 'chancel arch' of Bosham church.[40] Similarly, arcading and crosses are often found on ecclesiastical structures in manuscript art.[41]

37 It is possible (though rather unlikely) that the Tapestry shows a north (or south) view of the Abbey church: the three arches representing the nave and two aisles, with the ancillary buildings to either side representing the chapels of St Martin and that of Trente-Cièrges (which formed the foundation arms of the transepts). Allen Brown, 'Architecture of the Bayeux Tapestry', p. 217, made the interesting suggestion that 'it is perfectly possible – perhaps even natural' – that the Tapestry designer sought to depict the Carolingian chapel of Mont-Saint-Michel and not the Abbey church. More popular is the theory of J. J. G. Alexander, *Norman Illumination at Mont-Saint-Michel* (Oxford, 1970), pp. 16–17, that the Tapestry illustrates a novel system of decorative arcading, built around 1060, which seems to 'have caught the [Tapestry] artist's attention'. Richard Gameson gave historical credibility to this hypothesis, explaining that Abbot Scotland, the first Norman appointee at St Augustine's (1072–87) and formerly of Mont-Saint-Michel, would have been 'approachable as well as geographically convenient' for the Tapestry's patron – supposing that the Tapestry was produced in Canterbury: Gameson, *Study*, p. 172. Whilst this may be the case, there is nothing striking about the arcading in the Tapestry's rendition, which is typical of the general form of arcading elsewhere.

38 Examples include MSS Junius 11, p. 87, London, BL, Cotton Claudius B. iv, 32r (?Canterbury, St Augustine's, s. xi$^{2/4}$) and BL, Royal 15. A. xvi, 84r, (Canterbury, St Augustine's, s. xi$^{2/4}$): Temple, *Anglo-Saxon Manuscripts*, Cat. 58, Ill. 196 (and Ohlgren, *Illustration*, p. 574); Cat. 86, Ill. 267; Cat. 85, Ill. 211.

39 Cyril Hart, 'The Bayeux Tapestry and schools of illumination at Canterbury', *ANS* 22 (2000), 117–67, at 129, made the interesting comparison between Bosham in the Tapestry and the reliquaries in the apse of St Augustine's shown in Thomas of Elmham's history of St Augustine's Abbey. Whilst Hart believed that the designer of the Tapestry might have used the actual shrines for his model, these are unlikely to have been built much before 1091. However, the eighth-century Anglo-Saxon reliquary shrine at Mortain (Manche), France (*The Making of England: Anglo-Saxon Art and Culture AD 600–900*, ed. L. Webster and J. Backhouse (London, 1991), pp. 175–6), and a Romanesque example in the Metropolitan Museum of Art, New York (*English Romanesque Art 1066–1200*, ed. George Zarnecki (London, 1984), p. 282), demonstrate the use and subsequent survival of this form.

40 Junius 11, p. 84: Ohlgren, *Illustration*, p. 573.

41 Examples of such arcading are found in the *St Albans Psalter*, Hildesheim, St Godehard's Church, 1, p. 48 (St Albans Abbey, *c.* 1119–23), Cambridge, Pembroke College 120, 2v (?Bury St Edmunds Abbey, s. xii$^{2/4}$) and Cambridge, Trinity College R. 17. 1, 283v, 285 (Canterbury, Christ Church, *c.* 1147): Kauffmann, *Romanesque Manuscripts*, Cat. 29, Ill. 74; Cat. 35, Ill. 194. Examples of such crosses can be found in Florence, Biblioteca Mediceo-Laurenziana, Plut. XII.17, 2v (Canterbury, ?St Augustine's, *c.* 1120), Oxford, Bodleian Library, Laud, Misc 469, 7v (?Canterbury, *c.* 1130–40) and Cambridge, Trinity College R. 17. 1, 9r (Canterbury, Christ Church, *c.* 1147): Kauffmann, *Romanesque Manuscripts*, Cat. 19, Ill. 50; Cat. 54, Ill. 147; Cat. 68, Ill. 184.

The Real World of the Eleventh Century

We have seen from the three 'test cases' presented above that the reliability of the Bayeux Tapestry for eleventh-century material culture is variable. The design reflects a varying mixture of 'real life' and 'artistic' influences. Bearing these examples in mind and drawing on further research (which it is unfortunately not possible to present in detail here) it is possible to offer some broader thoughts and conclusions.

The accuracy of certain types of artefacts in the Bayeux Tapestry clearly reflects those of the eleventh century: the Tapestry's conical helmets are an example. Comparison with the archaeological evidence suggests that the same is true for some other aspects of its arms and armour, including swords, axes and kite-shields.

It is also apparent that there are elements in the Tapestry which could not possibly have reflected the contemporary world, and are more or less archaic. The churches of Bosham and Mont-Saint-Michel are cases in point. Generally, buildings in the Bayeux Tapestry – with the possible exception of Westminster Abbey – are fairly schematic. Their architectural forms and structural elements are greatly simplified. Most are constructed from a repertoire of basic architectural forms which are commonly found in manuscript illuminations and which can often be traced back, via carolingian art, to late antique exemplars.

Other elements of the Tapestry design broadly reflect the contemporary scene but have details which are less easy to understand and are perhaps of questionable veracity. The ships are an example. In general, they reflect a known eleventh-century form; however, certain characteristics are in reality diagnostic of the trading vessel, notably the gap amidships, which in the Bayeux Tapestry seem to be misappropriated.

Symbolism and Function

The accuracy, and inaccuracy, of many details, along with the extent and nature of the debt to inherited visual sources, shed valuable light on the designer and his work. Some anomalies in the material culture depicted in the Bayeux Tapestry seem to be purposeful. For example, many of the spears in the Tapestry are barbed and have small wings, which, according to the archaeological evidence, was not typical of contemporary weapons.[42] This characteristic was clearly borrowed from art, but the reason why it was not corrected should be considered. It seems that wings on barbed spears were an artistic convention, part of the 'iconography' of this particular artefact that helped convey its identity to the viewer. One might compare this anomaly with the image of the steam train that appears on road signs: it does not lead us to expect a steam engine; it has become an accepted convention for any type of train. Likewise, it

42 Rather, this feature is typical of hunting spears: S. H. Fuglesang, *Some Aspects of the Ringerike Style* (Odense, 1980), p. 137. It is noteworthy, therefore, that such spears are repeatedly depicted in combat scenes. Whilst barbed spears with wings might have been used for war, practical considerations argue against this: once embedded into flesh the weapon would be almost impossible to shift further forward to despatch the enemy, or to remove.

appears that to the eleventh-century beholder, wings on barbed spearheads were an accepted convention for depicting the spear.

The narrative of the Tapestry relies on imbuing certain artefacts with a symbolic value, and any attempt to evaluate the 'realism' of its elements must be alive to this fact. Certain items such as cloaks, long robes and certain types of armour, along with hawks, denote people of status. Similarly, some attributes, such as gaps amidships, certain haircuts and even the use of horses, seem to indicate race or affiliation. Many of these features seem to have a basis in real life, but common sense suggests that they will have been exaggerated for artistic effect. It is interesting that many of these usages are specific to the Bayeux Tapestry. Whilst the loss of other works undoubtedly accentuates the uniqueness of the Tapestry, it seems likely that the Tapestry designer developed his own visual repertoire to convey this narrative of recent events.

Production and Manufacture

The depiction of artefacts also sheds light on the production of the work as a whole. Certain artefacts, or ways of depicting them, only appear in particular sections of the Tapestry, and this may indicate that different teams of embroiderers worked on particular sections. Examples include the gap amidships, which has already been discussed. Alternatively, since many seemingly inventive details, such as the use of moustaches and haircuts as well as certain animals in the borders, only occur in the earlier parts of the Tapestry, this may suggest that the design was simplified as work progressed, perhaps to save money or time.

When trying to judge what the Tapestry designer may have actually intended, we should be aware of contemporary artistic conventions. For example, stripes on the Tapestry's ships and on the mound of Hastings Castle could be functional or decorative or, perhaps most plausibly, both. It seems logical to think that the stripes on the ships were meant to evoke clinker planking.[43] If this is the case then it is interesting that the designer does not depict scarf joins as found in later illuminations.[44] Conversely, although the stripes on the mound of Hastings Castle might have been intended to represent the layers of the mound, we know, thanks to excavation, that this was not the case; this mound was 'simply a dump of different sorts of sand, all of them very stable'.[45] One suspects, therefore, that the principal motivation here was pattern.

43 Clinker: a method of ship construction in which the hull planks overlap.

44 Scarf: a joint between the ends of two planks (which in art appears as a vertical line).

45 P. A. Barker and K. J. Barton, 'Excavations at Hastings Castle, 1968', *ArchJ* 134 (1977), 80–100, at 88. Mottes of multi-composition construction are known at Bakewell, Derbyshire, Carisbrook, Isle of Wight, Great Driffield, Yorkshire, Hallatton, Leicestershire, and York: E. S. Armitage, *Early Norman Castles of the British Isles* (London, 1912), p. 88; J. R. Kenyon, *Medieval Fortifications* (Leicester, 1990), p. 11.

Contemporary Art and the Bayeux Tapestry

Contemporary art, rather than 'reality', influenced many aspects of the Tapestry design, including architectural elements, vegetal decoration, mythical beasts and birds. It is well known that many of the best parallels for the Tapestry's imagery are found in manuscripts that were probably or certainly produced at Canterbury. These include such seemingly 'realistic' motifs as the ship figureheads, paralleled in the *Junius Manuscript* of Old English poetry (Oxford, Bodleian Library, Junius 11), and the bird slinger which is matched in the Old English *Hexateuch* (BL, Cotton Claudius B. iv).[46] We also see, for example, a double-storey house in MS Junius 11, and mailed hauberks similar to those in the Tapestry, in the *Harley Psalter* (BL, Harley 603).[47] For the most part, however, it seems that the Tapestry designer preferred, or was forced, to adapt visual models, rather than simply copying them.

Some elements of the Tapestry design are commonest in Romanesque illuminations. Examples include spurs and female garments with flared cuffs. These depictions suggest that the designer was – at times – in the vanguard of artistic fashion.

The tension between the need to show the 'real world' and that of following artistic conventions and using visual models is particularly strong in the Bayeux Tapestry. We will only advance our understanding of the reliability of its depictions of objects, and of its artistry, by the systematic exploration of individual motifs, as I hope to have shown here. Moreover, the exercise raises broader issues of considerable importance to art historians, historians and archaeologists, indeed to anyone who wishes to use art as a tool for understanding the past.

46 Junius 11, p. 68 and Claudius, B. iv, 26r: Wormald, 'Style and design', pp. 31–2, and Figs 7, 16–17.

47 Junius 11, p. 3 and BL, Harley 603, 73v: Ohlgren, *Illustration*, pp. 528, 248, respectively. Jennie Kiff correctly noted that the mailed hauberk in Harley 603, like that in Claudius B. iv, 24v, was not part of the original composition, and was added by a later hand: Jennie Kiff, 'Images of war: illustrations of warfare in early eleventh-century England', *ANS* 7 (1984), 178–94, at 190.

Index

The letters Þ and Đ (ð) are represented by th. Æ appears alphabetically as ae. Places are identified by their present country or English county. Icelanders real and legendary are indexed under their forenames, according to Icelandic practice, except for editors.